Compelled to Control

Also by J. Keith Miller

The Taste of New Wine

A Second Touch

Habitation of Dragons

The Becomers

The Edge of Adventure (with Bruce Larson)

Living the Adventure (with Bruce Larson)

The Passionate People (with Bruce Larson)

Please Love Me

The Single Experience (with Andrea Wells Miller)

The Scent of Love

The Dream

Hope in the Fast Lane (previously published as
Sin: Overcoming the Ultimate Deadly Addiction)

Facing Co-dependence
(with Pia Mellody and Andrea Wells Miller)

*A Hunger for Healing: The 12 Steps As
A Classical Model for Christian Spiritual Growth*

Facing Love Addiction
(with Pia Mellody and Andrea Wells Miller)

*Ten Minute Magic:
Uncovering and Achieving Your Dreams*

The Secret Life of the Soul

COMPELLED
TO CONTROL

Recovering Intimacy in
Broken Relationships

J. Keith Miller

With a Foreword by John Bradshaw

Health Communications, Inc.
Deerfield Beach, Florida
www.hci-online.com

Library of Congress Cataloging-in-Publication Data

Miller, Keith.
    Compelled to control : recovering intimacy in broken relationships /
J. Keith Miller ; with a foreword by John Bradshaw. — Rev. ed.
      p. cm.
    Includes bibliographical references.
    ISBN 1-55874-461-4 (trade paper)
    1. Intimacy (Psychology)   2. Control (Psychology)
3. Interpersonal conflict.   4. Interpersonal relations.   I. Title.
BF575.I5M55 1997
158.2—dc21   97-5376
                                          CIP

©1992, 1997 J. Keith Miller
ISBN 1-55874-461-4

Publisher: Health Communications, Inc.
            3201 S.W. 15th Street
            Deerfield Beach, Florida 33442-8190

Cover design by Iris T. Slones.

To Andrea
with much love

CONTENTS

FOREWORD

Reading *Compelled to Control,* I had the eerie feeling that someone had been describing portions of my life to Keith Miller. Control is a very covert form of interpersonal violence. It is elusive and easy to deny. I remember once saying, "I'm not into controlling," at which point my family hit the deck with laughter. Control addiction is a key to understanding toxic shame and the self-destruction that it creates. It is the major barrier to intimacy.

Keith Miller presents this problem in concrete terms. It is Keith's genius to take very elusive and complicated material and make it understandable. In order to break the trance of our own "control madness," we have to see it in an objectified manner. Keith projects it on a three-dimensional screen. His own rigorous honesty is a living mirror that can inspire us to let go of our own addiction to control.

Keith refuses to offer cures. He offers soulful alternatives that present us with some new choices. There are 12 Steps we can take that will allow us to live our life more deeply. Each step asks us to fiercely commit to emotional self-honesty.

The fruit of this commitment is the possibility of intimacy. This is what everyone says they want, but hardly anyone is willing to give up control so that they can get it.

Part 3 of this book shows us how we can be intimate. Few of us have models of intimacy from our childhood. Keith outlines a practical and useful set of corrective experiences. *Anyone* can learn these exercises.

These chapters are really more than exercises. They are contexts whereby we can find depth and value in our lives. This book offers a new view of living life more deeply and enjoying the sacredness of being with our loved ones.

The man you will intimately encounter in this book is the mature Keith Miller, writing with clinical exactness and a rich background of life experience. I recommend this book and I predict it will be around for a very long time.

John Bradshaw

ACKNOWLEDGMENTS

First I want to thank my friend Bruce Larson for his comment in a conversation over 20 years ago, when he said: "The question, 'Who's in control here?' is what problems in intimate relationships are all about." This book is a result of the seed planted in my mind that day.

Many of the ideas in this book came to me years ago through the work of the late Paul Tournier, particularly the notion of the development of the Person and personages. During our friendship of more than 20 years, Paul was a model and a mentor for me in learning how to try to live out the Person-dialogue in my life and work. One year I studied carefully more than 20 of his books in succession. Some of these are included in the References and Selected Readings. My gratitude to Paul Tournier is incalculable.

This project has taught me in a new way what a team effort can be like. Vicki Spencer, Earl Henslin, Chuck and Carolyn

Huffman and Brooks Goldsmith read all or parts of the manuscript in a long and rough form and gave me suggestions that were very helpful. I did not take all of their advice, so I cannot blame them for any errors or misconceptions you may find in the finished book.

Betty Bartlett gave invaluable assistance in researching and sorting material from all kinds of sources that helped bring some perspective to a potentially myopic approach.

I want to thank editors and friends Marie Stilkind, Barbara Nichols, Naomi Lucks, Laurie McClung and Roy Carlisle. I will always be grateful for their very significant and concrete suggestions and guidance through our "process."

Ann Tucker, our secretary, kept pulling chestnuts out of the fire with one hand (unobtrusively and with a wonderful disposition), while typing and retyping the manuscript with the other.

Finally, I want to thank my wife, Andrea, who, at my request, made some crucial editorial suggestions and at one point restructured a particularly convoluted section so that we could all understand it. I'm very grateful to be married to someone who could give me the help and support I needed without being "compelled to control."

INTRODUCTION

Something is wrong in America.

A great, unseen vibration is shaking the country, causing ripples—then waves—of anxiety, stress, anger and shame. These waves sweep across boundaries of race, gender, class and education into the lives of almost everyone. Even those apparently protected by wealth, power and religion are not immune.

The vibration that threatens to shake us apart is fear.

We are a nation of people who fear we are not "enough." Deep in the recess of our hearts, in places we rarely reveal even to ourselves, we feel shameful and inadequate—and we're terrified someone will find out. We live in constant fear that our shortcomings will be exposed to family, to friends, to the world. We wake up at night reliving a mistake and feel overwhelmed with shame.

We worry. Our personal relationships don't satisfy, nor do other aspects of our lives. We are lonely and frustrated, our marriages often end in separation or divorce, our children are estranged. In an effort to "fix it" we may turn to compulsive or addictive behaviors, only to find that our unconscious attempts to cover the pain are unsuccessful, too, and bring only more loneliness and fear.

We look everywhere for someone or something outside of ourselves to blame or complain about, for something to kill the pain and bring us peace. But when we increase our efforts to find happiness, we come face to face with the uncomfortable feeling that we are "not doing it right." Our desperate strivings leave our fundamental issues untouched. Blaise Pascal, the French philosopher, viewed this phenomenon another way: "We are complaining about the ants at the picnic when the bears are eating our children."

Life in the last decade of the century has changed our experience of time. Our grandparents seemed to live a life of relative serenity, moving at a steady pace down the quiet river called Time, on a strong but invisible current. As they paddled downstream, they heard the sounds and felt the pulse of life in the river and on the surrounding banks. The slower pace of life allowed them to live more in harmony with the flow of the water, the chirping of birds on shore, the scudding of clouds overhead.

But in today's world, we race downstream as if on a giant speedboat, ignoring the natural current of the river that flows, we think, too slowly for us to do all we must do. We grapple with time, try to expand it in our accelerating race to get more and more accomplished in a day, a week, a year, than anyone in the past ever dreamed of doing. In our race against the clock, we have created a fast-paced reality in which a person who elects to work "only" an eight-hour day has little chance to get ahead or climb the corporate ladder. As we zip through our days and nights, all we see and hear of the river bank is an unrecognizable blur.

By some miracle our minds can move faster and faster—but our feelings cannot. They still conform to the steady flow of the river. When our minds and feelings don't match up, we learn to disconnect from our feelings. We believe our feelings hamper us in keeping up our overcommitted, accelerated pace.[1] Our emotions become sealed off or grossly exaggerated, and "emotion" becomes a dirty word. Even people related by the close bonds of family pass each other in the halls of their lives numbly, without really connecting.

Couples may eat together or even "make love," but our lives seem to be happening to other people. Gradually we move into our heads and live there, exhausted and alone, walled off from ourselves and from those closest to us. We vaguely hear the voices of our loved ones but tend to lose touch with their tender feelings—and with our own.

Our answer is to try frantically to gain control of our work, our schedule and our relationships. Our control attempts leave in their wake some very unhappy mates, lovers, children and parents who make up our nuclear families. Even our friends and co-workers are affected. There are few truly happy campers in the world of a controller.

There are millions of controllers—and we are burning out at an incredible rate. Our relationships are hollow, ragged, distant. We're exhausted and feel totally alone inside, even though we may be surrounded by people. Instead of achieving that serene and happy life that our frantic, controlling activity was supposed to produce, we have tense stomachs and bruised or broken relationships.

Fortunately, there is a way out and many controllers are taking it. It begins by emotionally disembarking from that speedboat. Some of us can step back and make a rational decision to jump off. Others are hurled off when our overcontrolling gets out of control, leaving us with unmanageable lives. To our horror, we discover that no matter how hard we try to tighten our grip, we are truly powerless.

For some controllers a light comes on. Gradually we become aware that we don't need another degree, a promotion to president of the corporation or a net worth in the millions to find serenity. We make an astonishing discovery: The only possible way to get control is by giving up controlling. It's a paradox that is not easy to comprehend. But it is so.

I know firsthand. In recent years I have traveled the United States on speaking engagements and have met thousands of people. Everywhere I go, I find concerned professionals and disturbed lay people who want to know how to solve problems in intimate family and romantic relationships.

My journeys have given me many opportunities to investigate the causes and cures of dysfunction in intimate relationships. Addiction is blamed, and co-dependence. But what is the underlying cause of addiction and co-dependence? I find that the culprit is usually the compulsion to control. It is a disease and it is reaching epidemic proportions.

This book is the culmination of my search to isolate the causes and cures of painful breakdowns in intimate relationships. Since 1987, I have written and coauthored four books exploring these issues.[2] *Compelled to Control* focuses specifically on the tragic loss of intimacy, and points to principles of healthy intimacy and new ways to live creatively.

In this book I will explore the process of recovery from the control disease and describe a way to make your way back to reality-oriented, loving relationships with spouses, lovers, children, parents and friends.

The recovery process brings the hope of living sanely—with courage and serenity.

THE 12 STEPS OF ALCOHOLICS ANONYMOUS

1. We admitted we were powerless over alcohol—that our lives had become unmanageable.
2. Came to believe that a Power greater than ourselves could restore us to sanity.
3. Made a decision to turn our will and our lives over to the care of God as we understood Him.
4. Made a searching and fearless moral inventory of ourselves.
5. Admitted to God, to ourselves and to another human being the exact nature of our wrongs.
6. Were entirely ready to have God remove all these defects of character.
7. Humbly asked Him to remove our shortcomings.
8. Made a list of all persons we had harmed and became willing to make amends to them all.
9. Made direct amends to such people wherever possible, except when to do so would injure them or others.

10. Continued to take personal inventory and when we were wrong promptly admitted it.
11. Sought through prayer and meditation to improve our conscious contact with God, as we understood Him, praying only for knowledge of His will for us and the power to carry that out.
12. Having had a spiritual awakening as the result of these steps, we tried to carry this message to alcoholics and to practice these principles in all our affairs.

PART ONE

The Compulsion
to Control

1
Falling Out of the Speedboat

Discovering the
Compulsion
to Control

"You're controlling my life!" Sue shouted at Roger.[1] Her face was contorted, beams of hot, red anger shooting from her eyes. "You interrogate me about every dime I spend and then *you* go out and buy a brand new set of golf clubs.

"Every weekend that football is on TV, we *have* to stay here so you can watch. You don't like my friends who don't like football, so we never see them any more. We only see *your* friends.

"You control what we eat by only eating beef and potatoes and making fun of vegetables in front of the children. I suppose you think it's *funny* when you say that if you wanted to eat a bush, you'd get a plateful from the side yard hedge!" Sue glared at her husband.

Roger stared back in disbelief. What was she talking about? *"I'm* controlling *your* life?" His voice began to rise. He could not believe she was serious. It seemed to him that they always did what Sue wanted. The voice that repeated over and over in Roger's head always seemed to say, "Make your wife happy. Be unselfish. Do what she wants and she'll love you."

"For God's sake, Sue, I've gone where you wanted to go on vacation, gone to movies, plays and symphonies because you wanted to, made love the way you wanted and deferred to you about how to raise the kids—including what and how much they can do at each age." As he spoke, Roger felt a rumbling rage churning up his stomach. This was the second most controlling woman he'd ever known—next to his mother. And Sue was saying *he* was controlling *her* life! Roger's face was flushed as he tried to get his voice under control. He said evenly, "You try to control me every chance you get. You've done it through our whole marriage and you're doing it now. I'm sick of fighting with you all the time. I don't know, maybe we should just call this whole sorry marriage off."

Now it was Sue's turn to look at Roger in disbelief. She turned and stalked out of the bedroom, slamming the door.

"And that," Roger told me, "was how the great war was declared that finally brought us to you for counseling."

Given my experience—with my own compulsion to control and that of many other couples equally as sophisticated and intelligent as Roger and Sue—I suspected that they were both controlling, but that each could only see the *other's* control behaviors. At any rate, neither of them knew how to stop. They told me that intimacy had gone completely out of their relationship, except for the occasional sex-truce when they were both frantic to make love. Roger said sadly, "I love Sue and want to be close to her again. But things are so screwed up now that we can't even talk without fighting, let alone begin to like each other again."

Although they didn't have the words for it yet, what Roger and Sue wanted to know was this: What is this compulsion to control that blocks our communication and pushes us farther and farther apart? How can we become intimate again? Do we even know what authentic intimacy is? Apparently most of us do not. A divorce rate in America of more than 50 percent attests to our lack of understanding about what makes relationships work—and what causes them to fail.

How I Fell Off the Boat

Several years ago, having finally achieved the kind of success I'd always hoped for, my life began to fall apart. I had been an executive in the oil exploration business, a marketing consultant, a personal counselor, a writer and lecturer. I had a degree in psychological counseling, and I had been told that I was intelligent and sensitive. I enjoyed my work and was recognized in my field, and I had an attractive and loving family.

Then, seemingly out of the blue, the people closest to me began to tell me that I "controlled" them. I didn't know what they were talking about. After all, I was generous with them, I loved them and I dreamed of their being beautiful, successful people—like I wanted to be. I was a serious Christian trying to live a good life. What I didn't see was that my controlling presence was like a giant amoeba that slowly spread over my intimate relationships, oozing silently and inexorably across other people's boundaries, until *my* vocation, *my* ideas and *my* expectations crowded out the space for their identities and growth. My controlling behaviors were somehow occupying their emotional territory. Instead of focusing time, attention and love on them, *my* life had become the central life in our relationships. My vocation and dreams absorbed my thinking and took up the space where their lives would have been free to develop.

The discovery that I had a compulsion to control everything and everybody in my life came as a real surprise to me—I had always seen myself as a sensitive person who wanted everyone to be free to do what they needed and wanted to do. Since I couldn't see that I was always taking up more than my share of relationships, I was angry when others didn't appreciate the good things I thought I was bringing them. The results were bewildering arguments, separations and the frightening sense that my life was out of control. I felt emotionally depressed and lonely, with an even stronger need to "get things under control"—although the idea of "control" never consciously crossed my mind.

I accelerated my social drinking to kill the pain of this bewildering turn of events and what I regarded as false accusations. I tried desperately to get some sanity and closeness back in my life and relationships. But the harder I worked to create a life in which we could all be happy, the more people around me seemed to rebel. As I tried to cover the pain of my bruised ego and sense of inadequacy, I worked even longer hours to get away from the pain.

Of course, I didn't see myself as compulsive; I just thought I was able to get more done than other people. I couldn't see that what I thought was a desire to get the most out of life was really a deeply rooted compulsion to control, which I manifested by working most of the time. I worked more and more and became increasingly irritated and defensive. The fear that my life and relationships would become unmanageable increased. I feared that my inadequacies would be revealed and cause my loved ones to leave. As my feelings became more intense, I felt that a giant spring was tightening, forcing to the surface deeply submerged fears of failing, of being alone and ashamed—fears I'd held in check since childhood.

As my loneliness progressed, I began to seek ways out of my dilemma. I kept reminding myself that I was a loving father and husband, a writer and counselor who had helped many people. But evidently those with whom I thought I had the most intimate connections saw me as a self-centered and controlling egomaniac. It was very disturbing.

The degree of resistance to seeing my own control issues is almost unbelievable to me now. I simply could not believe that I was a controlling person in my home, when all I wanted to be was a good husband and father. Yet the clear evidence of my family told me otherwise. Finally, after several personal tragedies—including a divorce, some serious financial reverses, and much loneliness and pain—I sought professional treatment. As my denial cracked open, I discovered that my controlling attempts to cover my pain had turned into compulsive behavior that qualified as an addiction in itself. I was using this behavior to "fix" my life and was only making things worse. Only when I became aware of my contribution to the problem could I begin making steps toward a new way of living.

That was more than 10 years ago. The help I received in treatment, and later in 12-Step programs, has transformed my life. The quality of my inner experience and personal relationships has changed so much that I often find myself awake in the middle of the night, weeping with gratitude.

All this time I have continued to work the 12 Steps and attend meetings several times a week. I live an increasingly comfortable life that suits what I feel is the *real* me. For the first time I feel a serene settledness about who I am and how I can relate intimately to those close to me. Although I fail often, I now have the tools to move from separation back to intimacy with people and with God.

Understanding the Compulsion to Control

When I decided to write about the insidious compulsion to control other people and how it destroys personal relationships, my friends either grimaced or smiled as they recognized themselves. "Oh my gosh, it's true. Hurry up and write that book. I need it."

As I listened to people, it soon became apparent that control problems have an impact on more than personal relationships. Many people offered examples of their self-defeating attempts to control business associates, medical practices and church groups. The resulting destruction of relationships and morale was devastating.

As I began the project, I intended to survey psychological abstracts on the compulsion to control to see if my research would turn up anything that would verify my idea that control is the major factor in destroying intimate relationships. But I ran into a stone wall: there was almost nothing. Though many psychologists and counselors were convinced that the attempt to control was the major issue in many dysfunctional relations, none could recommend anything in the literature to explain it satisfactorily.[2]

In the past few years, several writers, such as John Bradshaw and Pia Mellody, have noted that childhood abuse and the resulting shame, guilt, anger, pain and fear in adult children lead to controlling behaviors that, in turn, have a profound effect on people's ability to have functional intimate relationships. I could find no one who had put forth the notion that there may be a dynamic "disease-like" factor in the compulsion to control that could have an enormous influence in the destruction of relationships.

The compulsion to control infiltrates like a cancer, destroying not only intimate relationships, but the health and happiness of people in educational, religious, political and business institutions. I had the sense that we were a nation of controllers. But how was I to write about a truth that everyone suspects yet no one wants to admit?

The words of psychologist Carl Rogers helped me tremendously:

> I came to a conclusion which others have reached before, that in a new field, perhaps what is needed first is to steep oneself in the events, to approach the phenomena with as few preconceptions as possible, to take a naturalist's observational, descriptive approach to these events, and to draw forth the low-level inferences that seem most relative to the material itself.[3]

This is what I had done, albeit unconsciously. I had steeped myself in the experiences of recovery and dealing with the pain in the disease processes involved in addictions, compulsions and broken relationships for 10 years. And now, in a secular context, I was going to write about what I had discovered.

My first question was basic: What is the underlying inner struggle for control all about? And from where does the compulsion come?

2
What Is Controlling All About?

The Need to Do Things "Right"

At the very foundation of human experience there rages a silent hidden battle for self-esteem, for the unique identity and soul of each individual. We experience the combatants in this inner struggle as different parts of our selves, almost as two warring factions or personalities. One combatant is our private, inner person who wants to be authentic and develop into the best we can be. The other combatant is experienced as a shaming voice that seems bent on frightening and embarrassing us to keep us from risking intimacy and taking any action that might free us from itself. This powerful, hidden controlling faction sometimes seems to speak with more than one voice, as if it were an entire committee of shaming voices that seeks to run our lives and convince us that we have little or no value.

As the struggle between our childlike inner person and the powerful shaming voices is heightened, we become afraid that we will be revealed as being inadequate, as having no self-esteem. Although the source of this fear may be repressed, it often surfaces in close relationships. And the pain leads us to try to "get control of ourselves" and stop the pain. To do this we often get into compulsive and even addictive behaviors, including attempts to control people and their feelings about us, so we can feel better.

We try to present the "good side" of ourselves—the inner person of integrity—to the world, and to control and limit the shame voices. Sometimes we have remarkable success. But when we are alone or in intimate relationships—particularly with lovers, mates or family members—the controlling, shaming side often takes charge, and we feel anxious, insecure, blaming and ashamed.

When we try to relate to someone, we may even hear the shaming inner voices speaking to our loved one through our own voice. We wind up trying to control others by using the same abusive tactics as those used on us by our inner committee. We are astounded to realize that *although we fear and hate those shaming inner voices that cripple our self-esteem, we actually use those very same shaming tactics on others in attempts to control them.* The result is that our relationships are bruised and broken, and we fail to achieve true intimacy and happiness. Whether our style of controlling is openly aggressive or passive-aggressive, apparently *all of us* use the same control techniques from our own inner warfare to control those around us.

What is operating to bring us, however unwillingly, to such an impasse? I believe it is a condition I will call the control disease, which comes from an impaired ability to express painful emotions appropriately, especially shame, and the fear of being revealed as inadequate.[1] This fear is created by our shame voices as they engage our inner person in a battle for self-esteem, integrity and identity.

What Are Feelings For?

Some of the primary feelings are anger, pain, fear, joy, sadness, guilt, loneliness and shame. When allowed to function normally, our feelings constitute a signal system from the unconscious awareness of our body to the consciousness of our minds, telling us what our reality is. When we pay attention to these signals, we can make congruent, reality-oriented decisions about our lives.

Why is it so difficult to claim these feelings and see them for the positive, nurturing forces they are? I have come to believe that this is because many of us in this country have been trained to believe that feelings, especially painful ones, are "bad." As a small boy I remember being told, "Don't be angry with your brother. It's not nice to be angry." This was after he had just kicked me very hard. Anger was not okay at our house. Where this is our experience, we often try to get rid of, tranquilize, or talk ourselves and other people out of unpleasant feelings.

If you have ever participated in a small meeting, perhaps in a school or a religious learning group, you may have noticed that when a member begins crying, the rush to stop the person's pain is immediate. People hop up like a bunch of rabbits, patting the weeping person and handing him or her tissues. We often do this not to make the person feel better, but because *we* can't stand to *see* pain.

When we are allowed to sit in our pain and weep if we need to, however, a curious thing happens. At the bottom of the pain, we frequently find the insight we need to solve the problem that caused the pain.

Pain can be the doorway to healing. In that sense, pain is valuable because it helps us discover important insights. Yet, when we are in the compulsion to control, we try to control tears and deny pain—ours and everyone else's.

So many of us have come to believe that feelings such as anger, pain and fear are "bad" and signs of weakness. We think that the job of our therapy or recovery is to get rid of the pain as quickly as possible. But the Swiss psychiatrist, Dr. Paul Tournier, said he hoped that his patients would not get rid of their pain until they knew the meaning of it.

Our inner pain acts like an alarm system to warn us of impending danger. Unfortunately, we tend to turn these messages off. For example, let's suppose the fire alarm went off in the building where you are right now, and you say to someone near you, "Would you please turn that alarm off? It's interrupting my reading." Because you don't acknowledge the meaning of a fire alarm, you are likely to get burned. In similar fashion, when we take tranquilizers for our pain, we may turn off the "alarm" without attending to the message it may have for us.

When things seem to go wrong in our lives and our thoughts are scrambled or uncertain, if we can learn to listen, our bodies and feelings can tell us how we are being affected by what is happening. We can hear messages from the deepest part of us that can save our lives and bring peace and healing into our relationships.

The pain of a stress-related disease or the emotional distress of living is trying to tell us something that can help us or even save our lives. Unless we listen to our pain, it will get worse, until we either die or deal with the problem. But it is not the *pain* that will kill us; it is the disease or the stress issue it is pointing to. The feeling of pain is our friend trying to save us, to lead us out of danger into recovery.

Pain also burns through the outer shell of an experience to reveal the inner kernel of truth about life itself that we cannot grasp by ordinary learning methods. For instance, until the pain in my life and relationships became very intense, I could not face my denial about being an almost totally self-centered controller.

Now I have to share a strange occurrence. As I was writing the above, I suddenly became alarmed. I had a pain in my chest. I thought it was either acute indigestion—which I almost never have—or a heart attack. I began to imagine that I was dying. I even wrote a note to my wife telling her I love her. But then I remembered what Paul Tournier had taught me. I stopped working, lay down and "listened to the pain," asking my Higher Power what the message of pain was for me. As clear as a bell, the answer came: "Your body is screaming at you that you have more commitments than you can handle! Change! Do something to cut some of those commitments."

The clarity and truth of this message struck me so forcefully that I got up and made notes on how to change my schedule. Then I called and put off the deadline for this book. The relief from the pain was almost immediate. But my former habit would have been to take something to silence the pain so that I could keep writing.

Shame: The Monster Behind Control

The feelings most relevant to the compulsion to control are *shame* and *guilt.* Guilt is the alarm signal that allows us to be moral beings. A feeling of guilt tells us when we have transgressed an ethical principle that is important to us. When we do so, an alarm signal goes off in our minds and we have an uncomfortable feeling. We "feel guilty." Guilt happens to "good" people who have done "bad" things that are contrary to their highest values, and it allows them to make corrections.

Shame feels like guilt, but there are two basic differences. First, to feel shame it is not necessary to have transgressed an ethical value. If we just make a mistake—an error of any kind, revealing the fact that we are imperfect—an overwhelming feeling of shame, of feeling less-than or worthless, can come over us. Shame is often a pervasive feeling that can be activated by another feeling. For example, I might become angry at my wife and have shame about the anger because I was told as a child that "good" people don't get angry.

Second, the basic feeling of shame is one of being a bad, defective person or worthless. With guilt we feel like a good person who has done a bad thing; with shame we feel like a bad person for being imperfect. Shame, then, is about one's self-esteem.[2]

An appropriate level of shame reminds us that we are not

God, but fallible people. This signal can give us humility and keep us from offending others. It doesn't take much of a shame feeling to get our attention, since it is so strong and is attached directly to our pride. When our feelings of shame threaten to overwhelm us, then we have too much.

The fear of being revealed as a failure, as not being "enough" somehow, is a primary feeling that leads to the compulsion to control other people. When we were children, the fear of being inadequate and shameful was tied to our terror of being deserted or rejected and we had little control over getting what we needed. To counteract that basic terror, we have evidently been trying all our lives in various ways to "get control" of life. This includes controlling other people.

Exaggerated Feelings Are Destructive

When our feelings, especially our feelings of shame, are too big, they are no longer beneficial. For instance, anger is good but rage is destructive. Fear is healthy in the face of danger, but panic attacks are not. When the feelings are greatly exaggerated, their signals are no longer effective and they frighten us. The experience of exaggerated feelings is what can give feelings their bad name.

If we are not in touch with our feelings, we are like ships without radar, moving through the fog. We have the volume turned off on the signal system from our unconscious, which would tell us when we were drifting into abusive, addictive or otherwise dangerous behavioral waters. It is no wonder we jump back and forth in this feeling-intensive disease, since our feelings are either exaggerated, inaccurate or unavailable. One minute we smile and try to please people, the next minute we are furious with them. We bob around in our emotional sea, seeming to change direction every day.

Some of us may have been afraid, angry or ashamed all our lives. Others may have felt inferior, abnormal or defective and had no idea why. We may have been so angry constantly that we could barely keep the lid on, or so filled with shyness or shame that we could barely function. Yet we are not sure where this anger, shyness or shame came from. When somebody says something mildly irritating, we over-react and blow up. If our mate burns the toast, we may find ourselves showing our displeasure by throwing it across the room.

At other times we may shame the people around us by pointing out their mistakes, thereby controlling them with anger or shame. Though we are horrified at these outbursts, we can't seem to control our swollen feelings. Life gets fearful and chaotic.

We say to ourselves, "Why am I so angry? There is nothing to be mad about." Or, "Why do I feel so embarrassed about a simple mistake like being late or failing to return a telephone call?" When we have exaggerated feelings, we may be carrying feelings from another generation that were dumped into our lives by caregivers who weren't handling their own feelings responsibly. The magnitude of our swollen feelings threatens to overwhelm us, and we become baffled and fearful. We fight like crazy to "keep things under control," to not be angry or not be so embarrassed at mistakes. We fear what might happen if the enormous load of feelings we are carrying should ever get out of hand. We fear these feelings may destroy us.

But how do feelings get to be too big?[3]

Carried Feelings

There is a symbolic sense in which we can "shovel" our unwanted feelings into other people's lives, as you might shovel coal into a wagon. If the other people have no boundaries, they may wind up "carrying" (experiencing as their own) those strong feelings for us. Here is a very simplistic example of the way we sometimes have exaggerated feelings because we are carrying the feelings of someone else.

Let's say I have been sending my son to college and he is about to graduate. It's his last term. In fact, his last final exam is tomorrow. He calls me about 7:00 P.M. and says, "Dad, I'm sorry, but I'm going to fail my final exam tomorrow. You told me to be honest. I've been out drinking this week and I didn't study. Oh, and I just checked at the registrar's office, and if I don't pass that test, I have to go to college for an additional year because I have to pass this course to graduate, and they only offer it in the spring."

All of a sudden he has my total attention. I'm paying for his college and I can envision his failure costing $20,000 for another year. I feel fear. I say, "Listen, I'll tell you what you do. You hire a tutor. I don't care what you have to pay him. Hire the tutor and stay up all night studying. It won't hurt you one night." I cheer him on. "Go for it! You can do it, son! You can make it!" But he says, "Naw, Dad, I think I'll just do what you told me when I was a little boy—just turn it over to God and get a good night's sleep."

I say with a frantic edge to my voice, "Not tonight!" But he says, "Naw, Dad, I'm just gonna go to bed."

"No, wait!" I plead. "Call me tomorrow and let me know how you did." Clunk. He hangs up.

All night long I lie awake, staring into the darkness, filled with fear for my son's future. I picture this kid as a 45-year-old man. He is sitting in an old rocking chair on a rickety front porch of a broken-down shanty. People are passing by, but nobody looks at him. The elbows have worn out of his sweater. He's got a big dirty beard with bugs in it. He smells bad, and he's alone in this little cracker-box house. (We controllers have an amazing imagination when it comes to fantasizing awful things that we fear are going to happen to people we love.)

I'm scared to death. I feel panicky. *And it's not even my exam!* All the next day I'm upset and my anxiety level is off the chart. By evening he still hasn't called me, so at about 7:30 P.M., I call.

"How did it go?" I say as calmly as I can.

"How did what go?"

"What do you mean *what?* Your exam!" By this time I'm a wreck. My nerves are almost shredded from no sleep and 24 hours of anxiety.

He says happily, "Oh, I made a 96."

A 96? Now I'm furious. "A 96!" I exclaim. I am about to chew him out for scaring me so much, when he interrupts me and says, "You know, Dad, I want to tell you something. You really are a good counselor. Last night after I talked to you, I went to bed and slept like a baby."

You know what that kid had done? He had taken the fear that he wasn't willing to handle responsibly, dumped it into the telephone, and I had caught it and carried it for him for 24 hours.

An imaginary story about a college kid is sort of funny. But it was not funny when your parents or mine did not handle feelings responsibly. They may have been "macho and in control" or maybe even very religious, moral and ethical, but they seemed to have no "bad" feelings. They had been taught that people who were *really* adequate were not supposed to have feelings like fear, shame and anger. So what did they do with these feelings? They dumped them unwittingly into the nearest handy receptacle: children with no boundaries. *Us!*

In recovery, we learn to give excessive feelings back symbolically to the person from whom we got them. When we do this, our normal feelings can become positive guides that move us toward embracing reality and experiencing authentic intimacy. My own experience of symbolically returning such feelings to my parents was one of the most transforming of my life.

On the other hand, you may not have seething emotional chaos. You may instead be the kind of person who reacts by repressing the whole problem, sealing your feelings off and becoming numb. You don't have many conscious feelings at all.

People who are not conscious of their feelings may come from the same kind of dysfunctional family as chaotic "over-feelers." The difference is that "non-feelers" may become *like* the "shameless" caregivers who victimized them, causing others to keep on feeling their fear and shame. Most people who attend Adult Children of Alcoholics meetings have identified with the *victim,* the child they were who was victimized. But the people most likely to dump feelings unconsciously on those around them are the ones who repress strong feelings themselves, and who think of the "feeling" group as weak and immature.

Reactions to the same abusive treatment by the same caregiver can be entirely different. For example, let's say that twin boys are abused by their father so that both are victims of his rage. One grows up and lives as a fearful victim all his life, while the other identifies with his father, the abuser, and becomes a macho abuser himself, unconscious of any of his victim feelings. While at a conscious level such people feel superior and believe that they can handle things, their fear of being seen as inadequate and out of control often runs deep. They "get rid" of their denied negative feelings by dumping them on unsuspecting wives, children or co-workers. But the abuser's repression may lead to physical illnesses.

The numb abuser-type has more difficulty entering recovery than the victim who feels the pain, because the abusers don't even know anything is wrong. Victim-type co-dependents often marry these numb abusers and create frustrating pseudo-intimate relationships called "love addictions" or "co-addicted relationships."[4]

What We Do When the Pain Is Too Big

Until my last few years in recovery, I was afraid almost every day. Yet I was so out of touch with my feelings that I thought my fear was just excitement. I have experienced a lot of fear about my adequacy. I have been afraid of you, the reader. I have been a lonely boy and man, who felt both inadequate and grandiose. I felt I was supposed to be great and outstanding, but at the same time I was filled with feelings of shame when I didn't do exceptionally well at something I set my mind to do. Above all, I have been afraid that you would find out that I was afraid.

I became a dedicated athlete, playing basketball for many years. I was only six feet tall, yet I played very hard with enormous men so that I'd be "the man." I broke my ankle playing basketball; my ribs were torn loose from the sternum while wrestling when I was a college student. As an adult in business, I had to prove I wasn't afraid so that I could continue to hide my shame and the fear that it engendered. To do this, I drove myself physically and emotionally, and took unnecessary risks.

I've talked to several professional athletes who are still performing to please a father or somebody important they felt they never impressed in childhood. They hear their fathers' voices inside sending shame messages to their frightened little persons. They expend superhuman and courageous effort to prove themselves and avoid facing internalized shame and condemnation.

The amazing thing about our denial of the "control disease" in this country is that it often causes us to see emotional sickness as spiritual health. For example, a minister who is a religious work addict often looks like a saint to his congregation. But the disease is progressive. After a while any addiction quits working and the pain and shame return. When this happens, the addict or controller must switch to another chemical or addictive behavior to cover his pain.

A look at some notorious televangelists illustrates the point. When they were caught in sexual escapades outside their marriages, people said, "Oh, they have been awful and immoral all the time." But the truth may be that when work failed to quiet their pain, they stopped using religious work addiction and began using sex instead. Their behavior was so out of character that it surprised everyone, sometimes including themselves, and their misery was so profound that they usually chose to blame others—even Satan, that ultimate negative force outside themselves.

My Own Introduction to the Control Disease

Although I have written several books on relationships, I have a difficult time living them out at close range. I have a special problem with commitment because I now know I am a control freak. I find it difficult to convince the people around me that when I am controlling them, I am really only trying to help them. They just don't buy that. I have a sneaking feeling that I am not alone among counselors, writers and speakers in being in denial of my compulsion to control. Perhaps there is an unconscious conspiracy of silence that would explain the lack

of information in the literature about some of the problems
caused by the compulsion to control other people. Although I
can't speak for others in the helping professions, I believe that
an unusually strong need to "help" may, in itself, spring from or
lead to the control disease. For me, it was certainly true.

Who has more control than a counselor? When you come in
as a client, you have an hour to get help and then you must
leave. You soon realize that you must be vulnerable or you can't
get relief from your pain. If you challenge us or are rude, we can
refuse to see you, claiming that you are resistant to therapy. We
have to be nice enough not to drive you away, so we can't be
too overt in our controlling. We learn to use passive-aggressive
control techniques as we guide people through their emotional
and spiritual diseases. We are in a very controlling role even if
our espoused method is "nondirective," as mine is. In my case
the nature of what I was doing fit perfectly into my need to control, combined with my need to be seen as a nondirective, loving helper of people. This may have worked in my vocation, but
this passive controlling was devastating when I brought it
home at night.

A Vivid Picture of the Control Disease

The Judeo-Christian Bible, along with some of the writings of
Buddhism, Hinduism and several other major religions and
philosophies, concurs with the Big Book of Alcoholics
Anonymous when it says that even an alcoholic's basic problem is not alcohol but control. The description given in the Big
Book describes the mindset of all kinds of controllers, not just
alcoholic ones:

> Each person is like an actor who wants to run the whole
> show. He is forever trying to arrange the lights, the ballet, the
> scenery and the rest of the players in his own way. If his
> arrangements would only stay put. If only people would do as
> he wished, the show would be great. Everybody, including him-
> self, would be pleased. Life would be wonderful. In trying to

make these arrangements, our actor may sometimes be quite virtuous. He may be kind, considerate, patient, generous, even modest and self-sacrificing. On the other hand he may be mean, egotistical, selfish and dishonest, but as in most humans, he is more likely to have varied traits. What usually happens? The show doesn't come off very well. He begins to think life doesn't treat him right. He tries to exert himself more. He becomes, on the next occasion, still more demanding or gracious, as the case may be. Still the play does not suit him. Admitting he may be somewhat at fault, he is sure the other people are more to blame. He becomes angry, indignant, self-pitying. What is his basic trouble? Is he not a self-seeker when trying to be kind? Is he not a victim of a delusion that he can get satisfaction and happiness out of this world if he only manages well? Is it not evident to all of the rest of the players that these are the things he wants? And do not each of his actions make each of them want to retaliate, snatch all they can get out of the show? Is he not, even in his best moments, a producer of confusion rather than of harmony?[5]

The primary problem of an addict is not a chemical, behavior or person. It is the compulsive tendency to play God and control other people's lives. This spiritual control disease is seen clearly in people who have an identifiable addiction such as alcohol, food, work or sex.

You may say, "But I'm not an addict." If this is true, I'm glad your circumstances haven't taken you in that direction. *But I believe that the same spiritual control disease often exists in people who have not identified a specific addiction.* It certainly is evident in the lives of those who are co-dependent.

Co-dependence is the name Pia Mellody and other therapists have given to the emotional and spiritual disease that underlies all other addictions and that fuels and accelerates the addictive process. This disease (discussed at some length in chapter 5) accounts for much of the personal dysfunction that must be dealt with after the chemical or compulsive behavior is stopped during the recovery process. Being addicted to a person, particularly an addictive person, is considered "love addiction."[6]

The same control disease that is evident in the lives of readily observable addicts strikes co-dependents and love addicts with the same devastating results. Those who are hooked into a relationship with an addict lose themselves to a great degree. They bring suffering or dysfunction upon themselves and others as a result of focusing excessively on someone else's needs. Partners of alcoholics, sex addicts, gambling addicts or drug addicts usually fall into the co-addict, co-dependent or love addict category. These are serious diseases and can be fatal, since they lead to lack of self-care and "careless" accidents.

The Underlying Cause of It All

It seems evident that there is an even more basic compulsion than the compulsion to ingest alcohol or other chemicals, or to act out the distorted, immature symptoms of co-dependence or love addiction. Beneath the addictions, and even beneath co-dependence, is a spiritual "disease" that sets people up to be controlling.

The cycle seems to start this way: When people become parents, their need to control their children and make them into a preconceived image sets up the cycle of co-dependence as the child builds an unreal personality to please them. This stifling of the child's natural aptitudes makes the child feel shame about his natural self. Because of a deep sense of disempowerment, this "manufactured" personality leads the child to attempt to control others' reality—the way they feel about the child—and possibly to addiction in adult life. It is a horrifying downward spiral with shame, low self-esteem and the compulsion to control at its center.

This disease of the spirit is nurtured by the crippling, self-defeating shame voices and feelings within us. Insidiously, our disease leads us to try to control others in a shaming or "fixing" way that destroys our personal relationships. This can be true even for those who have never engaged in a pattern of overt addictive behavior.

How Controlling Others Bruises or Breaks Our Relationships

I believe we are compelled to control by the nature of our own inner struggles and the shame that fuels them, and that the attempt to control others is the basic factor in the destruction of love between us and them, God and our inner child. Sometimes in the middle of the night, I wake up feeling scared, inadequate and worthless, convinced the whole world will condemn me as "less than" and shameful. My automatic, initial response to these fears is to try in whatever way possible to get control of myself, my circumstances and the people from whom I need love and affirmation. The compulsion to control is a powerful but invisible force that causes conflict and can leave a trail of destroyed relationships.

Sooner or later those we try to control respond negatively, either by openly retaliating or by withholding love and attention as a more subtle act of revenge. But what we often cannot see is that our *own* control issues may be at the bottom of the painful loneliness we experience. If we are involved in an addiction, we may think that stopping the addiction will heal our relationships. But experience indicates that this is not true.

Whether addicted or not, I believe that those of us who have the control disease have a very low tolerance for painful emotions such as shame, fear and pain. When these intolerable emotions threaten to surface, we have urgent internal drives that kick in automatically to help us find a way to cope. We try one or more of the following emotional pain relievers:

1. Intensifying our attempts to control others
2. Engaging in one or more addictions
3. Perfectionism
4. Acting out other characteristics of co-dependence

Each of these attempts to cope is an attempt to cover or tranquilize our pain. All of them bury our feelings deeper in denial and distort our reality more completely. We then cannot hear the messages our pain could give us to maintain our health and win our inner battle to live in reality and self-esteem.

Intensifying Our Control as an Emotional Painkiller

Since we can't see our own denied feelings and don't know where they come from, it seems natural to project the cause of these outbursts onto those around us. We figure that what the people around us are doing is causing the outsized anger or shame, and we set out to change *them* so we can be more comfortable. In this way, these denied feelings and projections lead to increased attempts to control others so that our own pain will let up.

This underlying compulsion to control people is a distorted version of the natural, healthy and basic drive to control our environment. The problem arises when we focus our need to control the environment onto *people.*

Engaging in Addictions as an Emotional Painkiller

When changing other people doesn't work (or while the control attempts are going on), we may take up addictive substances to quiet the increasing pain—"just until things get under control." The addictive behavior becomes a kind of ritual we perform to blot out the reality of our fear and shame. We appear to ourselves to be winning the inner battle for worth because our addiction temporarily blots out the shame voices.

It seems to work like this: When our control attempts lead to rejection and inner turmoil, we have increasingly intense feelings of shame, pain and fear. When these powerful feelings threaten to overwhelm us, they lead us to choose (or increase the use of) addictive substances and behaviors that will quiet the pain. Our bruised inner person can then hide in the addictive behavior. This process of hiding one's true person and running from pain into a behavior that feels good often culminates in a full-blown addiction.

We can use alcohol, food and work in addictive ways to blot out awareness that we are not in control when we think we should be. Substance abusers learn to drink or take drugs at the first hint of depression, pain or any hint of rejection. Many people use food as a way to block out the shame of the control disease. Spiritually, overeating is the same as drinking to oblivion: food is just a different painkiller. Working is another common addiction, an attractive one—our culture loves work addicts, often rewarding them with extra status, respect and money.

When we engage in these addictions and compulsions, we numb our feelings so that we can't see or hear what's happening to us in our lives. Since we are not in touch with our reality, we can't be intimate. Although society blesses work addicts, it curses the results of pain-solutions like addictions to chemicals, overeating, sex and gambling. But in every case the underlying issue seems to be an attempt to stop the pain, to feel good, to be somebody—even if only for an hour.

Unfortunately, attempting to alleviate our pain with an addictive chemical, behavior or relationship only makes the problem worse. One of the most profound changes that occurs when an addiction takes control is that all other intimate relationships are immediately distanced. It is as if the addict had taken a totally absorbing lover in the midst of a good marriage relationship. Addicts seem to put on blinders and become oblivious to the dysfunctional and selfish things they do to people, and to the exclusive nature of the priority given to the new "lover," be it a chemical, behavior or person.

Addicts not only lose contact with their primary intimate relationship; they lose any good relationships they had with their inner selves and with a Higher Power or God.

Men and women in this condition have cried out since the beginning of time, "How can I get rid of this haunting and lonely feeling of being separated from peace and happiness, from other people—and from myself?" They often feel that any sense of a good life—happy, intimate relationships particularly—is impossible. Unfortunately, we often try to overcome this sort of isolation in the most self-defeating ways imaginable: we either exaggerate or become increasingly subtle and intense in our attempts to control people. Whatever style we choose, we become more compulsive about the need to control, until we destroy the intimacy and sometimes the relationships themselves that we long for.

Prescription Drugs Can Become Addictive

Some people take tranquilizers to kill the pain of the control disease. Many doctors either aren't aware of or are in denial about the fact that some common tranquilizers are addictive. Yet many people who wouldn't touch alcohol or illegal drugs take tranquilizers regularly to calm the pain of unsuccessful controlling.

I'm *not* saying one should not take tranquilizers that have been prescribed by a physician, since they can stabilize those who have chemical imbalances and can help overwrought people get calm enough to begin therapy or treatment. But the *continuing* use of tranquilizers to "calm feelings" *without additional therapy* can be addictive and disastrous. The tragedy is that the tranquilizers sometimes numb the pain that might lead the sufferer to recovery.

Even Our Emotions Can Become Addictive

I believe it is possible to use a strong, painful emotion to distract oneself from other, more threatening realities. Even resentment can be addictive.

Let's say that my Aunt Minnie criticizes my children and my wife, and looks around the house as if she has a dirt detector, noticing everything that isn't perfect. I don't like Aunt Minnie. Now she is coming to our house and I think, "I am in recovery. I'm so grateful I don't have to resent Aunt Minnie this trip." I am a person who prays, so I say, "God, thank you for making it possible for me not to resent Aunt Minnie. She is coming for Thanksgiving and I am *not* going to resent her."

Yet she walks in the house and suddenly—against my will— I'm *filled* with resentment!

What does that sound like? It sounds like an alcoholic. "I'm *not* going to drink; thank you, God, for making it so that I don't have to drink anymore; I'm not giving in to drink." Then *pow*—

I've taken a drink! The exaggerated feelings themselves can become addictive: the pain, fear, resentment, shame, guilt, anger, self-pity, sadness, loneliness. It is possible to make one feeling, such as fear or jealousy, into our Higher Power, and to focus on that feeling, blotting out the other painful feelings.

Perfectionism: A Major Symptom of the Control Disease

If we were trained not to feel or express our feelings in order to be accepted, then they may be too threatening to face at all. If so, we may not have any "bad feelings," and we may tend to look down on people who do. For instance, in my family anger was absolutely unacceptable. Fear was acceptable if it was combined with enough sadness, but males really weren't supposed to experience either one. In such families, perfectionism often creeps in. We may get obsessive and try to make sure everything and everybody at our house is perfect. People had better hang their towels straight and put things back where they got them in our homes, or they are in big trouble when we become perfectionists.

Perfectionism is a primary symptom of the compulsion to control. By controlling all the tiny details that we can see and keeping them all in "perfect order," we can temporarily avoid facing the deep feelings and relationship issues in our lives that we fear may get out of control. But if we can't "do it perfectly" (whatever "it" is), we may experience a great deal of fear. We become obsessive about everything we do. For example, I was so afraid I would fail in school that I made A's to avoid F's. I was overkilling constantly to make sure I didn't fail at anything and "lose control." I did almost everything like that, while trying to look cool and masculine. I was keeping my perfectionism carefully hidden. This dishonesty and unreality became more extreme until I practically read Shakespeare behind a *Playboy* so I wouldn't appear to be a "sissy." Naturally, with this fear of being revealed as inadequate and shamed, being authentically intimate with a girlfriend and sharing my reality was out of the question.

Perfectionism is the *opposite* of trust and faith. Faith is surrendering the outcome of our efforts and our lives to a Higher Power. Perfectionism is compulsively having everything under control and *not* surrendered. And yet, ironically, obsessive religious perfectionists are sometimes considered outstanding models. People who feel great shame and fear if they do not pray with clockwork regularity, read the Bible, help at church, and constantly help feed and clothe people are often held up as saints.

It is not the *doing* of these things that is a problem, but the *motivation* for doing them. Rather than responding to love and serenity received from a spiritually healthy connection to God, many religious people feel *compelled* to participate in religious activities in a rigid manner because they unconsciously fear their inner shame voices if they do not. They have no idea that it is just another denied aspect of the compulsion to control.

Perfectionists trapped in the control compulsion often feel very lonely and isolated—even if they are affirmed by parents, teachers and communities where they live. When perfectionistic children grow up and begin to seek intimate relationships, their perfectionism may backfire. The stress of living with a perfectionist's standards is intolerable to most people. The perfectionist is often baffled and confused by the fact that others seem unable to see the light about being neater and prompter, and working harder. It is very uncomfortable to be close to a person compelled to control every detail in his environment.

Figure 2.1 summarizes what I have said so far about how the control disease operates.

When we controllers experience the painful consequences of our behavior, one would think we would end our own misery by simply stopping our controlling. Yet it seems that more often, we do the opposite. This is because other factors are at work, such as denial and the resulting state of being out of touch with many aspects of reality. Also, our concepts of both intimacy and spirituality are often distorted. In the next chapter, we'll look at how these additional factors affect the control disease.

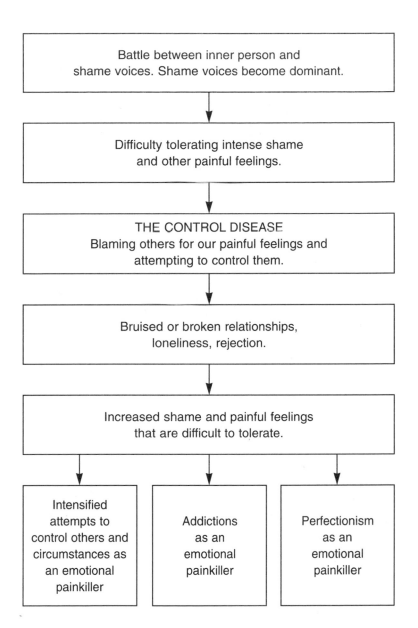

Figure 2.1. The Control Disease

3

Additional Factors That Operate in the Control Disease

As we have seen so far, the control disease is set up by our inner battle with the shame voices, combined with our low or nonexistent ability to tolerate shame and other painful feelings. We blame other people for our pain, rather than recognizing the source as our own inner battle, and try to control them to make ourselves more comfortable.

One factor that keeps us caught in this misery-producing process is *denial*. Denial is a process by which we take thoughts and feelings that are not acceptable to our conscious image of who we have to be and bury them in our unconscious. We do this by a sort of mental sleight of hand so that we aren't aware that we ever *had* the thoughts or feelings.

It's as if our unacceptable feelings were giant beach balls that we stuff out of sight beneath the surface of our consciousness. Once the ball is hidden, we can pretend—and come to believe—that all is well. But it takes a lot of emotional energy to hold these repressed feelings down. So when the pressure in our lives and relationships gets too great, the beach ball—our repressed feelings—may suddenly pop up into our consciousness. Now our overblown feelings of fear, anger, sadness, guilt, shame or loneliness suddenly feel as if they may overwhelm us.

Conversely, if our denied thoughts and feelings do not jump out in exaggerated forms, our feelings about those close to us may instead disappear into the numbness of an emotional fog bank. Since our shame voices do not want us to share our feelings, as this would lead us to our reality (which is that we are not shameful people), they tell us that our feelings are not acceptable and that they will reveal our weakness and inadequacy (as our parents had once told us). So an unconscious part of our inner warfare is the battle to hide our painful feelings from ourselves. Yet the hiding of feelings enervates us and keeps us from the healing and love we could receive from sharing intimately.

Because of denial, we are out of touch with all kinds of reality. Frederick Buechner has said that "reality is the way things are." We who have the control disease are out of touch with the way things are in our lives; not only our feelings but our perceptions about ourselves, our value, even some of our attitudes and dreams, as well as the effects we have on other people.

The way we comprehend our personal reality is often skewed and stunted very early in life. As children, almost all of us are mistreated one way or another—physically, emotionally or intellectually. When children are abused, they react by shutting down and finding a way to adapt. Usually they hide thoughts and feelings that are too dangerous and develop coping behaviors to try to gain their parents' approval. They exert an extraordinary effort to obtain this approval. In the extreme, the struggle to control themselves and their parents' responses to them means that many children lose touch with important parts of their own personal reality. They bury the "dangerous" thoughts and feelings that disturb them or their caregivers. The result is that choked-off emotions never develop in a healthy way, remaining at a very childish level.

Our chronological age is often far ahead of our emotional age. We walk around in adult bodies doing grown-up things like graduating from college, getting good jobs and getting married. But we may have lost sight of what we really wanted to do or be, what we truly feel or think.

Internal conflict can create full-time stress. Our shame voices prevent our facing the true thoughts and feelings of our inner person for fear we may be judged inadequate. Overcontrol may gain us a certain kind of acceptance, but something incredibly valuable is lost in the process. The tragedy is that what we lose may be the best thing about us, our unique contribution to the world.

We may be out of touch with reality in three areas: ourselves, our relationships with others and our relationship with God.

Our Reality About Ourselves

You may be familiar with the parody of a lost-and-found ad that Barbara Johnson talks about: "Lost: Dog with three legs. Left ear missing. Blind in right eye. Tail broken. Recently castrated. Answers to the name of Lucky." Some of us have been living like that for years, out of touch with the reality of our own lives.

Several years ago I read an article in *Esquire* magazine about Paul Newman, written by one of his best friends. The author, who'd been out to dinner with Newman before he wrote his article, said:

> Paul Newman makes a lot of money. He gives to charities when he wants to, he loves his wife, he makes movies when he wants to, he drives race cars when he wants to and he has that face that looks like it did when he was 23. God, by the time I got home (from dinner) I wanted to shoot myself.[1]

The article was written by Robert Redford.

It seems all of us, no matter how exalted by society, may have a distorted view when it comes to seeing our own reality.

Our Reality About Our Relationships with Others

Our perception about ourselves is not the only thing that's not clear. Our reality about the way things are between ourselves and other people, especially in intimate relationships, is also skewed. Because of our inner shame and fear, we give others power over us that they otherwise would not have. Grown men in the prime of life cower before their wives or aging mothers and fathers. We may run, emotionally or physically, from people we give power to.

Sometimes we look down on, victimize or abuse other people who give power to us because of *their* shame and fear. And although we can seldom *see* ourselves doing these things, we may do them with grown children, lovers, mates, parents, friends and co-workers. In all these ways and others, our skewed reality about people around us can cripple our lives— and theirs.

Ultimate Reality: Our Reality About God

We who have the control disease are also unclear about the Ultimate Reality. The idea of a loving, supportive Higher Power or God is very important for recovery from addictions, co-dependence and the control disease. But having been abused by our first "Higher Powers"—our parents—we consider the idea of surrender to God to be abhorrent and sometimes terrifying.[2] For this reason, many people don't want a Higher Power or spirituality to be a part of recovery or of the 12 Steps.

Addicts get this part of their reality further twisted. When addicts get hooked by their chemical or behavior of choice—be it alcohol, drugs, food, work, gambling or a specific person—that chemical or behavior becomes the most compelling intimate relationship in their lives. It *becomes* their Higher Power or God.

Love addicts tend to make other people—wife, husband, child, lover—their Higher Power. These are natural shifts from having had a dysfunctional parent as an abusive Higher Power. If we don't make some person our Higher Power, we may make some goal or profession, our appearance, money, or even an addiction our Higher Power. Because this spiritual disease beneath all our addictions is progressive, our reality eventually gets so out of balance that we are finally controlled by the harmful Higher Power we have selected. Since this Higher Power is not God but an addiction or dysfunctional relationship, our serenity and intimate relationships are destroyed or seriously bruised. This is one reason why I believe the disease underlying addictions is a spiritual disease. We surrender our lives to a false and destructive god.

On the other hand, our reality can become skewed about who God is in a way that leads *us* to become a Higher Power and to try to control others' reality. We may even have or be several Higher Powers at once. For example, my wife may make me her Higher Power and defer to me and also to her parents, and I may make our children my Higher Power. When she's gone, I let my children work me over and get their way. But at the same time, I may make my parents or alcohol or making money my High Powers; this controlling works in all kinds of ways. When we have more than one Higher Power, we experience painful soul-ripping dilemmas, when the will of one Higher Power conflicts with that of another.

We Cannot See That Our View of Reality Is Skewed

Because our conception of reality is shrouded in denial we are not aware that our reality is skewed. Here we are, grown people, and our perception of reality in the crucial relationships of our lives is not accurate. But we can't *see* this fact because of denial. Since we are honest people, we look at our lives and say, "I don't see that I am doing anything wrong." So we blame *other* people for our unhappiness and sense of separation from our inner selves. We blame people close to us whose reality—about

us, about them, about God—is different from ours. We're impatient and resentful about their failure to understand the way
things are (*our* perceptions and expectations), never seeing that
we are the ones in delusion. When this situation exists, it seems
only natural that we should try to control people in order to get
them and their reality straightened out.

Reality, Intimacy and Spirituality

It's interesting how the meaning of significant words in a culture can change over the years. Piet Heim, the Danish philosopher, once said that important words are like old houses at the
beach with the windows knocked out: meanings blow in and
out of them like the wind from the sea. With that in mind, I
want to define two terms that help delineate the major symptoms of the control disease. The meanings of these words have
changed in the past few years, perhaps because of the denial
present in the control disease. The terms are "intimate" and
"spiritual."

What Is Authentic Intimacy?

The term *intimacy* has lost its original meaning. Many contemporary people equate intimacy almost exclusively with sex.
If I said I was intimate with my wife last night, you would
probably think I had sex with her.

But more accurately, intimacy means that I *share my personal
reality* with you—especially my thoughts and feelings—and *you
do not try to "fix" me,* or try to adjust my reality by telling me that
I "shouldn't feel" what I have expressed. Then you share your
personal reality with me, and I do not "fix" you. When this
mutual sharing of reality in a nonjudgmental and caring atmosphere is taking place, the participants are emotional equals, not
teacher-student or doctor-patient.[3] One of the primary consequences of the compulsion to control is loss of the ability to be
intimate in this way.

When our shame voices threaten to overwhelm our fearful

inner person with messages about our worthlessness, the last thing we want to do is to share *that* reality. When the fear and shame symptoms are flaring, authentic intimacy seems out of the question because sharing our "failure to be adequate" is terrifying. The shame voices inside tell us we would surely be rejected if our secret—that we are not enough—were known.

The Relationship of Sex to Intimacy

Intimacy is one of the key experiences and goals of the institution of marriage, which allows two people to participate in the creation of new human lives. This being true, what would be a good way to design their physical bodies? If you were an engineer designing bodies, how better than male and female, since you can actually—physically and symbolically—be inside each other in sexual intercourse? In human beings, sex can be seen as an outward physical symbol of the shared intimacy of a couple's life together.

But many men and women, even in marriage, can't be intimate. They are either not in touch with their personal reality, or they are terrified to share that reality because of the fear of past rejection as a child by parents or siblings when they attempted intimacy. So many relationships include very little true intimacy, even though the partners think the sort of guarded interchange they experience *is* intimacy.

Men in our culture seem to have an especially difficult problem with sharing feelings and being intimate. When men can't share their intimate feelings, they often compensate and go for sex instead, thinking sex *is* intimacy. But we Americans have demonstrated convincingly that "having sex" will not make us secure as men—or women. In the long haul, sex does not create the atmosphere of acceptance that sharing one's reality does. So sex without intimacy doesn't solve the basic inner warfare to determine if we are valuable.

What Does Spirituality Have to Do with Authentic Intimacy?

When I use the word *spiritual* in connection with this compulsion to control, I do not mean "religious." In recovery programs, the term spiritual deals with the degree to which we are in touch with reality. Spiritual people are in touch with their own reality (thoughts, feelings, behaviors, physical and sexual reality), with the reality of the people, places and things around them, and also with ultimate reality, God. For example, a religious person may know a lot *about* God in an intellectual, once-removed sense, but a spiritual person is *in touch* with God on a deeper, more intuitive and interactive level. As we shall see, in the life of a spiritual person, a relationship with God becomes increasingly personal and central to growth and personal development.

The best traditional Christian spirituality, for example, has always included the idea that a truly spiritual person is trying continually to put aside all dishonest, immoral and "unreal" aspects of life to stand before God as a person unencumbered by the unreality of false, grandiose and self-defeating behavior. The remarkable thing about those judged to be truly spiritual is that they are able to discern the unreality in situations and people around them as well as in themselves. The Hebrew prophets Jesus and Paul are classic examples in biblical history.

In other religious traditions, too, spirituality manifests as an ability to recognize reality. For example, Gandhi discerned that passive resistance by a nation of people would be stronger than military forays of fanatic but outgunned zealots. He was able to see that a groundswell of self-esteem coming from the cooperation of weak people could be stronger than the mighty will of the British Empire. This sort of discernment concerning what's real in a situation is fairly common among authentically spiritual people.

The recovery movement, in producing a people who must connect with God and share intimately the reality of their lives and relationships in order to survive, has unwittingly created a powerful contemporary spirituality.

Sharing our reality through authentic intimacy is one of the most tender experiences in human life. It is the basis for spiritual communication and recovery. In intimate sharing we feel accepted *just as we are*, without having to earn that acceptance through perfect performances. Feelings of gratitude and love often grow spontaneously in an intimate encounter; when intimacy occurs, there is seldom a sound from the shame voices.

Authentic intimacy is spiritual. Sex may or may not be. And when sex does not "fix" our feelings, we often blame that failure on our partner and switch to another partner, claiming that "intimacy" isn't working. Many people who cannot share their personal reality tend to think the problem with the relationship is that they have the wrong partner. It doesn't occur to them that *they* may be the ones who do not know how to be intimate.

The compulsion to control blocks us from being spiritual and intimate by keeping us in denial about our own reality, and in fear about sharing it. We must deny any reality that might affect our ability to control others and their feelings about us.

What Happens When We Can't Be Spiritual?

We tend to become controlling and abusive when we cannot be spiritual. We are not only out of touch with our own reality, but we teach our families to be out of touch with their reality in order that we look adequate, pious or religious. Because we are out of touch with the reality that we are not perfect, we often judge and condemn people who make mistakes, and try to straighten them out and control them.

I have done this. I was so in denial and so afraid of being discovered as inadequate that I went along with the judgments of family members, friends and institutions when they condemned and rejected certain people because they weren't "doing it right." I was out of touch with my thoughts and feelings and I didn't trust my own perceptions. My need for acceptance was so great that I was afraid to trust my reality when it conflicted with that of powerful people I depended on for emotional and financial support.

Those of us who are not able to be spiritual or intimate are not in touch with *many* aspects of our reality, including our compulsion to control. But these inhibiting and dysfunctional fears and behaviors are often alive and hiding in our inner basement, buried far beneath—and yet affecting—the private conversations of our close relationships.

What Heals Our Bruised and Broken Relationships?

As we shall see, an important part of recovery is to learn to experience our feelings and to read the signals of our bodies better. Each feeling brings us a beneficial tool for living. Our fear brings us wisdom that can keep us from many catastrophes; our sadness gives us our healing; our anger gives us strength. At the beginning of this century, American women finally got angry enough to do something about their status as second-class citizens without even the right to vote. Their anger gave them the strength to stand up and fight for their rights. This is true of every social change that I can think of in this country's history. At the heart of the movement for change was a group of angry people whose anger gave them the strength to face the powers in control. This is also true in abusive relationships. When we get angry enough, we will confront an abuser or find the courage to leave and get help.

But many feelings have a bad name. And our carried feelings are often so strong and frightening that many of us don't even want feelings. But a large part of recovery is getting back in touch with our *own* feelings in a functional way so that they can stabilize us. When we pay attention to them, our feelings tell us what's going on that we might not be aware of. Like the colors from a color chart, feelings add vividness and richness to our lives. When we cannot experience our feelings because of denial, life may seem like a black-and-white movie with a scratchy soundtrack. But when we are in recovery and get back in touch with our feelings, life can explode around us in Technicolor with Surround Sound.

The further we go toward being fully functional human

beings, the more we are in touch with our reality and the reality of others, and the more spiritual we can become. If we are spiritual, we can respond in sane and caring ways to the realities of our lives and the lives of those around us, even when they differ. But when we are not in touch with reality, then we cannot be spiritual.

4
The Child's Journey
How We Develop the Urge to "Get Control"

The secret journey of each person chronicles the battle between the inner person and the fear of not being enough. This journey shapes almost every aspect of our lives as we attempt to gain control of our inner selves, our environment and our relationships. My own story is one example of how such a journey can begin.

The Beginnings of My Own Need for Control

My first awareness of wanting control and not having it had to do with my father. I desperately wanted him to love me and play with me. But he evidently couldn't love me—at least not in a way I could understand. He appeared to love (and like) my brother, who was five years older and was named after him. Dad took Earle hunting and fishing. I wanted to go too, but he wouldn't let me. He said, "You're too little and you're liable to get hurt, son. You stay home." I would cling to his leg as they left, but he would shake me off and leave with my brother, while I howled in shame and anger. So I went to my mother in tears. I just ached. I said, "What's the matter with me that Daddy won't take me, Mom? I want to go with Daddy and Earle."

"Don't worry, son," she said. "In just a few years your brother will get interested in the neighborhood kids and he'll want to go out and play with them. Then it will be your turn, and Daddy will take you."

Although I tried unsuccessfully to get to go each time, I continued to hope that someday Dad would take me. Sure enough, as the years passed, my brother went out to play baseball with the neighborhood kids. My time had arrived. But when that day came, my dad had lost all interest in hunting and fishing. He took me once that I can remember, and he invited a friend of mine whose dad had died when my friend was a baby. I was very resentful because I had always dreamed of this day alone with my father. To say the least, I was not nice to my friend when Dad paid more attention to him than he did to me. I remember with intense pain that my father rebuked me severely for "being so selfish when my friend didn't even have a father." I wanted to scream at him, "I don't either!" But I didn't. I just felt filled with hurt, anger and shame, which my father had unwittingly dumped on me rather than face his absence as a father. As far as I remember, he never took me out fishing again. I had no way to tell my father that my bad behavior was about my love for him and my ache to be loved by him as a son. I thought, "I must be a horrible person. Even my own daddy doesn't want to play with me."

I must have made an unconscious decision at about that time to go for achievement. Getting affirmation for achieving was a lot more controllable than getting love. Affirmation for doing well felt like love. People paid attention to me and seemed to want to be around me when I was successful. I could study hard and make good grades. I could practice all day and become an athlete. And when I did well, coaches and other men would say, "Good boy!" and it felt as I imagined love from a father would feel.

But inside I was terrified of love and intimacy and didn't feel as if I had it or deserved it. "After all," I reasoned, "if my own dad doesn't love me, why would anybody else?"

I became an overachiever. Looking back, it was as if I had a jet strapped to my back. When I woke up in the morning, that jet would fire and I just hoped I didn't hit a wall! I was going *somewhere,* but my compulsive power far exceeded my ability to make choices and steer rationally through the opportunities for achievement. I was what poet Robert Bly calls an upward climber, a golden boy. I went for it.

Although I was outwardly a star, I was secretly afraid of people. My mother had enmeshed with me and became a brilliant resident coach in my life. She taught me that I could—and should—be a great man. Though I was basically shy, for her benefit I had to "look like" I was good with people and at ease with them.[1] With her help, I discovered some bizarre ways to achieve the appearance of people-control. For example, in my high school of 3,500 students, I memorized almost everybody's name from the yearbook—and spoke to them by name. I was elected to many high offices at school, including president of the senior class and "king" of the school. And why not? I was often the only one running for office who knew all the voters.

Imagine a teenage kid being lonely and driven enough to pay that kind of price. I was on top and never appreciated it. I felt I had arrived there through deceit, not because I was lovable. My shame voices worked me over inside. The amazing thing is that many of my fellow students probably *did* like me. I was sincere about liking them. But sealed inside my perfectionism and my compulsive need to achieve, I couldn't *receive* the very affirmation I was working for. And of course, authentic intimacy was out of the question. Whom could I allow to see the scared little boy under "the king's" robes?

The Person and the Personages

In spite of the reams of pages that have been written about child development, we do not know exactly how a child develops through the maze of dysfunction present in many homes into a functioning, interdependent person who can be authentically intimate.

As the study of co-dependence and addictions has progressed, it is apparent that we need new ways to describe the development of the human personality. These new ways of thinking must take into consideration the family systems model and the almost universal existence of co-dependence among contemporary Westerners. Further, this co-dependence leads to intense stress and increases the compulsive controlling and addictive behaviors that have been adopted to quiet the pain and fear of being shamed.

To take a fresh look at how a child may develop into a functional intimate person, I want to present a model formulated by Dr. Paul Tournier, founder of the worldwide movement among physicians and counselors called *Groupe Medicine de la Personne.*[2]

Tournier's work is particularly appropriate to the issues of a child growing up in the midst of two opposing forces in a family: (1) the strong (though often unrecognized) need in parents to control; and (2) the powerful need in the child for intimacy and close relating that ideally becomes the matrix in which healthy spiritual and emotional development can take place.

Since virtually all parents with the control disease have a tendency to try to make their child into their own image (or the image the parents have chosen for the child), their unconscious attempts to change the child's inherent reality threatens the child's basic integrity. Developmental psychology makes it clear that crucial experiences can happen to different children at different ages. But I want to present a rough and simplistic picture of how a child may develop in a home in which the parents, however well-meaning, have the control disease.

From the time it is born, a child responds naturally and openly to people and events with tears, anger, contentment or laughter. Dr. Tournier calls this natural responding self the child's Person. (This natural Person is very like the precious inner child described in recovery literature. From this point on in this book, I will capitalize the "P" in Person when it refers to that inner consciousness of self who is the protagonist in the story of each individual's battle for self-worth and integrity.) Along with the needs for food, water, air and sleep, the child has an inherent need to be loved by its parents or caretakers. All goes well as long as the natural responses of the child are not in conflict with the desires or beliefs of the parent figures.

For instance, a guest may be entranced with the cooing noises baby Herkimer is making in his highchair while waiting for breakfast. His mother is delighted. But five minutes later, when Herkimer blows a mouthful of warm oatmeal all over the guest's face and clothes—a trick very similar to cooing, from the baby's perspective—the mother, furious, says "No!" and slaps the baby's hand. After a few more tries the baby realizes that he will not get love from Mother by blowing oatmeal on guests. So the child learns to hide the urge to blow oatmeal. This is a part of civilizing the child.

But there is a problem: the child has never hidden anything. Remember that the little Person responds naturally and honestly. How, then, do we learn to hide our unacceptable feelings and desires?

Tournier says that something begins to happen at this point that allows us to hide our feelings and thoughts from others. We develop what he calls *personages*.[3] A personage is like a mask painted with expressions of the various thoughts and feelings that I believe will keep me from being rejected by caregivers and that will bring me their love and acceptance. As we grow up, all of us develop several of these personages/personalities, each with its own language.

For example, a child develops a "parent" personage for dealing with parents complete with a language all its own. As the child grows older, other personages come into being to deal with teachers (the "well-behaved, good student" personage), peers (the "macho athlete" personage) and other significant groups.

Developing personages is a normal coping behavior. But when we are disconnected from our inner Person, we often try frantically to identify with one or more of our personages. Some years ago my wife, Andrea, wrote of how she realized she had unconsciously developed different personages as an adult in order to cope with life as a single woman:

> I discovered that I had developed different versions of myself which reflected the different personalities or lives I was living. At work I was supposed to be the competent businesswoman from 8:00 to 5:00 weekdays. On the social scene, however, I wanted to be a fun, swinging date, so on evenings and weekends, I was a different person with a different look and a different sound.
>
> The third version was the regular church-attending Christian on Sunday. And at church my clothes, attitudes and style of relating were very different from those of the businesswoman or the swinging single. To my parents I was yet another person as I tried to appear to be the capable, optimistic daughter who was still the same sweet girl but more mature. They were 950 miles away and couldn't really know, so I would write letters that were carefully worded to portray this image, and on my visits home I would try to be that person.
>
> I wasn't consciously dishonest in being these different people. It was just that I had unconsciously developed these personages to help me deal successfully with the various roles I found myself in—in a way that would win approval from the people to whom I was trying to relate.
>
> Down inside was the real me, trying to pull all the strings and remember all the rules—codes of behavior, styles of dress and so on, in each of my lives. In reality I was often scared, hurt and lonely, and I was almost desperate. But somehow these different facades helped me appear to be in control and to cope for a while.[4]

In every major area of our lives, in order to counteract our parents' original attempts to control, we develop a personage to portray to the people in authority in our group the proper image for gaining love or approval—regardless of what the actual feelings of our inner Person may be. Unfortunately, when we are in our personages, we cannot be intimate because we cannot share our real feelings.

The personage is not opaque like the "mask" of the persona we speak of in our society. A personage is partially transparent: I am afraid for you to see through my personage for fear that you'll reject me, yet I also long for you to see through the personage to the person hiding behind it, hoping that we can be intimate. But in actual experience we are usually not conscious of the fact that we even have personages. We just vaguely notice that we speak and act differently in different situations, and that we hesitate to be vulnerable and transparent.

Developing the Protective Personage and Learning to Keep Secrets

Children learn to develop personages to keep controllers from destroying their private integrity. Often this begins when we learn that we can have a secret life. Let's look at one example:

Sally is four years old and living in a small town. Her mother walks with her to nursery school. For the first few days, they walk a certain way by the park. Then Mom says, "You can also go around another way, behind the stores." Finally, when Sally has learned how to get to and from nursery school well, Mom sends her off one morning on her own.

At this point in life, Sally thinks her mother knows everything she's thinking because she says things like, "Sally, you've got to go potty," and she's right every time.

When Sally comes home from school by herself, her mother says, "How did you go to school?"

Sally replies, "By the park."

"How did you come home?"

"Behind the stores."

"What did the teacher say?" And on and on.

In a few days Sally gets very sick of this probing—after all, Mom knows what she's thinking, so why all the questions? After a week she longs for a little privacy.

So one day when Sally gets home from school her mother says, "Which way did you go to school?" Well, she really went behind the stores, but she's desperate for some relief from the probing. So Sally is going to do something today she's never done before—lie. She takes a deep breath and says, "I went by the park," and grits her teeth, getting ready for the ax to fall, because she still thinks Mom can read her mind.

But instead her mother continues as usual "What did the teacher say?" All of sudden Sally realizes that her mother *doesn't know everything she's thinking!* This opens up tremendous possibilities. Now she can lead two lives, and her mother won't even know about one of them. She can have unacceptable feelings and think unacceptable thoughts and not be criticized. But she can also dream her own beautiful and creative dreams about the future without being laughed at or publicly shamed. Suddenly she has realized that she can *keep a secret!*

Keeping Secrets

The ability to keep a secret is one of the first steps to developing the protective boundaries that allow healthy people to own and develop their own aptitudes and abilities, and a private spiritual life. Tournier felt that learning to keep a secret was the first movement toward becoming a mature Person capable of authentic intimacy.

When children are able to keep a secret, they can hide those impulses to do things that are unacceptable to controlling parents and that might lose their love—like the urge to blow warm oatmeal on visitors. But this ability to hide thoughts and feelings can also lead to some frightening misunderstandings that may shape the child's life in a dysfunctional direction.

For example, let's say that our little oatmeal-blower, Herkimer, is a few months older. He is out in the backyard playing in the rain. In the mud near the neighbor's driveway he finds a rubber dolly. He thinks, "Aha, a treasure!" He doesn't even know what a rubber dolly is. He doesn't have any sisters and has never seen a dolly up close.

So he brings this one in to his daddy, who is a professional athlete, and says, "Look, Daddy, look what I've found," and hugs the dolly to his face. But his father's reaction is bewildering and strong.

"Put that dolly down!" he shouts. "Real boys don't play with dollies!" His neck is very red and his eyes are glowering with a strange look. As adults we can see that the father is afraid the child will grow up to be gay, or that someone might think the father isn't masculine if his son plays with dolls. But all the little boy realizes is that he has been rejected for sharing his real feelings.

He now knows it's dangerous to show your treasures to your daddy: he'll hate you. The child may begin to get the idea that his daddy hates boys who like anything feminine. So he may reject girls and have trouble relating to them or even to his own feminine side. This boy may develop a personage of a macho athlete to display around his father or other boys in order to win the father's love. He may hide his *anima* or feminine side altogether, including his artistic or poetic ability, and may even be ashamed to reveal it by the time he is a young adult— though secretly he has kept his Person alive through his thoughts, dreams and reading. If he had lost touch with his Person because of his father's shaming abuse, then he could have wound up a lonely, separate and lost person who could not be intimate. So being able to keep secrets can be valuable. Without intimate feedback, however, unexamined secrets can lead to being irrationally ashamed about authentic aspects of one's personality.

Personages Can Be Helpful as Well as Isolating

It is good to remember that not only are personages psychological defenses, they can also be healthy social costumes. Although personages are developed in reaction to caretakers whose expectations are threatening to the child's innate personality, the conscious use of personages will always be necessary to some degree for healthy social interactions. For example, it is appropriate to wear conservative clothes to a formal business meeting, even though we may feel that our *real* selves are more comfortable in blue jeans and well-worn sneakers.

Personages become dysfunctional when they are opposed to the Person's moral values, or when we are so separated from our Person that we are no longer aware that we are not being ourselves when we adopt a certain personage. This can happen when we have unconsciously adopted as our basic identity a personage that is far from that of the true Person within—who has been deserted and replaced. Any time a personage is seen by an individual as being his authentic self, then denial is taking place and true intimate relationships are virtually impossible. For instance, a social leader may see himself as totally honest and committed to justice and truth, when in fact he is acting unethically. Such a person probably finds being authentically intimate very difficult because a significant part of his reality is not available for him to choose to share.

How the Rewards of Affirmation Shape Personages

Since children must have love and approval, or at least attention, they are very likely to repeat certain rewarded behaviors when the price is right.

Let's say, for example, that our little Herkimer, who doesn't get much attention from his parents at home, is sitting in church one morning between his parents as they are listening to the sermon. He is looking around and trying not to go nuts from boredom while waiting for the sermon to be over. Suddenly the preacher makes a very dramatic point and there is a hush in the room. The little boy says in a clear resonant voice, "A-men!" And in that instant a minister is born.

Little Herkimer begins to realize that he can get the love he's starved for by praying and saying religious things, whether or not he feels religious inside. And as he hears his daddy tell a friend how well his boy prays at home, the religious interest is set. He is only three years old, but when he prays, magic takes place: his daddy loves him. By the time Herkimer is 35, he may be the senior minister of his church.

But the danger of these hidden love transactions is that when Herkimer hits mid-life, he may feel very anxious and go to counseling, only to realize that he wasn't *called* to the ministry by God, but *sent* by his mother and father. *They* wanted him to be a minister. He needed the love so much, first from them and then the others in the church, that he never stopped to consider what he, the Person inside, wanted to do and be in life, apart from their wishes. It was his religious personage who got ordained, and in mid-life his true Person, who got repressed as a child, is now crying out for some attention before it's too late. The dysfunctional behaviors that he may engage in to feel good and have intimacy constitute what is sometimes called a mid-life crisis.

Many people appear to get their vocational identities the way little Herkimer did. Bank presidents sometimes have bank president sons who may wind up 30 years later hating money and banking. The same thing can happen to businesspeople, housewives, teachers, lawyers, doctors, nurses—anyone.

Making Unhealthy Choices to Win Love

If children do not develop a strong Person-identity of their own, they may make all kinds of bad choices in order to win their parents' or other people's love. For instance, let's say that little Millie grows up having been trained to be a "mommy." Everything is all right until she passes a certain age when young women in her parents' culture are "supposed to be" married.

A year or so after that age, if young Millie is not married, her mother gets very tense. She is threatened because her own ego is on the line. After all, Millie is her daughter; if Mother has done a good job, Millie should have caught a husband by now—or so the co-dependent script goes. So the mother may start putting pressure on Millie to get serious about somebody she's dating.

Millie is not thinking about marriage at this time—or wasn't until her mother began saying things like, "You aren't getting any younger, you know," and "Look how many of your friends are getting married." As a result, although Millie isn't really sure her boyfriend is whom she ought to marry, she accelerates the relationship. Since she does want to get married someday, she falls in love with the idea of marrying the boyfriend. Six months later the wedding takes place.

It's no wonder thousands of women—and men—have not only marital problems but identity problems in their marriages. Many of them got married to get love or approval from a third party, a parent or a social group.

If the marriage does break up, the daughter may come home and become a child again under the loving but controlling and crippling rule of concerned parents she has never broken with—even though this "child" may be 35 and have four children. The Person of the divorced daughter may be filled with shame and anger as the voices outside and inside scream in the night that she is a failure and less than everyone else.

On the other hand, some children who don't make the adolescent break stay single because, whether subtly or openly, their mothers or fathers communicate the controlling and shaming message that they need the child in order to survive. Some parents get sick and want the child to stay single and take care of them. Often a daughter gets this assignment. This may happen even though the parent says (although with a long face), "No, no, you go on and live your life. Don't worry, I'll get along somehow." But the child receives a very different message at a subconscious level. And the interior shaming voices complete the welding of the chain to the parent. There may be situations in which not living one's own life in order to care for a parent is justified. But except in rare cases, I know of very few instances where the "child" who feels coerced into staying single is able to develop into a whole Person with a strong identity who can maintain an intimate relationship. The parent usually says the child made a free choice. But the question of how free the choice was is a crucial issue in the inner battle for integrity in the development of the Person.

If you have never been married, do not think I am saying, "Your parents kept you from it." I am only saying that in some cases, crippling co-dependent behaviors take place as a result of unspoken control messages from parents. The person who remains single wonders how it all happened and why intimate relationships are so difficult.

Some of the most serious adjustment problems in adult life spring from such unspoken control messages sent between parents and children. The children are filled with the fear of being worthless if they do not meet their parents'—and their friends'—expectations. Because of child abuse this fear of being shamed is often greater than the strength of the stunted inner Person, longing to live as a free individual. The tragedy is that since most co-dependent families are stuck in the secret-keeping stage, the children can't check out the reality of their feelings and fears.

Choosing to Reveal Your Secrets

Being able to keep a secret is only the first step in this process toward becoming an intimate and interdependent Person. If you can keep secrets, you can become an individual. But to be a whole Person with an identity who is capable of intimacy and spiritual growth, one must move to a second stage. The secret-keeper must become free to choose to tell another person his secrets, what is inside the Person. This sharing can be the doorway to a life of intimacy and creative spiritual growth. This is not to say that to be a whole Person you *must* tell all that is inside. (I agree with those who think that if you are *unable* to keep a secret or have private areas of your own, you may be neurotic and have no boundaries.)

But to be a whole person, one should be able to *choose to* tell his secrets if and when it seems appropriate. Many people simply can't tell their true feelings or personal thoughts under any circumstances. The threat of the inner shame voices is too scary.

For example, for many of us, our first perfectly normal questions and comments about sex were unacceptable to our parents. The horrified looks on their faces and the way they shook their heads deluged us with their shame. So even as adults, many people feel shameful—worthless or guilty—when engaging in sexual thoughts or sexual behavior of any kind, even within a marriage.

Not only did we feel shame about "bad" things (like sex), but we also may have been shamed by having parents ignore or put down our dreams about a vocation of which they didn't approve. Such personal vocational dreams are often plunged into secrecy and hidden from the world forever because when we were little our parents said "no," or we thought they did when we mentioned being a writer, a football player, a business tycoon, a doctor or a ballerina. So we hid our dreams inside. And those "unacceptable" thoughts and dreams become a secret nest of disappointment in which our thwarted Persons often hide.

The Fear of Being Known as We Really Are

Since we only remember the emotional impact (at age two or three) of our parents' rejection, we tend to grow up with inordinate fears of showing anyone else our true inner Person, that part of us with all of the cherished feelings and dreams that we felt were unacceptable. This inability to share our true feelings keeps us from the intimacy by which we could verify that our true identity—our true Person—is actually okay and even lovable. As we grow up physically and achieve marks of status in our vocational worlds, sometimes we are even more afraid of intimacy because it might reveal the vast chasm between the adequacy of our vocational personage and our fearful and inexperienced Person inside, haunted by the fear of failure.

Hiding Feelings and Thoughts Can Cause an Identity Crisis

As we grow up, we often polish our outer personages until we honestly believe they are the real us. But when the personages get to be substantially different from our inner Person, we become worried and afraid that our "deception" will be discovered. Andrea, who in the earlier illustration told how she separated her life into four personages, put it this way:

But then the four neatly divided areas of my life started getting fractured and tangled up. I started having trouble remembering where I had met people when I saw them in a different setting. If I had met a man at work and saw him at church, I couldn't remember where I'd met him. But if I saw him back at work again, I'd know who he was instantly. And I also got caught if one person knew me in more than one setting because she could see differences. And that made me uneasy. If someone knew me at work and then saw me out at a singles party, I felt the differences presented a shocking contrast. The contrast between my church self and my social self *really* seemed great. And the harder I tried to make all these parts of me fit together, the more inadequate, shaky, empty and incomplete I seemed to be inside, since I didn't know who the real me was. It felt like I was looking at my reflection in a broken mirror with the pieces of my four lives overlapping, but not really presenting one congruent picture.[5]

It's easy to see why control of people and circumstances was so important to Andrea and why intimate sharing was so difficult. To keep peace within ourselves and to still the discounting voices, we often repress our true feelings, keeping them out of sight in our unconscious. When we do, we may find ourselves feeling numb, out of touch with the beauty and joy of life going on around us. We may also see ourselves living by values a part of us doesn't approve of. Sometimes we find to our dismay that we don't know what our true Persons are really like anymore, or what we want to do or be, even as physically mature adults.

These repressed honest feelings, good and bad, seem to have a great deal of emotional energy connected to them. Certainly it takes a lot of energy to hold such feelings down; and like pushing beach balls under water, the further we push them under, the greater the pressure and psychic energy it takes to keep them out of our sight. This can be experienced as an anxious "stress" feeling. Almost everything about this process keeps us from the very intimate sharing that could bring perspective and reality-checking into play. Without intimate sharing, the pressure builds inside.

Many people who have "beach-balled" their true Persons become very anxious "for no reason at all" and feel "out of touch" with themselves. Pretty soon the anxiety may become unmanageable, and they may experience all kinds of neurotic and unreasonable fears. The feelings that accompany this sort of experience can constitute a real identity crisis.

Andrea describes such an identity crisis, in which she realized that she was almost completely out of touch with her Person's needs, wants and dreams:

> It was morning and I lay in bed, eyes wide open, realizing that I was alone in the house. It was raining outside and still dark. My husband had left early and would not be back until late that evening. It was a Saturday, and I didn't have to go to work or get out of bed or do anything. So, as I lay there staring at the ceiling, I started imagining what I would do if I didn't have to do what anybody else expected me to do—my mother, my husband, my boss. I expanded the fantasy in my mind to include more questions like: What if I had all the money I needed or could go anywhere I wanted to go, then what would I do?
>
> There was absolutely no answer. I couldn't even make a list to choose from. My mind went blank and I panicked. There I was, with a whole long day ahead of me, and I couldn't think of anything I wanted to do, either on a grand scale or a small scale, like brush my teeth or make a cup of coffee.
>
> I finally got up, automatically got into my robe and made coffee. I walked around the living room holding a cup of hot coffee and thinking about that blank in my mind. All I could think of doing was to fantasize asking my mother or husband or boss what to do, imagine an answer from one of them, and then to do it. I was stunned that morning to realize that I'd never dared to think of what I was really like and what I might want to do or be as a person apart from my family's expectations.[6]

Later on we will deal with ways we can begin to shuck off the control others exert over us and begin to choose appropriate ways to express our personages and free our repressed Persons.

At this point, however, I want to describe the intentional and unintentional child abuse that keep the precious little Person in each child from developing its potential, and make the child repress his true Person who lies beneath the personages that dominate the lives of so many adults. This separation from our true Person leaves us feeling lonely, uncertain of who we are, afraid of being controlled and terrified of authentic intimacy.

5
The Many Faces of "Child Abuse"

How Controlling Parents Set Up
the Compulsion to Control

What Is a Mature Adult, and How Does a Helpless Child Become One?

What are the characteristics of a fully functional adult, one who is able to have satisfying intimate relationships with others, self and God? How does a helpless child get to be such an adult?

The answers to these questions for many people have come through an understanding of the "disease" of co-dependence as contrasted with the characteristics of a healthy, non-co-dependent adult.

According to Pia Mellody, a mature, healthy adult has at least these five characteristics:

1. A sense of being valuable along with the ability to experience self-esteem.

2. A sense of personal safety and security in normal relationships because one can set good physical, sexual, emotional
   and spiritual/intellectual boundaries (and can also respect
   others' boundaries).
3. The ability to own and express one's reality honestly,
   especially imperfection.
4. The ability to determine and take care of one's adult needs
   and wants without exaggerated shame or fear, and to ask
   for help when needed.
5. The ability to express one's reality moderately (not in
   extremes) in a way that is age-appropriate.[1]

These mature adult traits develop out of natural characteristics with which every child is born. These early characteristics
are related to the mature traits of adults as seeds are related to
flowers:

1. Each child is by nature valuable.
2. Each child is by nature vulnerable.
3. Each child is by nature imperfect.
4. Each child is by nature needing, wanting and dependent.
5. Each child is by nature immature.

The job of the parents is to nurture these natural characteristics, so that by adulthood the child will have learned the skills
necessary to live freely and creatively, embodying the five characteristics of a mature adult.

But when parents don't respect and nurture these traits
properly, and instead try to force the child to meet the parents'
expectations, then the child's emotional and spiritual development is arrested. The child develops "unnatural" coping
behaviors, an unnatural personage, to please the parents, avoid
punishment and get approval and attention from others. These
personage behaviors are often not consonant with the child's
natural characteristics, abilities and inclinations. When the
child grows up, these unnatural behaviors become the primary
symptoms of co-dependence.

Co-dependence, then, is basically a condition of immaturity, a dysfunctional way of living that inhibits intimacy and spirituality. It is these co-dependent personages we are likely to meet when we set out to have adult intimate relationships. In the experience of closeness, the co-dependent has great needs to control reality lest he be revealed to the other as not being "enough" or not doing life "right," and being shamed or rejected. This makes intimacy elusive and usually destroys or deflects any intimacy bridges coming from another.

Although some co-dependent adults fear being revealed as inadequate, and thereby rejected, others, having experienced the same abuse, almost totally repress any feelings of inadequacy or fear of rejection. They believe they were born superior, and that they should "be in charge of," control or fix others. These are usually much harder to treat because they have buried their fears of shame and rejection so deeply and are not as aware that such overt control is inappropriate. But neither kind of co-dependent is able to live comfortably as a mature adult experiencing intimate relationships with others, self or God. This discomfort in relationships drives both kinds of co-dependent to get control of others through whatever means available, thinking (or hoping) that this will alleviate the discomfort. For both kinds of co-dependent, the compulsion to control others is central, whether or not the feelings of fear or inadequacy are denied.

How Co-dependence Develops from "Child Abuse"

The five natural characteristics of a child constitute a matrix out of which a healthy person grows. If the caregivers nurture these characteristics and let them develop naturally, then the child will have feelings of self-esteem and a sense of the value of his natural inner-child Person. The child can learn to trust and develop his natural aptitudes and gifts. The nurtured Person develops (1) self-esteem, (2) healthy boundaries, (3) awareness of reality, (4) the abilities to satisfy his needs and wants and to ask for help, and (5) the ability to act moderately and appropriately at his own age level. Healthy parenting allows a child to grow into an adult who is congruent, the same person inside as out. The developing Person moves through life toward the realization of his potential and is increasingly able to relate intimately and lovingly, and increasingly more congruent.

But if the child is raised in a dysfunctional family and the parents are operating in the control disease, they try to make the child behave according to their expectations of what he should be. When the child reaches a certain level of awareness, and the self-centered parental control reaches a certain intensity, the child becomes afraid of losing the parents' love by "not being enough." This fear becomes so great that the natural Person-child is cut off, locked in the basement of the child's psyche. The child then proceeds to build an other-pleasing or other-dominating personality (usually several personages to meet the expectations of different authority groups). Most of this building of other personalities is not obvious to the future co-dependent, who thinks he is just growing up naturally—though painfully.

Even though the parents may be well-meaning and the expectations not conscious, their dominating attempts to mold the child into being some preconceived "type" are abusive. *When a child is not assisted in developing mature mechanisms in the areas of its five natural characteristics, and is instead constantly "shaped" toward the parents' unnatural (for the child) expectations, child abuse is said to have taken place.* The child is filled with shame at not being authentic and filled with fear when he doesn't please the parent. This happens even though the child may not have any idea what the source of the shame is, which may be triggered by any perceived mistake or imperfection.

Every Child Is Valuable: How a Child's Value Is Abused

By the very virtue of birth, every child has value. A child is a precious gift of God and does not have to prove her value. Value is not determined by what the child does or earns in life; rather, it is essential to her being. But when, through excessive discipline for not "doing it right," a child is punished severely or is emotionally or spiritually abused, her sense of value does not develop. In fact, such a child usually develops a low self-esteem that colors almost every aspect of life and sets up the shame voices. The child develops an overwhelming sense of shame about any perceived imperfection or mistake.

For example, let's say a father is taking his little three-year-old boy, Jimmy, shopping with him on Saturday morning. The father is a big man, dressed in blue jeans, a denim jacket, a black cowboy hat and boots. He has gone to pick up some chewing tobacco. The little boy wants something to chew, too, and pleads loudly with his daddy for some chewing gum. The father doesn't like his son shouting in the store, so he shames the child by saying, "Shut up. You're not going to get any chewing gum. You had chewing gum yesterday. Just shut up and be quiet!" They are standing in the checkout line waiting to pay for the father's purchase. When the little child sits on the floor pouting, he sees a piece of chewing gum that has been stepped on many times. It is round and black and flat. The child begins to peel it up off the floor with his thumbnail.

There are two nice-looking women about the father's age standing behind the child and the father, watching this take place. As Jimmy peels the chewing gum off the floor and pops it into his mouth to chew, one of the women wrinkles her nose, involuntarily exclaims, "Euuu!" and puts her hand over her mouth in disgust. The father looks and sees what has happened. He notices the woman's reaction and has a shame attack—this attractive woman thinks his boy is disgusting. Instead of dealing with his own shame, he hits the little boy in the face saying, "Spit out that chewing gum. That's the dirtiest thing I've ever seen. You're a dumb little jerk!"

All Jimmy knows is that he wanted a piece of chewing gum, saw it and tried to get it. But his father, by not handling his own sense of shame appropriately, has telegraphed (dumped) that shame into the child's life through his hand. Now the child feels an enormous sense of worthlessness.

Some parents for whom physical violence is abhorrent can get the same shaming effect without ever raising their voices, simply by looks of distaste accompanied by slight shakes of the head or a certain disgusted sigh.

Children who have been disciplined like this, or with any other wide range of shaming or abusive behaviors, grow up doubting their own value. They tend to develop in one of several ways. They may become perfectionists in an attempt to win a sense of worth (and avoid shame). They may develop into people-pleasers or over-strive for power or fame to prove they are worth something and to avoid the shaming voices. Or they may develop into extremely controlling people when any imperfection or mistake comes close to being revealed.

This sort of devaluing parental behavior leads to co-dependent symptom number one: difficulty experiencing and expressing appropriate levels of self-esteem. As adults, they will either adopt a "better than" posture to hide the low self-esteem or a "less than" stance to avoid having to compete and be proved worthless. In either case, the person desperately tries to control relationships in order to avoid being revealed as inadequate. These internal shame struggles to "look okay" and be acceptable to oneself make spirituality and intimacy very difficult.

Every Child Is Vulnerable: How the Child Becomes Abused by Not Being Taught to Have Healthy Boundaries

All children are by nature vulnerable—that is, they cannot protect themselves from physical, emotional, spiritual or intellectual attack. Children are not born with the skills or defenses they need to protect themselves. If they are to have security, a sense of safety in their interactions with other people, they must be taught by their primary caregivers to have boundaries.

A boundary is like an invisible, protective fence around our personal space.[2] Boundaries keep others from abusing us, from bursting into our space and controlling us, or from getting us to do things not in our best interest before we have a chance to think or say no. Our boundaries also keep us aware of others' boundaries, so that we do not break into their personal space to control or abuse them.

Children learn boundaries by observing how their caregivers behave, and will usually adopt a boundary style from one or both parents. For example, some parents walk around the house naked and don't close the door when they are using the bathroom or being sexually intimate in their bedroom; or they walk in on the child in the bathroom; or they insist that the child "tell everything" to the parent. All of these cases indicate that the parents' own physical, sexual and emotional boundaries are damaged, and these behaviors and attitudes may be adopted by the child. Similarly, if the parents never communicate about feelings, always stay isolated from the children and have walls between each other, the children may adopt rigid walls instead of healthy boundaries. In these and many other ways, the parents model either healthy boundaries, damaged boundaries or walls.

Children who are not taught to have strong functional boundaries become either too vulnerable (victims) or invulnerable (offenders—meaning someone who transgresses another person's boundaries). Victim-type co-dependents lacking boundaries are unable to say no and hence are continually over-committed or are isolated and do not interact with other people. In any of these cases, the result is usually the second primary adult symptom of co-dependence: difficulty setting and maintaining appropriate boundaries.

In adult intimate relationships, damaged boundaries or walls set up a strong need to control the reality of the partner. A person with no boundaries may want to enmesh, to relate totally to another, with no boundaries in the relationship. A person with walls may want to be with someone who has no boundaries in order to observe sharing without having to be vulnerable and actually engage in sharing. Or a person with walls may want another person with walls, so that no one has to risk sharing. In all of these cases spirituality and intimacy are virtually impossible, and it becomes very important to control the other to keep from being dominated and shamed.

Every Child by Nature Is Imperfect: How a Child Is Abused by Not Being Allowed to Be Imperfect

Children learn by trial and error. When it comes to learning to live, as Philip Parham has said, "Experience is not the best teacher—it is the only teacher."[3] A child doesn't just decide to walk one day and then do it. He struggles to pull up, then later lets go first with one hand, then with both hands. Eventually, the child takes a step, usually falls at first, but finally, after many failures, moves forward, and walking has begun. The process is filled with failures and mistakes. Almost everything a child learns to do takes place through this experience of trying, failing many times and adjusting.

A child who is allowed to be imperfect, and who is encouraged to try again and again without being shamed, grows up learning that imperfection is natural. It is the matrix out of which new learning takes place. In many families, however, children are shamed and criticized when they fail or make a mistake. This may be an open shaming, like laughing derisively at a child who falls down while trying to walk or learning to ride a bike, or it can be subtle. I remember that the first grade I brought home on a paper from school was an 86. I had no idea what an 86 was except that I'd done my best. My well-meaning mother, who was a perfectionist, said, "Hmmm . . . 86 . . . what did you miss?" Something about the way she said it triggered my shame, and I believed that an 86 wasn't good enough to get her approval. I tried never to make such a low grade again, though I often did.

When imperfection is treated as a liability instead of the natural condition for growth, and a child is ridiculed or *not* taught that being imperfect is natural, this becomes spiritual child abuse. Such a child may grow up having a terrible time sharing his reality for fear it "won't be enough" and the inner shame voices will be unleashed. This keeps a child from intimate relationships with God or other people. Further, if the parents don't admit their own imperfections to the child in an age-appropriate way, the situation is made worse. When the parents act as if *they* don't make mistakes, they are behaving as if they are gods in the family. This may teach the children to be their own Higher Power, to deny their imperfection and play God, the Perfect One, repressing and denying the imperfect parts of their own reality. Like the parents, these children may criticize and judge the imperfection of others, trying to control by shaming them for mistakes, just as the parents shamed the children. Children do need help to overcome their imperfection, so they can fit into society, but the help needs to be respectful and beneficial. Shaming and punitive *techniques* for addressing imperfection are the problem, *not* the fact that the issues are being addressed.

Children who have such shaming experiences usually choose one of two responses or vacillate between the two. They may become "bad" or "rebellious" if they feel they can't measure up to the parents, or "good" and "perfect" if they choose the perfectionist route and deny their own imperfections. Either way, as an adult the person often exhibits the third primary symptom of co-dependence: difficulty owning and expressing one's reality, especially imperfection.

When a child is not allowed to be naturally imperfect but is instead criticized, ridiculed and rejected, problems with spirituality and intimacy will follow, as sure as the night follows the day. A healthy relationship with a person or a Higher Power may be virtually impossible, since early sharing of reality with the parental Higher Powers brought criticism, ridicule or rejection.

Every Child Is by Nature Needing, Wanting and Dependent: How Abuse Takes Place When a Child Is Not Taught How to Meet Legitimate Needs and Wants, and to Be Interdependent and Ask for Help

Human beings evidently do not have as many instincts that enable them to meet their own basic needs as some animals do. Some examples of human needs are: food; clothing; shelter; medical and dental care; emotional and sexual needs, including the knowledge of how to be a woman or man and how to relate to members of one's own and the opposite sex. Children must also be taught what to do about their "wants." They need to learn what is socially acceptable to want, what wants are financially feasible and what is safe or appropriate to want in relationships with others.

In learning to meet legitimate needs and wants, a child must be taught by the caregiver that it is all right to request help directly and how to ask for that help appropriately. Children need to learn all these things if they are to become fully functional adults. Furthermore, if the parents or caregivers don't take care of *their own* needs and wants, *that* is abusive for their child as well, since parental self-care modeling is necessary for the child to learn to meet his needs. For example, parents who don't take care of their own medical needs are abusing their children by modeling neglect, implying it is not important for adults to meet such needs.

If children are not taught how to meet these needs by their caregivers, as adults these abused children will often repress their legitimate needs or take a dysfunctional approach to the whole issue. For example, if a parent does everything for a child and does not teach the child how to meet her own needs and wants, that child will likely become too dependent and continually look for someone to take care of even simple matters. Because I was not taught how to take care of my clothes I have discarded many clothes and shoes that I now know could have been cleaned and repaired to look practically new. And not knowing how to take care of one's personal needs and being too dependent can have a disastrous effect on an adult relationship, since the abused adult child expects his mate to take care of all kinds of personal, medical and financial needs.

This sort of abuse can be tricky, especially when mothers or fathers are extremely close to an opposite-sex child and help the child with everything. My mother was this way. She made me the little king of her life and taught me wonderful things about music and storytelling. She encouraged me to try things and showed me how to succeed in them—for instance, how to sell magazines door to door. But the problem came when I had more school work, basketball and dramatic competitions than I could handle and was about to fail to get a major paper in on time. Instead of letting me take the consequences of my over-commitments, she delivered the magazines and helped me with the paper. I made it through one crisis after another and looked like a superhero. She did this many times because she could not stand for me to have the pain of failing. The only trouble was that she was abusing me by not teaching me how to meet my own needs. What she unwittingly taught me instead was to overcommit continually in order to be a star (so I'd be "enough"). She was also teaching me that I should find a woman whose life's work was to take care of me and bail me out of my overcommitted schedule so I could keep being a star.

There is little question in my mind that this made me expect that the job of the woman in my life was to be my support system and clean up my messes (behind the scenes). If my wife did not choose to make me and my success the central focus of her life, as my mother seemed to, then she was "copping out" on her responsibilities.

At one level I recognized that this wasn't right, but when I first got married, I deeply resented my wife's "selfishness" in wanting to have a life of her own. Since that was the only kind of parenting I knew, I tried to rescue my children from pain by fixing them and keeping them from any failures. This kind of over-parenting can be very serious abuse—all in the name of being a loving (super) parent.

On the other hand, if a child is not taught how to meet needs and wants and is *attacked* for expressing them, that also is child abuse. Such children will likely grow up being anti-dependent and may not ask for help even when in need.

I had a friend who was continually advised by a doctor that his smoking cough sounded serious and that he should have a chest X ray. But my friend never had time—until suddenly one day he couldn't breathe and in a short time died of lung cancer. Unfortunately, this is far from being an isolated case.

If a child is not taught how to meet needs or wants and

parents *ignore* the child's needs and wants, that, too, is child abuse. Such children may grow up denying their needs and wants altogether.

For example, a person I know, who was successful in his profession because of outstanding abilities, had only a couple of shabby old suits because his clothing needs were ignored when he was a child. In recovery he learned to meet his needs and ask for help. Among other things, he bought some new clothes. This awakened the realization that he could also have intimate relationships because now he felt he could dress suitably and be responsible.

I remember as a small child telling my mother I wanted a new bicycle—any bicycle would have been fine. But it was during the Great Depression and our family couldn't afford a new bicycle for me. My mother had a shame attack because she couldn't get me a bicycle. Instead of simply saying we couldn't afford it, she said, "There are children *starving* in Armenia—and you want a new bicycle." I felt ashamed of wanting a new bicycle and grew up feeling shame and guilt when I wanted something nice for myself.

Last year we bought a new car and I experienced great joy in driving and owning it. But I was surprised that for a day or two I would relapse into feelings of shame when I saw certain people because I didn't want them to know that I was driving a new car. I realized what was going on and worked the first three Steps on those childhood feelings of shame about buying something nice for myself. (We'll see how to use the 12 Steps in this way, beginning in chapter 8). But I was amazed as I realized where my ambivalence about getting nice things for myself came from. I was taught that it was not okay for me to want anything nice for myself as long as anyone else was poor, anywhere. This was never said directly, but it was the message I interpreted that set up my internal shame reaction. This quality of not knowing how to meet my wants has meant that I'd buy nice things for everyone in my family, claiming I didn't need anything. But then I'd feel hurt if they didn't see through my false position and buy me nice gifts. This has affected my ability to be intimate because I couldn't be honest about the reality of my wants and needs. I wasn't even in touch with them.

The tragedy of child abuse in this area of meeting needs and wants is that it leads adults to despair when they don't know how to get their needs met in the normal acceptable ways. As a result, many of them turn to *addictions* to kill their pain and frustration, and as an easier way to get the good feelings they would like to have by meeting their needs and wants.

For a while addictions may mask their pain, not only about the unmet need, but also about the shame they feel because they don't know how to meet those needs directly. Other people abused in this way turn to lives of physical or mental illness, because chronically ill people have their needs met by others.

Children who are not taught how to meet needs and wants are filled with shame introjected from the parents, and hide their own reality. They cannot be spiritual or intimate. As they grow into adulthood, such children are driven by the control disease to all kinds of passive-aggressive control methods in their attempts to have intimate relationships. But the bottom line is that a child abused by not being taught to meet needs and wants and to ask for help appropriately has great fear of being shamed, and intimacy becomes very difficult. Such a person develops the fourth primary adult symptom of co-dependence: difficulty taking care of one's adult needs and wants, and asking for help.

Every Child by Nature Is Immature: How Abuse Takes Place When Age-Appropriate Behavior Is Neither Allowed nor Encouraged

One of the little-recognized forms of child abuse takes place when a parent pushes a child to do more than is age-appropriate—for example, when parents try to urge a seven-year-old to play baseball or dance as well as a 10-year-old. Unfortunately, such pushing is often considered good parenting in our culture, with children feeling shame at not being able to perform as well as parents expect. In fact, they sometimes feel shame when only performing at the top of their own age group.[4]

Because our society puts such a high premium on super achievement, children who are pushed hard at an early age will often grow up to be very successful outwardly. But on the inside they may be miserable, feeling shame, believing they don't deserve to be where they are or just being exhausted and frantic about failure in trying to continue to keep a pace that is always stressful.

The other side of the coin of this abuse is to allow or encourage an older child to act like a younger child. A seven-year-old girl doesn't get her way, so she throws a tantrum, kicking and screaming in the living room filled with guests. As she cries and thrashes around on the floor, her father laughs and says, "Isn't she cute? She acts just like her mother. Can't do a thing with her." That is very abusive—to the mother as well as to the child. This girl will almost certainly grow up with a chaotic inner life, trying to get her way by throwing fits.

Children treated in these ways may grow up with a highly controlling, overly mature lifestyle if pushed to be superachievers; or into a chaotic, out-of-control style of living if not taught to act at least their own age. Both types will likely think and operate in extremes: "If you don't like everything I do, you probably hate me," or "Since I can't be perfect, I won't try at all."

Both will probably have trouble with spirituality and intimacy issues because they can't afford to share their reality, which is either never enough, or bizarre and out of control. In close relationships, such people are often stone-cold or else they act impulsively, like children, since they can neither experience nor express their normal emotions as an adult. Such people often try to resolve intimacy struggles by performing the "grand exit" (exploding their feelings, stalking out, slamming the door) or even by leaving the relationship altogether.

This is the fifth primary symptom of co-dependence: difficulty expressing one's reality moderately and acting one's age.

The helpless feelings such people have lead to an intense need to find ways to get things (and people and their reality—particularly concerning the controller) under control. Intimacy for a person abused in this way is not a happy thought because it would reveal the self-perceived inner inadequacy.

The Bottom Line

If children are abused regarding their five natural characteristics, they cannot flourish as mature adults. This lack of maturity and the shame it causes will lead them to be closed and hide the fact that they don't feel valuable, that they don't have good boundaries, that they can't express their reality for fear of being shamed, that they can't meet their needs and wants and can't ask for help, and that they don't know how to express their reality appropriately.

Their denial, fear of shame and lack of training as to how to relate intimately with the opposite (or their own) sex will make intimacy frightening. Control—however they can get it—will seem like a necessity for any stability in close relationships. All of the mature characteristics listed at the beginning of this chapter are necessary for fully functional intimate relationships and for true spirituality to take place. But when parents control children through the abuse we have been examining, it sets the children up for the kind of immaturity that makes intimate relationships almost impossible. It also re-creates the co-dependence in the next generation, and trains the adult children to do the dominant or passive-aggressive kinds of controlling that they are compelled to do in order to keep the enormous shame and fear subdued in their lives.

That is a frantic and lonely way to live.

6
The Lonely Way

How an Abused Child Grows into an Adult Controller

A child who has been abused in the ways we have been examining is often headed for a lonely and frightening experience when it comes to intimacy in close relationships.

From early childhood, I have been virtually terrified that people would find out about me—that I am not very interesting, smart or fun to be with—and would not want to be around me. When I was about to take an examination, try out for a team or set out to win a sweetheart, I was horrified when it looked as if I wouldn't make it. All of my inner shame voices would scream at me, telling me I wasn't going to measure up. And if I *didn't,* I was going to be a "shameful, rejected piece of dirt!"

My expectations of myself were so high that anything less than number one, perfect, totally accepted, seemed like a failure. That brought shameful replays in my imagination of the things I did wrong, so that even if I made a 94 on an exam, we won the district championship in basketball or I was elected president of my fraternity, I recalled the ways I had failed or how close the election had been.

In my marriage, when I had any sexual failure and wasn't able to make my wife totally happy, I felt enormous shame and fear. In writing this book, I have seen how desperately I have had to control people and circumstances all my life not to be destroyed by the powerful, almost overwhelming inner shaming voices—even though I was not consciously aware of them as "voices." I have seen how I have struggled to try to find self-acceptance, integrity and congruence that would bring some kind of serenity in my life and intimate relationships. This was all true, although I was not aware of it at the time. I just thought I was high-strung and had a bad case of pre-game jitters when I was faced with possible failure.

Because abused children feel as adults that they must hide their true reality to be safe from shame and rejection, it feels as if their own inner Person's reality is not acceptable in some objective sense. Many abused children develop a frantic need to control other people's reactions to them, or to direct the communication in their relationships. They fear that expressing their own reality will lead to rejection and trigger feelings of inadequacy, lack of self-worth or being an "imperfect idiot."

As the abusive parents were trying to control the child's reality, either consciously or unconsciously, the parents were using the abusive behaviors just discussed as part of this control. Even if the parents adored the child and were trying to make her grow into their idea of a successful adult, the child often didn't receive the intended direction as positive guidance but as an attack on her real self. This reaction (especially if exaggerated) makes the child's developing inner Person feel inadequate, somehow wrong or less than, filled with shame for not being enough or "right" in some way.

Something subtle happens inside the child, who picks up an urgent, nervous need to get control of his reality in order to gain the necessary love and approval from the parents. Later, the child broadens the control focus to include other important, frightening people out in the world who are also seen as possible sources of affirmation or rejection and shame. But when the child first starts to try to control any of these big people directly, the rejection is likely to be strong and defeat almost certain. So the child walks a tightrope when approaching close relationships: wanting acceptance and success, but fearing rejection. As adolescence begins, there are little horror-show vignettes for the blossoming co-dependent when situations begin to arise in which some degree of intimacy is expected.

I'll never forget the first time I kissed a girl on a date. We had been to a movie and had been taken in an older friend's car. I prearranged for him to drive down the block while I walked my date to her front door. I had planned the kiss, hoping she wouldn't turn her head, causing me to miss her lips. I was afraid she might laugh at me or draw back in disgust. No one had given me any clues about how girls felt about kissing. I was terribly afraid I'd fail and be shamed. I could feel my heart beating in my throat.

When the moment came, the kiss was accurate and fast. I turned and ran up the street, elated that I hadn't "failed." Now I realize that was hardly an intimate encounter for my date—or me—but I was totally fixated on controlling the experience.

I lived through a series of such "approaches to intimacy" involving the various stages of asking for dates, touching and proposing "going steady." I experienced lonely times in the shame-pit of my soul when I failed to be what I wanted to—or was rejected, wasn't invited, or came home and masturbated. I cursed myself for being a no-good degenerate and an inept fool. All in all, adolescence was a grim and pressured time.

It shouldn't take long for most children to see that it is impossible to gain the kind of control of people they desire, but the persistence of the delusion that enough effort will bring people around is incredible. Since the prospect of intimacy is so threatening, however, many young people turn to other avenues in the futile attempt to get control of their lives—through increased amounts of education, money, power, prestige, social position, professional or sexual conquests, or even religious work.

Unfortunately, all control strategies fail to bring peace in the inner warfare with shame. Furthermore, they eliminate the possibility of authentic intimacy because when we are trying to get control of others (or to beat them out competitively), we cannot share our reality for fear of almost certain rejection by the other party. Also, we cannot admit our own weakness, fear or pain for fear of the loss of control.

Why "Enough" Is Never Enough

This almost universal need to get control of life and relationships is certain to fail because the unconscious presupposition is a delusion. This is the unfortunate notion that once one gets *enough* power (or control, education, money, sex or prestige), then the basic sense of being "enough" will take place. Since the difficulty is an inner one stemming from childhood abuse, no amount of outer success can get close to the deeper inner issues.

After a while some of these children, now adults, begin to realize that they are not going to get enough control to make them have good feelings about themselves and solve these basic deficit needs. At this point many people switch tactics.

As the pain swells and threatens to get out of control, these children becoming adults must do something to quell these feelings that threaten to overwhelm them. Remember, besides their own painful feelings, children often carry feelings from their parents that can add an overwhelming intensity to their own natural feelings. The combined feelings can become *enormous*. Such children feel that their feelings are irrational, are too much to bear and may drive them crazy.

Take, for example, the family of a physician who is not facing her own fear, anger, sexual needs and so on. She feels that she simply "doesn't have" such needs and feelings because of her knowledge and training, when in reality she has repressed them because they are "not acceptable" for a person of her stature. Because those feelings have to go somewhere, she may unconsciously dump them into her children's lives. When children carry these feelings for the parent along with their own feelings, it can become overwhelming, and the child may act out through addictions or other unacceptable behavior. The fact that the highest suicide rate is said to be among teenagers may not be unrelated to the pain caused from the delusion that we should be able to get our relationships and lives "under control."

Addictive-Compulsive Behavior: A New Pain to Calm the Old Pain

At this point many people turn to some sort of compulsive or addictive behavior or chemical, because as they are working compulsively, for instance, or drinking, all else is blotted out. Painful feelings are temporarily subdued, along with the shame voices. As we engage in a compulsive or addictive behavior, the pain from the deficit needs caused by the child abuse is temporarily calmed, and the good feelings resulting from the addictive agent or behavior become the focus of one's life.

Since almost all addictive and compulsive behaviors of this sort have a positive payoff, they are effective at first. For instance, if we have a few drinks or "help" the family get organized, our fear may diminish. But later, in all addictions, an increased amount of the chemical or behavior is necessary to do the same painkilling job, so that we have to drink six drinks instead of three, work 12 hours instead of 10, act out sexually outside of the marriage instead of just often in the marriage, or monitor and attempt to control *all* the activities of the loved one. As this acceleration takes place, a new kind of pain emerges, coming from the addictive behavior itself. For instance, alcoholics may get debilitating liver disease; or get drunk in front of the boss and get fired; or be deserted by their spouse; or embarrass their children, who reject the alcoholic parent. The family of the workaholic or compulsive controller may reject her after living for years with the compulsive behavior. The examples are infinite.

Ironically, since the purpose of all addictions is also to gain control of one's good feelings as well as to calm the pain, they are sure to fail. This failure is assured because addictive and compulsive behaviors increase in intensity and lead one to the condition of being out of control. A workaholic begins to have ulcers or heart trouble, can't sleep, or has other physical symptoms. An alcoholic begins to be irresponsible about money, sex or other relationships, or her vocation. The person with a food addiction gains (or loses) an enormous amount of weight and endangers his health. A compulsive controller winds up isolated and alone, even in the midst of his own family. The good feelings promised by each addiction vanish—leaving only the imperious compulsion to continue the addictive behavior.

The Addictive Agent Becomes the Addict's Higher Power

The tragedy is that all of these compulsions and addictions, by the nature of the way they operate, eliminate authentic intimacy. The focus of the addict's life—the addict's Higher Power or God—*is the addictive substance or object. That* reality is too threatening to share, so one withdraws to "worship" one's Higher Power: alcohol, work, sex, food or the control of people.

The addict cannot see this happening, and, in fact, thinks it is *not.* This is true because, as we have seen, the primary characteristic of all addictions is denial. The person who is behaving compulsively can't see the addictive symptoms and rationalizes her actions so that they do not look "serious enough" to the addict to be marks of an addiction.

For example, a person who is drinking a quart of whiskey a day may tell people, "Oh, I have a couple of drinks in the evening"—and will really mean it. The addict thus minimizes the amount he is drinking—a form of denial. A man who is a work addict will say in defense of his working all the time that he is "only doing this in order to earn a good living for the family," or "This is only temporary, and when we get things under control at the company, then I won't work so hard." A controller of people says, "Listen, I'm just helping my family. If I don't see that people around here do what they are supposed to, this family would fall apart!" These are often delusional statements. Take the work addict, for instance. Once a demanding project is finished, the work addict takes on another one (often just before the first one is completed), and this new project also becomes "absolutely essential" to the welfare of the family or to the addict's vocational future.

Since all addictions and compulsions are progressive—becoming more intense and less effective in calming the pain as time goes on—the addict is led to more frantic attempts to deny and control his feelings and keep the shaming voices quiet. All these attempts fail at a certain level, and all put up increasingly sturdy walls of separation between the addict and his own reality. So the frantic search for effective ways to control his own and other people's lives and reality, in order to feel accepted and at peace, is doomed to failure in every case.

Denial Blots Out Positive Hopes and Desires

Denial has another side effect. Besides hiding the reality and extent of the *addictive* behavior and the exaggerated feelings that led the person to the addiction or compulsion, denial also blots out the positive hopes, dreams and aptitudes that are impossible to face because of the threat of failure and the shame it would bring. The person quits experiencing important positive and negative feelings and "stuffs them" to eliminate both the painful feelings and the positive, hopeful feelings.

With regard to the effect of denial on spontaneity and intimacy, the trouble is that all of the denied feelings and thoughts are potentially important parts of the *content* of authentic intimacy and spiritual growth. If I am not aware that I am having strong feelings, then I certainly cannot share them openly and vulnerably with another person. Attempts to control through addictions constitute perhaps the most effective block to authentic intimacy, because addictions even remove the consciousness of the addicts' true inner reality as they focus on the addictive agent or behavior. Not only can addicts and compulsive controllers not share their reality intimately with another person, but after a certain point, they can't even share intimately with themselves or with God.

Intimacy involves two Persons dealing with and sharing the reality of their own lives and accepting the reality of the other's life. When addictions or co-dependent control issues are in action, even if one party is being intimate and is sharing, the controlling person cannot participate. Intimacy is further blocked because the "reality" an addict does share is skewed and dishonest; in many cases it is an attempt to gain the approval of the other in order to feel worthy—the need that lies at the root of the controller's life. So in some "intimate relationships," one party is trying desperately to be intimate and is baffled by the continuing failure of the other party to participate wholeheartedly.

Where are we on the journey toward maturity, happiness and intimacy? How can we reclaim what is rightfully ours? In part 2 we will explore some techniques that have helped many people on their journeys to recover their inner Person and find authentic intimacy.

7

The Person-Dialogue

Doorway to Healing
and Intimacy

The way of healing in intimate relationships is paradoxical. Directly attacking the problems of a bruised or broken relationship may give some temporary relief, but unless the parties temporarily turn away from the relationship problems—which invariably involve blaming the partner—and turn to the inner warfare—the personal problems *within each one's own life*—there is little hope of either healing or intimacy. Separation and fear come from that inner conflict between the positive voice of the Person who calls to us to become all that we can be and to have integrity and congruence, and those introjected shaming voices of abusive caregivers, perhaps long dead, who tell us that we are not worthy of success and not worthy of being loved—or that we are better than others and were born to control them.

At each step in growing up we heard these opposites calling, struggling for control over us. We long for some support for our vulnerable authentic Person. When we find someone to love romantically, there rises in us the hope that here at last is a playmate and an ally for our private inner-child Person. But when we get in a close long-term relationship, the control disease rears its ugly head as our partner's and our own abusive family-of-origin patterns unfold. We run for cover inside ourselves and hide behind our personages. To our horror we are again alone in our "wonderful relationship," fighting for our value and self-esteem in the face of outer as well as inner voices we hear as abusive and condemning.[1]

Authentic Person-Dialogue: The Beginning of Hope

As we have seen, the ability to keep secrets is a lifesaver. The ability to hide our personal reality behind our personages is the first step toward becoming a functional and free person. However, our development takes place not in isolation but in relation to other people. As I once heard psychologist Rokelle Lerner say, "Since our relational problems are born in relationships, it seems they must be healed in relationships."

When we encounter the presence of a Person who is not veiled by his dysfunctional personage, a new possibility for connection and healing is born. A helping Person who is present rather than hiding in a personage creates conditions for intimacy and deep dialogue about the problems and joys, the awesome secrets of life. Something like this, or the hope for it, often happens in romantic relationships that become long term, even though a lot of protective hiding may take place to ensure the continuance of the relationship. At least we feel hope that here, with this loved one, we can find a nonjudgmental home in which our Person can at last live and grow.

But after the "honeymoon period," the old familiar fears of loneliness and worthlessness often surface again. Unexpectedly, our partner changes and becomes in some ways like our abusive caregivers. Actually, most people revert to the behaviors of their own caregivers as they unconsciously try to re-create their family of origin. But the change appears to the partner as being a change from the "deceitful loving facade" maintained during courtship. The result is a re-creation of the past generation's intimate warfare and hiding. When the partners try to fix the relationship, they often focus on the hiding and abusive controlling of the other. But this is jumping into the control disease big time. Now the relationship looks pretty hopeless.

Often only when committed partners begin to focus on their own issues and deal with their own inner warfare can they begin to get some insight into their struggle with shame and self-esteem, and why their relationship is stuck. But even good traditional therapy that leads to some healing of the past often does not free the client to become an authentically intimate Person in relationships outside the therapeutic situation. She can share emotional and intellectual reality *with a therapist,* but unless there is a Person-dialogue involved in the healing process, in which the counselor shares something of her own inner struggles, the patient doesn't have a model for the natural process of intimate sharing.

It is this dual sharing that constitutes a Person-dialogue. Paul Tournier pointed out that a healing dialogue takes place when one individual, such as a counselor, listens to another person. Then the counselor begins to reveal his Person by sharing the painful, frightening, lonely feelings and experiences that are normally hidden behind the personage. This mutual sharing in an appropriate atmosphere of trust can lead to a wholly different order of dialogue. In this intimate exchange, a matrix of healing is created in which the pain and fears of both persons can interact in a creative way.

For example, a man with low self-esteem whose marriage is on the rocks engages in a Person-dialogue with a counselor. The client shares the fear and pain of the separation and loneliness and the sense of failure that he is experiencing. To the client, the counselor seems to be capable and intelligent, operating out of a position of self-esteem. When the counselor begins to share his own pain and fear encountered in some past intimate relationship, a new dynamic enters the situation. The patient knows at a feeling level that the counselor understands what is going on. But a dawning hope is also born. "My gosh, if this counselor is able to cope and has been through what I have, maybe I can cope, too. . . ."

By exposing relevant parts of his own inner conflict, the counselor may take away the client's fear of inner warfare. The counselor's integrity in sharing supports the ascendance of the authentic Person inside the patient, who is so lonely and afraid to share in the face of the shaming inner voices. This deep identification of two Persons on the journey through the pain of life provides the spiritual ambience in which psychological and emotional—and in some cases, physical—healing and growth take place. The presence and acceptance of another Person on the same journey can channel a transcendent and healing force into both Persons in the dialogue.

It is not possible to describe precisely what Tournier did in his therapy sessions because it varied according to the nature and development of his patient's Person. As one who took counsel with him, I can say that he seemed simply to join me in my situation. He did not reveal secret things about his life that were not relevant to my issues, and he did not reveal confidences or the identity of others. But in sharing his reality, he became a companion on the journey through life with me. He told of his own loneliness and of the fear in his life and relationships.

Although we spoke of possible directions in which I might move, he was never "directive" in the sense of giving advice. As I shared my shame about being a failure as a husband and father, he shared his shame about not being able to be what he wanted to be at home and in his intimate relationships. As he shared and then listened, I had the feeling that I was finding my own way, that he was along as a helpful, more experienced companion on the journey. Yet his presence and insights, his experience and obvious strength, made all the difference.

It was a paradox. Here, with this world-famous psychiatrist, I found hope and the creative energy to find a new life as he took *off* the mantle of famous author and lecturer. He shared the loneliness he felt as a young boy whose father had died, his fears of failure, and his lifelong desire to succeed and control his destiny. The paradox lay in the fact that the things he was sharing, that I would have thought would make me lose respect for him, became like a drawbridge he put down into my life and loneliness. Sometimes he would listen and be still with me for long periods; sometimes he would come out and share.

Slowly, tentatively, I came out of my fear-filled cave of isolation and pain. As I shared more deeply under the protective umbrella of his sharing, I noticed that my shame was lessened. I felt as if I was temporarily okay, even though my life and marriage were not okay at all.

Becoming a Carrier of Intimacy

Not only did I come to some decisions that I needed to make about my life and my marriage, but I realized—contrary to anything that my background and education had taught me—that Paul Tournier's sharing of weakness and pain actually increased the strength and capability I experienced in him. As we continued the Person-dialogue, I made a decision to be as intimate as he was, to also share my life in Person-dialogues. I was learning not only how to be intimate, but how to be a carrier of intimacy.

I discovered that a healthy Person develops as the result of a delicate balance between holding one's tongue and sharing one's reality. Tournier believed that one who reveals secrets too easily is not necessarily mature, for those who open their hearts too freely rarely tell secrets of a liberating nature. On the other hand, one who limits talk to impersonal ideas—even true and helpful ones—forfeits growth. The opposing actions of withdrawing and giving of self alternate throughout a healthy person's life.

When you open a secret area to another, something very basic has taken place within each of you: by means of such genuine encounters, one becomes authentically spiritual and intimate. Tournier was convinced that no one can discover the self in solitude. It is only by giving of self that one can find oneself. To tell a secret is to give one's self. It is the most precious gift, the one that touches the deepest chords of humanity. By overcoming the natural resistance to opening one's heart, overcoming timidity, fear, shame and constraint, the individual human being becomes a Person capable of intimacy and love.

Tournier advised choosing a confidant or confessor to share one's secrets with very carefully. If a person confides a precious secret to someone who can't keep it, the subsequent disclosure is a betrayal and may block personal growth as much as the telling might have encouraged it. The violated person may withdraw for years, or forever, from such personal encounters.

But what can we do if we are stuck in a relationship and hurt by another, yet we long to be known? What if we are blocked by the fear (or the knowledge) that our secrets might destroy the very relationship or dream of intimacy for which our inner Person longs?

A Higher Power: A Security Beyond the Relationship and the Inner Warfare

The fear of being abused and controlled in an intimate relationship is so great that the idea of being revealed keeps many people from ever being able to lay down the compulsion to control and trade it for the healing intimacy of a Person-dialogue. "What if I quit controlling my wife and share myself vulnerably with her, my hurts and dreams and fears? What if she thinks less of me or even uses these secrets to make fun of me or quits loving me or decides to leave me?"

These are not unusual fears. The Person reasons, "If I shared my true issues and feelings and the other person couldn't handle knowing those things and still love, respect and want to be with me, the lostness I would feel would be irreparable. The thing that my shame voices have been telling me all my life would have come true: 'See, you are *not* worth anything. We told you that if they really knew you, they wouldn't love you. Now you are all alone!'"

And sometimes the reaction of one hearing the intimate truth of another *is* a fearful withdrawal of some sort.

Tournier believed that only a greater security in God, a loving and supportive relationship separate and beyond the intimate relationship with a loved one, could give one the courage to risk laying down the compulsion to control. If one shared intimately and the relationship blew up, there would be a security to go to on the other side of the broken marriage. For Tournier, that relationship was a Person-dialogue with God.

When we cultivate a Person-dialogue with God, we acquire an ally in the inner warfare for self-esteem against the shaming inner voices. We learn in a Person-dialogue with God that we are a precious child of inestimable value because we are made in God's image. We have the courage to face the falseness of our dysfunctional personages and also the reality and positive potential of our Person. We gain great strength and even personal courage in our Person as we realize that even if everyone we know rejects us, God will not. So at least theoretically we may have the courage to lay down the compulsion to control along with the other addictions we develop to cover the pain and failure caused by our control attempts. We may find the courage to risk living lives of intimacy and serenity in spite of our fears.

But how do we do all this? Where and how can we find people to teach us these realities and show us *how* the Higher Power operates to give us this courage? Because evidently we *must* find a power beyond ourselves in order to become the whole Persons we long to be and to discover the wonder of loving intimacy.

Some years ago, as a frightened and isolated person who had alienated almost everyone close to me, I found some people who were living and sharing the integrity and intimacy I had always longed for. Very reluctantly, I joined them, for in my shame, I was terribly afraid of what I might discover about myself.

PART TWO

Healing the Compulsion to Control and Learning the Art of Authentic Intimacy

8
The 12 Steps
A Road to Healing

The group of loving and supportive people who helped me on my healing journey were in a 12-Step program that I began attending after my denial had begun to crack in therapy. Although it is not the only recovery program available, my own experience has shown me that the 12-Step process is a remarkable way of healing and transformation. At least two of the primary sources of human distress that pertain specifically to the compulsion to control and the breakdown of intimacy are routinely healed or improved dramatically in the lives of people "working the Steps."

The 12-Step program is a transrational spiritual process that deals with problems about which many people are in denial. For the purposes of this discussion, I want to show how the program affects the two underlying hypotheses presented by this book:

1. The compulsion to control is caused by the deep interior battle between the inner Person struggling for identity and self-esteem, and the powerful, often unconscious shaming inner voices that discredit and stifle the inner Person as she battles for authenticity and love. The problem is how to dismantle the powerful dysfunctional shaming "committee." Then the Person can develop her innate abilities and relate intimately, where appropriate—without the constant threat of inner rejection and shame—in a free and loving manner under a Higher Power.

2. Shaming blocks intimacy in close relationships. The developing Person is afraid to share his inner reality for fear of being discounted and rejected by those who are closest and most important. Since this sharing of reality in a nonjudgmental atmosphere is the basic dynamic of intimacy, the recovery of loving intimacy cannot take place until enough trust develops that the Person will risk sharing. Since most people were not trained to share their reality without disguising it to win love or using it to change others, many adults do not know how to maintain intimate love relationships.

The four major parts of every 12-Step program are: (1) meetings, (2) sponsors, (3) working the Steps and reading the literature and (4) relating to a Higher Power. We will look at these parts of the 12-Step program, with the focus on how each helps dismantle the abusive shame core and how each teaches the establishment and maintenance of authentic intimacy in close relationships.

How Meetings Affect the Shame Core

For a shame-filled person attending a 12-Step program for the first time, thinking about going to a meeting and having other people—people who might recognize us—see our shame is very fearful, a real threat to the delusion of control. Admitting that we are imperfect—or worse, "out of control" about anything, may result in an inner shame attack of major proportions. But in a 12-Step meeting *everyone* admits failure and inability to control *every time* a person speaks: "My name is Rebecca. I'm an alcoholic." "My name is Bob. I'm a co-dependent." "My name is Diane. I'm an overeater." "My name is Tom. I'm a sex addict."

When the pain gets severe enough and one actually attends a few meetings, a strange and seemingly paradoxical thing begins to happen. As the new person hears people stand up and admit they are powerless over their compulsion and that they didn't know how to live before coming into the program, a dawning awareness comes to the newcomer: "I'm not alone! That's the way I am." The fact that people share their deepest feelings and failures with strangers is overwhelming to the new person. Not only does no one reject the sharer, but they say things like, "Keep coming back," or "Glad you're here," or "Thanks for sharing." Then someone else may identify with the "shameful" things shared: "Boy, that really tells my story, too. But in this program I'm hoping that I can get well and quit trying to control everyone's life. My wife told me last night that she can't believe it's me. I'd just say to you newcomers, 'Keep coming back and . . . work the Steps.'"

Before long the inner shame about having problems seems out of place. It's as if the world one has always known and feared is being turned upside down. Here in 12-Step meetings people are actually rewarded—not shamed—for sharing their unacceptable feelings and for working on the kinds of problems that destroyed their relationships and drove them to powerlessness in the first place.

Not only are you not ashamed of being there and not feeling out of place, but you feel *accepted just as you are.* Some people feel at home for the first time in their lives. The sense of being accepted brings some grown men and women to tears. Far from feeling that you are with a "bunch of losers who couldn't control their lives," you realize that most of these people seem to be stronger than the people outside the meeting and stronger than your own parents, who were afraid to be intimate but had to be in control to have a continuing relationship. The control your parents exercised might have been a passive-aggressive nagging, picking, complaining, enmeshing kind of control or an offending, abusive control of always having to be right. But the results for the children were the same: an inability to be authentically intimate, and a loneliness—often acute—in the midst of people in one's own family. What you learn by listening in meetings over a period of months is sometimes like having someone show you a secret journal *about you* and some of your own family members.

Many of the people one meets in 12-Step meetings had almost lost all hope of building healthy self-esteem and intimacy. But they found that a miracle seemed to unfold as they began to be intimate with others who had this disease, and as they shared the reality of their broken and unmanageable lives. As they began to admit the shameful truth (that they were drunks, overeaters, controllers), and as they shared the intimate details of their inner pain and dysfunctional lives with each other, a strange thing happened. The people who were *doing the sharing* began to get well, as well as the people who listened. The *intimacy itself was healing,* just the *sharing* of their hidden, painful reality and the offering of intimacy without trying to fix each other. As this has happened over the years since 1934, when 12-Step groups started, a new manifestation of genuine intimacy in community has been born into our time.

Just as the first prehistoric communities were formed for survival, eventually developing into the matrix for intimacy and personal spiritual growth, so this new group of people came together in the 20th century to learn to survive. But they went on to develop an emotional space in which they could grow personally and spiritually. The first alcoholics went to meetings because they knew that unless they did, their consumption of alcohol would kill them. They would try again to take control of other people's lives to defeat their fear and shame, intimacy would cease, and the pain would become so great that they would drink or act out again, and lose everything they had gained.

These self-defeating patterns drove the founders of the 12 Steps to the end of themselves, so that they had nothing to share except their inner reality, which they perceived as being worthless to anyone else. They felt that they had nothing to offer anybody, but as they shared their pain and the details of their mostly dysfunctional lives, their Higher Power took it and made a healing "medicine" out of the broken reality and the hope they were finding together. An elixir of health was made from their intimacy and shared reality.

As they began to see what was working, they realized that this process was creating a fellowship that was like nothing they had ever seen or heard. The intimacy allowed them to see each other's needs and true condition. As time went by, the members could actually watch positive changes taking place in each other—they had an X-ray picture of their inner progress through their intimate sharing. This made them realize that in giving away their reality in the sharing, they could help each other find a new life.

As these men and women began to share, their denial receded, and they realized the sharing of reality called for change in their behaviors. The new values they had were not being expressed by their old ways of living, and they felt impelled to do something about that. But when they tried, they realized they were powerless to change anything. They had tried to stop drinking on their own but failed again and again. Now they saw that they could not quit controlling others, either. By themselves they couldn't create the intimacy *outside* the group that they were finding in meetings.

But some of them were getting well and their relationships were changing. As they had gained self-esteem, many were less abusive with their families. However, they didn't know how to help all the new people who had begun to come to them for help. The control disease reasserted itself. Everyone wanted to be a chief who knew the "right way."

Finally they wrote the 12 Steps that had led them to healing and to a Higher Power who *could* defeat both their compulsion to control and the shaming voices that powered it. They didn't understand *why* the Steps worked, but they understood from experience and observation *that* they worked. These Steps led them to a new intimate and creative life that was empowered not by control but by intimacy, the sharing of their reality with each other and with a Higher Power.

As new people began to try to take the 12 Steps to recovery, they soon realized that they had questions. Also, some things were not appropriate for sharing in meetings—things that might harm or incriminate others—but these things needed to be shared in certain Steps. The founders had discovered great support in sharing with each other personally as individuals, and the notion came about that each person who wanted to work the Steps needed a sponsor, a guide who had worked some or all of the Steps, who could see through some of the denial as he listened, and who could share his experience, strength and hope with the new 12-Stepper.

How Sponsorship Affects Shame and Intimacy

Newcomers began to feel safe and have real hope as they learned to trust the healing "experience, strength and hope" of people in 12-Step groups whom they could *see* changing from week to week. Then sooner or later, the new person would hear someone say, "I heard that if you want to get well in this program, you need to get a sponsor and work the Steps. And for me that was true."

As people share one-on-one with their sponsors, discussing the deeper and more shameful events in their lives that they couldn't share in meetings, a wonderful thing often happens. The sponsor's uncritical listening and acceptance becomes a stronger reinforcement than the inner shame voices, even if only momentarily, and the inner Person of the sponsoree begins to feel hope and courage. When the sponsor in turn identifies with the person sharing and shares his experience concerning the same issues, an authentic Person-dialogue is often born, along with a deeper sense of trust than the new pilgrim has ever known. Not only is the healing process accelerated, but the new person *and the sponsor* learn how to practice authentic intimacy in a one-on-one relationship.

Working the Steps gives sponsorees and sponsors something objective to focus on while they are reducing shame and learning how to be intimate. Since all sponsors are also recovering from the compulsion to control, the working of the Steps helps both parties avoid the tendency to get into their control games. Besides, the *content* of the Steps confronts both with their controlling and compulsive tendencies.[1]

After the sponsor tells the sponsoree what her own version of working the Steps is and what she expects of the relationship, the sponsor and the sponsoree usually tell each other their stories of how they came to the program. Then they are ready to begin to read the literature and look at the 12 Steps.

In the following four chapters we will take a look at the other two parts of the recovery program: working the Steps and the role of a Higher Power in the recovery process. We will look at the 12 Steps through the eyes of newcomers Roger and Sue, as they begin their journey through the program. Roger and Sue felt pretty hopeless about their relationship when they finally dared to try a 12-Step program. But when it was suggested that they might benefit from attending 12-Step *meetings* (separately), they were suitably horrified. Nonetheless, they each finally agreed to try a meeting and see what it was all about.

9
Steps 1, 2 and 3

Beginning the Journey to Freedom, Intimacy and Learning to Live

Steps 1, 2 and 3 put frustrated seekers in touch with their powerlessness to overcome the compulsion to control and the addictions it leads to.[1] Once they see that they do *not* have the strength to straighten out their lives, they are put in touch with a Higher Power who can give them this strength. They are amazed to discover that this Higher Power is loving and supportive. They find out firsthand that the Higher Power can help them focus a real source of strength and energy on defeating the shame voices and the dysfunctional behaviors that are destroying their lives.

Step 1:
Admitted that we were powerless over alcohol
(control, food and so on) and that our lives had
become unmanageable.

For newcomers, the doorway to healing the compulsion to control is to admit powerlessness and unmanageability, frankly facing the fact that our attempts to control others and our own happiness have not worked. For shame-based people like Roger and Sue, to even come to a meeting of "out of control" people was bad enough; but to *admit openly* that they were *powerless* and that their lives had become *unmanageable* seemed as if it would unleash an unbearable shame attack. But they discovered something quite different, as Roger recalls:

> I was really surprised at the people I saw at that first meeting. I thought they would be down-and-outers, real losers. But instead I found these intelligent, well-dressed men and women—I mean they were teachers, attorneys, sales clerks, mechanics, everything. Many of them were obviously coping well. Yet they had the nerve to stand up in front of all these people and admit, without shame, that they were powerless to quit their addictions and their compulsion to control until they started working this program.

The effect on Roger, as on most newcomers, was powerful. It began to dawn on him that maybe he had been living life on a false set of assumptions. As he listened to the old-timers talk about finding serenity and even beginning to like themselves, the message seeped in that maybe his shame-filled inner voices were wrong.

> I began to think, maybe I *am* a good person! Maybe I can like myself and quit trying to run the world to prove I am somebody. It was a real revelation.

As we break the silence barrier in a meeting and admit our own inner Person's powerlessness to fix ourselves or other people, a sense of peace and even self-esteem may come. At last we are being responsible by owning the reality of our human condition. We may spend less time in the inner "shame box" as we start to see life from a different perspective—humility.

At this point the early alcoholics realized that their behavior had been insane. They saw that for them to try to control other people's reality didn't make sense. It would never work for them. As they shared their reality with each other in meetings, they began to laugh as they saw the ridiculousness of their attempts to control their destiny and the destinies of other people in order to get love. It had brought only rejection, alienation, exaggerated resentment, anger, fear, pain, guilt and shame. Yet they had continued to do the *same* controlling things, expecting *different* results. It was crazy! With this realization, they formulated Step 2.

Step 2:
Came to believe that a power greater than ourselves could restore us to sanity.

Now we begin to see specifically how we have been living in an insane way and to hear the universal futility of control attempts to solve relational problems. We begin to realize that we need a Higher Power to help us change what we have not been able to change. So we begin to look to a Higher Power to help us out of our insane attempts to control the world, and to believe that such a Power will do so. As we take Step 2, we are being intimate with God or our Higher Power, as we share the reality of our "insanity" and our powerlessness.

For shame-based people like Sue, the first few Steps can be very difficult. Not only was she asked to go to a disgraceful meeting, and to admit in Step 1 that she was powerless and her life was unmanageable, but in Step 2 she was asked to admit insanity! As Sue recalls:

> At first I could not honestly do this. But I kept listening to other people. They were crying, laughing, as they talked about

the crazy, irrational things they had done while in the disease, and that helped me—especially since they mentioned some things I'd also done.

Sue began to see that openly revealing shameful behaviors and fears causes those shameful behaviors and fears to lose their power.

> People kept saying, "You're as sick as your secrets." Hearing the witness of others that a Higher Power had helped them change their behavior, overcome shame, and find serenity and self-esteem—well, after a while I wanted to try, too.

Sue, like many others, began to share her own shameful secrets and watch them lose their power. At the same time, she began to feel her long-lost inner Person come alive, and to experience some serenity and a budding sense of health and strength.

These beginning experiences of health and self-acceptance caused some of the early alcoholics to want to commit their whole lives to the One who has the power to overcome the disease that had driven them to a state of unmanageability. So they formulated Step 3.

Step 3:
Made a decision to turn our lives and our wills over to the care of God as we understood Him.

As we began to be intimate with each other and then began to get intimate with God, many of us learned to share our reality with God on a regular basis and to begin a Person-dialogue with our Higher Power. In Step 2, we had acknowledged the reality of a Higher Power and the fact that *we* were *not* God and that our previous Higher Powers (alcohol, controlling, compulsive working, people, food) had led us to misery instead of happiness and peace. At this point, some saw that the Higher Power was actually God and that they were powerless when it came to changing other people. They saw that they had tried unsuccessfully to play God in their own lives and relationships.

In our society, most of us get our foundational (though unconscious) grasp of the notion of what God is like from our relationship with our father. This foundational picture is reinforced or contradicted by the contemporary religious bodies we are exposed to. Many people had either abusing or deserting fathers. Such people coming into 12-Step programs are often atheists or agnostics. Roger was no exception. He hadn't given God a thought in years.

> The idea of deciding to turn my life and my will over to God seemed not only impossible, but stupid. The notion that I was going to have to take Step 3 in order to get well made me furious. I could almost hear God as being those shame and fear voices we talked about—and they sounded just like my parents yelling at me.

The founders of the program were wise enough to tell people like Roger that they didn't have to commit their lives to the abusive God of their childhoods; they could pick anything they wanted to for a Higher Power. The founders knew that the trusting *process* begins as one re-centers the control of the world outside oneself. This allowed the anger and the shame about "God" (connected with early experiences of abuse when trusting an imperfect parent) to subside long enough to let in a new experience of a loving, accepting and non-shaming Higher Power.

In my own journey, I had always considered myself a believer. But one day I heard a new man in the program talking to an old-timer about the 3rd Step, and I found that I had to rethink my entire belief system. The new man said, "No way I'm going to turn my life over to God! He'd ruin me—and I'd deserve it." He went on to say that for him God was a giant policeman—and his previous experience with the police had been pretty bleak.

The old-timer, a strong, quiet man, listened to the new man's description of God. Then in all seriousness he said, "You ought to fire that S.O.B. You ought to fire him! You've got the wrong god for this program, friend. The God who operates here is loving, forgiving and gives you all the chances you need to get the program; he's honest and will always be there for you. I had a god like yours when I first came in here, but I had to fire him and get me a new God."

"What can I do about a God if I fire mine?" the new man asked.

The old-timer thought a minute. "Well," he said, "I guess you can use mine until you get on your feet."

All my theological buzzers went off. I thought, *Fire God? We're dealing with Ultimate Reality here, friends. You just can't fire God and get a new one!* But I kept my mouth shut and listened, and I learned another one of the many humbling lessons that I have received while working the 12 Steps.

I realized that after 30 years of being a speaker, 8 years of graduate work in psychology and theology, being on the staff of a seminary and later a writer about God, I needed to do exactly what the old-timer had suggested so colorfully: I needed to fire my god! At least, I needed to fire my concept of a god who promises he will be with you and then really doesn't come through when you count on him. I needed to fire the god who says he loves you, but is gone out of town or is too tired to show up and teach you to be a man and teach you how to grow up, a god who leaves you filled with shame and feelings of unworthiness because he didn't have time for you. No wonder I didn't want to turn my life and will over to God: my unconscious operational image of God was an image of my human father as I had experienced him, not the God of the Bible at all.

My father had not been there for me when I really needed him as a little boy. I (like most people) had not understood that my relationship with an imperfect human parent was the unconscious foundation on which I would build whatever theology I could. So even though I had consciously believed God would take care of my financial security and my family, my stomach churned with fear and doubt when they were threatened.

The quiet witness of old-timers—who came to Step 3 as agnostics or atheists and discovered in the 12-Step community a Healing Presence and a reality that included an experience of intimacy and self-acceptance through a Higher Power—can help the newcomer replace the experience of a shaming Higher Power with a loving one. For many, this experience leads to a realization that God can provide an underlying security that frees people to risk being intimate with others and facing the most shaming truths about themselves. After all, even if others reject them, they have confidence that God accepts and loves them, continues to guide them and gives them the courage to know the truth about themselves and their relationships.

One striking by-product of the 12-Step movement that I discovered in traveling around America is that many 12-Steppers have gone back into religious institutions and become (anonymously) spiritual powerhouses for renewal there.

As the early members of Alcoholics Anonymous made the decision to surrender their lives, wills and futures to God, they started listening intently for God's reality. They invited God to teach them how to live and how to overcome the ravages of this disease, and hope began to be born. With each other, they faced who they really were. The fear of being revealed disappeared, and thus the fear of their shame voices. Some of their lifelong loneliness went away.

Many of us found we had been hiding from people as we tried to get control, always begging others to love us but knowing that if love was offered, we couldn't believe that love because we were hiding our true feelings and thoughts. Now we came out of hiding and presented our reality to each other. If someone loved us, we might believe it. We no longer had to fear that we would be discovered as inadequate. We had spoken these fears out loud. Now we could face the future with a group of loving people and with a new kind of serenity.

But the early alcoholics found it wasn't enough just to look to the future and walk on. They saw that they had to go back inside themselves where they had buried their most painful reality, where it was festering and causing bewildering guilt, shame, fear and resentment. Much of their past reality was in denial, and they couldn't even see it, much less present it to God—which they were now committed to do. They had to find a way to exhume their buried past, so they formulated Steps 4, 5 and 6.

READER/CUSTOMER CARE SURVEY

If you are enjoying this book, please help us serve you better and meet your changing needs by taking a few minutes to complete this survey. Please fold it and drop it in the mail.

As a special "**Thank You**" we'll send you news about new books and a valuable **Gift Certificate**!

PLEASE PRINT   C8C

NAME:_____

ADDRESS: _____

_____

TELEPHONE NUMBER: _____

FAX NUMBER: _____

E-MAIL: _____

WEBSITE: _____

(1) Gender: 1)_____Female 2)_____Male

(2) Age:
1)_____12 or under   5)_____30-39
2)_____13-15   6)_____40-49
3)_____16-19   7)_____50-59
4)_____20-29   8)_____60+

(3) Your Children's Age(s):
Check all that apply.
1)_____6 or Under   3)_____11-14
2)_____7-10   4)_____15-18

(7) Marital Status:
1)_____Married
2)_____Single
3)_____Divorced/Wid.

(8) Was this book
1)_____Purchased for yourself?
2)_____Received as a gift?

(9) How many books do you read a month?
1)_____1   3)_____3
2)_____2   4)_____4+

(10) How did you find out about this book?
Please check ONE.
1)_____Personal Recommendation
2)_____Store Display
3)_____TV/Radio Program
4)_____Bestseller List
5)_____Website
6)_____Advertisement/Article or Book Review
7)_____Catalog or mailing
8)_____Other_____

(11) What FIVE subject areas do you enjoy reading about most?
Rank: 1 (favorite) through 5 (least favorite)
A)_____ Self Development
B)_____ New Age/Alternative Healing
C)_____ Storytelling
D)_____ Spirituality/Inspiration
E)_____ Family and Relationships
F)_____ Health and Nutrition
G)_____ Recovery
H)_____ Business/Professional
I)_____ Entertainment
J)_____ Teen Issues
K)_____ Pets

(16) Where do you purchase most of your books?
Check the top TWO locations.
A)_____ General Bookstore
B)_____ Religious Bookstore
C)_____ Warehouse/Price Club
D)_____ Discount or Other Retail Store
E)_____ Website
F)_____ Book Club/Mail Order

(18) Did you enjoy the stories in this book?
1)_____Almost All
2)_____Few
3)_____Some

(19) What type of magazine do you SUBSCRIBE to?
Check up to FIVE subscription categories.
A)_____ General Inspiration
B)_____ Religious/Devotional
C)_____ Business/Professional
D)_____ World News/Current Events
E)_____ Entertainment
F)_____ Homemaking, Cooking, Crafts
G)_____ Women's Issues
H)_____ Other (please specify) _____

(24) Please indicate your income level
1)_____Student/Retired-fixed income
2)_____Under $25,000
3)_____$25,000-$50,000
4)_____$50,001-$75,000
5)_____$75,001-$100,000
6)_____Over $100,000

||||

BUSINESS REPLY MAIL
FIRST-CLASS MAIL PERMIT NO 45 DEERFIELD BEACH, FL

POSTAGE WILL BE PAID BY ADDRESSEE

HEALTH COMMUNICATIONS, INC.
3201 SW 15TH STREET
DEERFIELD BEACH FL 33442-9875

|ıı|lıııı|lıı|ıı|ı|ıı|ıı|ı|ıl|ll|ıı|ıı|ı|ıı|ıı|ı|ı|ı|lı|

FOLD HERE
((25) Do you attend seminars?
1)_____Yes   2)_____No
(26) If you answered yes, what type?
Check all that apply.
  1)_____Business/Financial
  2)_____Motivational
  3)_____Religious/Spiritual
  4)_____Job-related
  5)_____Family/Relationship issues
(31) Are you:
1) A Parent?_____
2) A Grandparent?_____

Additional comments you would like to make:

_____

_____

_____

_____

10
Steps 4, 5 and 6

A Journey into the Interior to Discover the Person Behind the Personages

After taking Steps 1 through 3, 12-Step pilgrims usually become even more eager to find out how to get well. The sense of support they have received from others, in meetings and from a sponsor usually enables them to face the fear of discovering what they are holding in denial. This prospect has been too fearful before. The shame voices have implied that at the very core of their lives is a rotten, worthless worm. But they are beginning to suspect that at the center of their lives may be a good Person who is worth saving and knowing. With the guidance of a sponsor—and the support of others who've been there—they are now ready to go in and locate the "bad" things about their lives, bring them out to face them, and then share them with God and another person. All this may seem impossible to shame-based people who are just starting the journey, but that is why Step 4 comes only after they have completed Steps 1 through 3.

Step 4:
Made a searching and fearless moral inventory of ourselves.

As Sue remembers her experience, "After a while it became clear to me that I couldn't make this journey alone, the way I'd always done in my life." She had found a basic truth: The movement toward authentic intimacy always requires a companion. At this point, 12-Step members turn to their sponsors, who are able to listen without judging them and share their own lives.

> My sponsor helped me begin the 4th Step, to look back inside and see how I'd harmed other people and had destroyed intimacy with them. This wasn't easy. I had to remember ways in which I had tried to control people, use them, shame them and manipulate them—I guess I had tried to play God in other's lives.
>
> My inventory also included the "good" things I'd done. My sponsor owned her own business, and she told me that if I was turning my life over to God, then my inventory should be analogous to turning a business over to a new owner: listing the positive assets would be as important as listing the dysfunctional behaviors and thought patterns. Looking for "good" things about myself wasn't so easy, either. I didn't have a very high opinion of myself.

But Sue tried anyway; she began to search for the positive, functional, loving things in her life. She found that as she began to list these items, she could see even more items—on both side of the ledger.

I felt as Sue did. As a person in the shame battle, I had always been afraid to look too deeply within. My shame voices warned me that I wasn't who I tried to make people believe I was. The idea of digging around and *writing on paper* the shameful things

I'd done was very frightening. I was in such denial that I didn't really know much to write, but I was told to write what I could see that I had done, and to list the resentments, fears and control behaviors I could get in touch with. Since many people in the meetings (including my sponsor) had told me that Step 4 is where the cleanup operation begins that leads to a new life, I began writing what I could see.[1]

As I did this moral inventory, my denial began to crack open at a deeper level. When I listed the first item and confessed to the harm I had done, it was as if I were pulling a thread out of my mouth. Tied to that thread was a string, a rope was attached to that, and a chain was fastened to the rope. Hanging from the chain was a bucket of garbage filled with all kinds of things I had denied and repressed for years. As I brought each new bit of knowledge to the surface and wrote it on paper, an amazing thing happened. Suddenly some of my lifelong fears subsided; some of the restlessness, the inner turmoil, the fear of intimacy and of love began to dissipate. Fresh breezes began to blow through the basement of my life, where all those hurts, pains, fears and resentments had been stored.

As I listed all these things and brought them out, I realized I was in a new place. My shame core seemed to shrivel. I was taking responsibility for my own actions, and I felt a sense of self-esteem. But now that these hidden inventory items were visible, something had to be done with them to complete the freeing process. For this, the early alcoholics formulated Step 5.

Step 5:
Admitted to God, to ourselves and to another human being the exact nature of our wrongs.

The original 12-Step pilgrims realized from the beginning that it wasn't enough just to discover their own reality as they took their inventory; they had to *share it* with another human being *in order to get well.*

All of the previous Steps—including the decision to come to

a 12-Step meeting—constitute a direct confrontation between the inner Person and the shame core, with its committee of shaming voices. As Roger told me:

> My fear of all the previous Steps paled as I faced the prospect of revealing to another, face to face, my very soul. I was going to show this person the throne room of my inflated, controlling self, my trophies of selfishness and abuse. As I did Step 4, I saw that I had perpetrated these hurts in order to fix and change other people, my wife included, and to cover the pain and other bloated feelings that might reveal the shame of my powerlessness and failure to be "enough." It was pretty painful to realize all this. But when my pain and isolation had gotten strong enough, and I shared my 5th Step, a kind of miracle took place.

I know how Roger felt because I remember how I felt in the same circumstance. I'll never forget the fear of judgment and rejection as I sat there in the presence of another person. Some of my sins were so petty they embarrassed me; some were so shameful I feared no one could accept me when they became known. Ironically, I had a fear that I didn't have "enough" sins in certain areas to be considered a real man. When I finished reading my 5th Step, I was so flooded with shame I was weeping. I feared looking up at the counselor who was listening. I could practically see the rejection and disgust that I knew would be on his face. But after what seemed like a long time, I finally looked up and met his eyes—and he was crying too. He said, "Good Lord, Keith, your list is just like mine."

In that moment something happened that was to change my life. I saw that I was *not* the shameful person I had always feared I was. This intelligent, sensitive stranger had seen my worst, my most shameful self, and he had not only *not* rejected me, but had *identified with me and accepted me just as I was!* Gradually it dawned on me that I wasn't uniquely awful, and that day I think I joined the human race.

I realized that the tide of my essential inner battle for integrity and identity had turned. My inner Person was going to win. I was going to become free to be the human being God made me to be before I had got buried in the life-and-death war with shame.

But there was another element that accelerated the blossoming of the seeds of self-esteem sown by doing the footwork for Steps 4 and 5. My sponsor had told me to list the *good* things about myself in my inventory. Strangely, as a shamed-based person, I found this even more difficult than cracking the denial about my shameful side. But my sponsor showed me how to make a list of my positive qualities and read them into a tape recorder.

Every day for several weeks I was encouraged to listen to this list the first thing when I woke in the morning and the last thing before I went to sleep. At first it was excruciating because I thought they weren't true. But then one day I wept as I listened. "You are a precious child of God, you love your family, you've done the best you could as a friend, husband and father, you try hard to have integrity and you love God. . . . " And the list went on.[2]

Gradually I realized that, notwithstanding all my failures, these positive things about my inner Person were true also. As a result, I became stronger and more confident as a man. I still saw my failures and the controlling abuse I'd discovered, but confessing and being forgiven was like having my inner slate wiped clean by the gentle hand of a Higher Power. Gone were the confusing, fearful, dysfunctional and controlling behaviors I'd stored inside myself—at least their power to shame and cripple me was gone. I saw that pointing out these old buried experiences had been a large part of the arsenal of my shame voices in the battle to control my Person and keep me from breaking free to fulfill my destiny as a mature human being.

Now I felt that I was standing on the brink of a new life. Maybe I *could* be intimate some day. Maybe I could be both vocationally and personally free to risk sharing my reality and going for my dreams without such an inordinate and shame-filled fear of failure.

Just seeing our denied material in the presence of another person has always lessened 12-Steppers' sense of shame about it. We learn a strange thing about shame: It loses some of its dominating power when the secret thoughts it threatens us with are brought out into the light voluntarily. As the early 12-Steppers shared their reality by doing Step 5, many of them found a peace they had never known before. The very fact of sharing these shameful hurts with another human being—and hearing the identification and sharing of the listener—itself constituted much of the healing they had waited for all their lives.

They saw that it wasn't "content," "answers" and "resolution" of all their relational problems that they needed. What they needed was to share these secret truths about themselves intimately with someone who could accept them as they were and who could then share from their own lives. The intimacy itself provided the healing. Intimacy with and acceptance by another person and God became the keys to the forgiveness they needed for their healing. After this, many began to share in meetings the deeper reality they had discovered through Steps 4 and 5, so that the sharing became deeper in the meetings. Other people were inspired to become more open, to share their reality at a deeper level.

As people face and share the shameful *and* the positive realities of their lives, several things often begin to happen. In bringing things out in the open, we are able to see them more clearly. Our denial subsides and we see that we really have hurt people.

We see that while we were accusing our mates and building a case against them, much of what our mates had been saying about us—which we had denied—was true. This begins to bring us some degree of humility. Humility doesn't mean being subservient or putting oneself down. Humility in 12-Step terms is more a matter of seeing things as they really are.

Then another paradox may present itself. Some of us begin to realize that even with all these faults and bad behaviors, we are somehow lovable and acceptable. God has made each of us a precious child who has faults and incompleteness and who has an addiction to controlling other people, but who, with God's power, has begun the process of being healed and made whole. This humility allows us to grow spiritually—to get solidly in touch with our reality and the love of God. Many people, through this process, have had physical healings as well. As they begin to get their repressed reality out, the symptomology that had formed in order to reveal their denied reality to their consciousness was no longer necessary. People have been cured of many stress-related diseases, including heart trouble, cancer and arthritis, during this 12-Step process.[3]

Somewhere in this stage of working the Steps, the early 12-Steppers began to realize that this program was leading them to happiness. As that happiness began to grow, the love and acceptance they received created an atmosphere of hope and a desire for more—more healing, more reality. They had actively sought to do away with the controlling character defects that caused pain in their own life and in other people's lives, and life was very different—and much better. As this consciousness grew, the founders formulated Step 6.

Step 6:
Became entirely ready to have God remove all these defects of character.

Essentially the founders were saying, "I have tried for 5 Steps and I have done what the people in this program told me to do. As I have done this I have found new life. I have found new hope that I will not be a loser in the inner warfare for integrity and happiness. I have found new acceptance. I am not bound by my past the way I was. The unacceptable and shameful reality I stored in the basement of my soul, which caused bad dreams, anxiety, controlling behaviors and mental, emotional and spiritual diseases, began to dissipate. These character defects all took place when I was playing God, hiding my reality without humility, intimacy or love. The beginning sense of relief from these experiences is enormous. At this point I was ready to consider giving God the 'rest of my life.'" As Sue comments:

> Shame and the fear of failure had been winning my inner battle all my life, so I was very careful about making commitments to change things. What if I decided to change and couldn't—or wouldn't—do it?

The inner voices are unrelenting in their shaming accusations. So to become ready to have God remove all one's character defects sounds at first like an impossible and scary decision
to be perfect. Sue says:

> I decided to take Steps 6 and 7 for two reasons. First, I was
> amazed by the new sense of self-esteem, the diminishment of
> shame experiences and the new feelings of joy and serenity that
> I experienced. It took me a lot of meetings over many months
> before I could work the first five Steps, but it was worth it. I real-
> ized that I had made a journey into my own interior and begun
> to discover my inner Person. And amazingly, I *liked* her! Second,
> those who had gone before me kept repeating that Steps 6 and
> 7 represented the spiritual watershed that put them in a whole
> new life of freedom.
>
> Inside I felt hopeful, free. I wanted more—in fact, I wanted it
> all! I finally thought, "If life can be as different as it is for me after
> getting some of my reality straightened out through committing
> myself to the program and to God, then maybe I can trust my
> Higher Power with my *whole future* by taking Step 7 and *humbly
> asking God to remove my shortcomings*. Then I can enlist God in the
> entire inner battle with my shaming self."

The founders knew that compulsive and addictive people
tend to jump out and make commitments without thinking
through what they are really committing. Step 6 gives us a
chance to decide whether or not we really want to put our
whole lives in God's hands to free us entirely from the baggage
and carnage of our inner warfare.

When we are ready, we are standing on the brink of a spiritual
watershed and are prepared for Steps 7, 8 and 9.

11
Steps 7, 8 and 9

Clearing the Decks for
a Whole New Life

Having established a relationship with our Higher Power and accessed God's power, we found the courage to begin to discover what was hidden from us in our lives. We wanted to bring it out of the shadow of shame so that we could hold it up to God before another person. In that person's eyes, we saw that our shame voices were wrong about us. Even with the awful things we'd done, we were acceptable and good people, with enough integrity to face ourselves and begin getting our lives cleaned up. After looking back at what had happened to us as we'd worked the program and realized the changes we'd seen, we became ready to ask God to take charge and make us free from all our character defects.

Step 7:
Humbly asked God to remove our shortcomings.

When I came to Step 7, I was afraid. I told my sponsor that I had always feared that someday I'd have to straighten up my whole life. But since I'd tried so often and failed, I was really hesitant to promise to do that.

My sponsor laughed and said, "Keith, you can't read very well. Step 7 doesn't say, 'I now promise to clean up my whole life.' It says you are going to *quit trying* to straighten out all your character defects." I said, "*Quit* trying? I can't do that. That's irresponsible!"

"No," he said, "it means that you are going to detach from trying to *control* your life and all your character defects. You're going to face them, name them and *turn them over to God* for healing, as you've done in the first five Steps."

When the truth hit me—that I could actually detach myself from my frantic and compulsive attempts to control my life— my inner Person wept with relief. *I was to show up, face reality, work the Steps on those things I was powerless over and commit my whole life to God, one day at a time.*

Roger's experience reflects that of many people in the program:

> It's ironic. As I quit trying to run the world, my life has become less stressful. After I humbly asked God to remove my shortcomings, some of the things about my behavior that I've been powerless over for years—I mean serious character defects that were ruining my marriage—have gradually disappeared.
>
> I don't pretend to know *how* this works, but I do know that because I *want* to see the truth about my life—because I know that this willingness will eventually lead me to freedom and serenity—I'm not so afraid to see my own faults and admit them.

Roger remembers that it wasn't easy for him to take Step 7. It wasn't easy for me, either. For most people who come to the 12 Steps, the only sense of security they know is in trying to control people and solve their own character defects themselves. By Step 6 they have usually realized that it was impossible for them to get their lives straightened out alone and have begun to depend on a Higher Power.

For many of us the spiritual watershed moment came when we realized that we were *no longer responsible for overcoming the control disease and our addictions,* that God had offered to do this. With a great sense of humility and gratitude, we then asked God to remove our defects of character as they appeared to us. Now when the defects come up, instead of wrestling with them and trying to beat them down through control, we surrender them to God, detach from them and go on with whatever we were doing.

This was an incredible experience for me, as I had always been super-responsible in order to avoid being shamed. But the shift from being in charge of all outcomes to one of doing our best and turning the outcome over to God puts many of us into a *spiritual* life, a life controlled by the reality and power of God's spirit instead of our own manipulations and controlling behaviors. In this shift we realize that good works aren't what get us God's approval; God *already* loves us and is offering to make us whole and free Persons. Our Higher Power is offering us salvation from the abusing introjected parts of ourselves and from being afraid to be close to other people. As we live with the fact that God is straightening out our lives, we are amazed to discover that we are beginning to relax with other people outside our 12-Step groups, and even with ourselves.

As this happens, we realize (or are told by a sponsor) that now it is time to begin straightening up our bruised and broken relationships from the past. Our shame has abated enough that we are able to turn outside ourselves and risk perhaps the greatest shame we have yet faced. We realize that the broken relationships caused by our playing God need to be tended to before we can let God teach us how to love people at close range. So we approach Step 8.

Step 8:
Made a list of all the people we had harmed
and became willing to make amends to them all.

It may be clear by now that a person who has been defeated in the inner shame war has a deep aversion to revealing any reality that may be perceived as less than perfect and therefore grounds for rejection from others, or for shame attacks from the inner voices. The first seven Steps represent a continual and ascending series of frightening confrontations of the inner shame voices. We have been asked to take more and more threatening and frightening actions in order to discover and claim our previously hidden reality. We have taken steps that put us in increasingly vulnerable positions of doing the *very thing we feared* would lead to shame attacks. We admitted power-lessness, then "insanity" and "giving up" to God. We faced unmentionable shameful situations, and revealed more and more of the shameful secrets that have kept us bound to the stake of shame driven into the middle of our soul. The program is structured so that not only are the situations more threatening and intimate as one goes through the Steps, but the content shared is more shameful and threatening to the shame voices. Nowhere does this become more clear than in Steps 8 and 9.

After the first seven Steps, the walls of denial have begun to crumble, and we can see more clearly what happened in our bruised relationships in the past. It becomes clear that intimacy had broken down in the first place because we weren't in touch with our true feelings and thoughts. We often projected our denied anger and need to control onto others, giving us an excuse to control them to "protect" ourselves. We were also afraid to share our reality for fear of rejection and losing control. Further, many of us realized that the pain we had caused other people had created a separation within ourselves. As Sue recalls:

> I couldn't become intimate with new people until I had somehow let God heal the separation in me. I had to face the

brokenness I had with other people in my past. I have to admit that I didn't know exactly *why* making amends would free me, but I was told that thousands of people working the program had discovered through experience that this was true.

So I made a list of all the people that I had harmed. I also began to remember additional people I had abused, resented, feared and controlled in what seemed like a zillion ways.

To face all of one's shameful stuff written on a list in Step 4 is one thing. To read the whole list to another human being in Step 5 is much more difficult for a shame-based person. But to face the dishonest, abusive and harmful things one has done to others *with them, face to face,* is to experience fear and the threat of rejection and shame of a whole different order. Now the very people we always feared would reject us if they knew what we were like are going to get a chance to do just that. The fear of that kind of vulnerability and intimacy, and of the confrontation it might lead to, are hard to describe to one who has not faced her own shame and fear of rejection.

Even listing the people I had harmed was hard to do. In my frantic need to be right, I started recalling all the wrong things the people on my list had done to *me.* But my sponsor reminded me that in this program we are not to take other people's inventory, only our own; we are not responsible for what other people did to us, only with clearing up our own mistakes. But the founders realized that just writing a list of these people was not enough, so they formulated Step 9.

Step 9:
Made direct amends to such people, wherever possible, except when to do so would injure them or others.

The early 12-Steppers realized that in Step 9 they had to go out and offer intimacy to the people with whom they had destroyed the possibility of trust. They were never to do this when it would harm another person, but other than that, they were to make direct amends—no matter what it cost. Says Roger:

I was scared when I contemplated taking this Step, but my sponsor had some good advice. He said that the responses of others to your taking this Step will vary. Sometimes people reject you; sometimes people accept you, and you can reestablish intimacy. But he made sure I understood that it is *not* the responsibility of the person doing the 9th Step to reestablish a relationship.

The response of the other person is not the issue as long as you have, in a nonmanipulative way, expressed the reality of the harm done to that person, expressed sorrow and regret, and made amends as well as you can. That is *all* you are responsible for. The other people's responses, whatever they may be, are about them, their own history and their own journey. If they don't respond to your sincere attempts to make amends or if they reject you, you've still done your job by going. Whatever happens, your life will be changed in a healthy way—because you are finally learning how to deal responsibly with failure and broken relationships.

When I had made amends to the people in my life whom I had abused, controlled and harmed in various ways (much of which I had previously thought was legitimate relating, or which I had rationalized and blamed on the other people's previous behavior toward me), I felt clean and strong in a way I never had. I couldn't think of anyone I had harmed that I had not either made amends to or tried to. I knew that making amends did not "make right" what I'd done, but I also knew that at some level I had done what I could. I no longer felt shame or guilt about my past. That meant that my shame voices *had nothing about past relationships to shame me with.*

It was like a miracle! My self-esteem increased and my sense of inadequacy and shame seemed, by comparison to my past experience, to have virtually disappeared. Since that time I have not been afraid to look people from my past in the eye. I have begun to experience much gratitude to God for forgiveness and for the whole reconciliation process, which I'd never fully grasped in my previous faith journey.

With regard to intimacy, I think I felt more comfortable being intimate with new people I had not known before because I didn't have to wonder if some event or person from my past was going to jump up and contradict the reality I was sharing. When people have done the first nine Steps thoroughly, God often begins to free them to relate to others intimately.

At this point a whole new pattern and possibility for living opened up before many of us. The Big Book of Alcoholics Anonymous describes this transition in what it calls "the promises," which the early alcoholics realized were coming true after they completed Step 9.

> If we are painstaking about this phase of our development, we will be amazed before we are halfway through. We are going to know a new freedom and a new happiness. We will not regret the past nor wish to shut the door on it. We will comprehend the word serenity and know peace. No matter how far down the scale we have gone, we will see how our experience can benefit others. That feeling of uselessness and self-pity will disappear. We will lose interest in selfish things and gain interest in our fellows. Self-seeking will slip away. Our whole attitude and outlook on life will change. Fear of people and economic insecurity will leave us. We will intuitively know how to handle situations that used to baffle us. We will suddenly realize that God is doing for us what we could not do for ourselves.[1]

As these promises became true for the early alcoholics after they had completed Step 9, they realized that they had taken the Steps necessary to lead them to a whole new life—a life with the potential of sanity, sobriety, self-esteem and authentic intimacy; a life in which any block to intimacy and to claiming their reality became the enemy. Any block to intimacy was seen as one step toward controlling again, and getting trapped in the control disease and the addictive behaviors it sets up.

But they also knew that this control disease is insidious and addictive in nature, and that it would keep coming back with the inner shame voices to get control of the precious, developing inner Person. They could only count on temporary healing unless they continued to practice daily the principles they had learned in doing the first nine Steps. So they formulated Steps 10, 11 and 12.

12
Steps 10, 11 and 12
Maintaining Integrity and
Moving Out into the World as a
Carrier of Intimacy and Reality

The last three Steps are often called the maintenance Steps because only by doing them at
deeper and deeper levels can we maintain sanity,
integrity and self-esteem. Only by doing these
Steps can we continue to grow into the caring,
intimate people we have the potential to become.
Step 10 reveals how to stay in touch with our
reality and keep being intimate by sharing it.

Step 10:
*Continued to take personal inventory and when
we were wrong, promptly admitted it.*

From the beginning of the program, many people
who have been through the Steps have continued

every day to walk through them in their minds and face anew their powerlessness over the disease. As they meet new challenges, they see and claim the insanity of their behavior, offer their lives and their wills to God, and do daily inventories on the specific new and crucial problems that come up. They list their major character defects and watch them to uncover new examples of their dishonesty and manipulation. When these things show up, they confess them at once. They make amends and try to keep short accounts with God and with people so that the new, honest relationships they are experiencing do not get clouded over again by outbreaks of the control disease.

Shame has always been a patient and silent adversary in my inner struggles. When I realized that I was being compulsive, selfish or controlling in the past, I would become enveloped by shame. Then I'd swear off the harmful behavior and make firm resolutions not to do whatever it was again. The determination in my mind would keep me from the controlling habit or the addictive substance for a while. But my shame voices would wait patiently until I got too "Hungry, Angry, Lonely or Tired," (or HALT, as they say in the program). Then in an instant I would try to run someone's life or fix them, and would be right back in the hot grease of my shame again. My inner voices would tell me mercilessly that I was a failure and would let me have it when I failed to be what I knew I "should" be.

But the structure of making a daily short inventory and a periodic thorough one has meant that I now have some tools to keep me honest and to bring me back to the principles of the Steps every few hours.

This discipline of taking a few minutes before going to bed to think back through my day to find instances of self-centeredness, self-will, exaggerated self-satisfaction, controlling people and other character defects helps me to make amends the next day and not store more denied material in my unconscious. This habit bleeds off my overall sense of shame and the need to keep a tight control on my behavior to avoid being shamed. Since I am choosing to do something constructive about my character defects and compulsions, I feel more acceptable and worthy as I do my daily inventory and meditation time.[1]

With regard to intimacy, when I am handling my current harmful behaviors and sharing my reality, my life of intimate relating is no longer fraught with the fear of being discovered and not being accepted. I take deep breaths, exhale with relief and somehow feel closer to people everywhere. I know that many of them are bound to be like I was, filled with the fear of not being enough and shamed by their failures to be perfect. And I can sometimes make allowances for others' behaviors I would not tolerate before.

Some people at this point in the 12 Steps may realize that they are happier, stronger and less afraid to share personal reality. People talk about the "miracles of the program," but the truth is that almost anyone who commits his life to God and works the Steps in the context of the 12-Step program is a candidate for one or more of these miracles.

Most people are aware that they are stronger after doing Steps 1 through 9 because they have a way to keep the channels of intimacy open between themselves and other people, God and their inner Person. Many of us, however, came to realize that this whole way of life depends on getting to know God by sharing our reality with God. Now that God had supported us in taking Steps to know ourselves, some of us have found a great hunger to know how to relate to our Higher Power more intimately. As we think about God, some of us find ourselves expressing our gratitude; in fact, one of the marks of 12-Step people is the gratitude that we feel to God and to each other for our healing and for the fact that we are not as afraid of life or being close to people. To express this new awareness of the need to know God more personally, the founders formulated Step 11.

Step 11:
Sought through prayer and meditation
to improve our conscious contact with God,
praying only for knowledge of God's will for us
and for the power to carry that out.

Having come this far in the 12-Step process, we have improved our ability to be intimate with others and with ourselves. Through increasingly intimate and threatening self-revelations, we have confronted our shame voices and begun to free ourselves from their control. Whereas we had been convinced that such revelations would destroy us with shame, now we have seen shame's biggest lie: that "keeping everything secret is our strength and security, so we must not share deeply." We have moved from Tournier's first step in becoming a functional person—that of being *able to keep* secrets—to the second step—that of *choosing to tell* our secrets in a safe, appropriate atmosphere.

The experience of going to meetings, sharing with sponsors and others in recovery and working the Steps gives us an increasing awareness that all kinds of shameful secrets lose their power over us when we share them. As the shame voices lose their domination over us, our authentic inner Person gains confidence and strength to risk expressing its secrets, dreams and hopes (as well as the shameful facts about our past and present) with others in the program.

At this point many begin to experience a longing to share freely with people who are not in a 12-Step program. After a few unproductive or painful attempts, a new problem becomes apparent.

Sue speaks of this common problem voiced by many people in recovery.

> I found that it was one thing to be intimate with people in 12-Step meetings, but it was vastly more difficult to feel secure enough to go back to my marriage and my other painful relationships and to share honestly and vulnerably there from

within my Person. I had all this freedom, this new power, and I wanted to express it in all aspects of my life, but it was pretty scary.

Sue had discovered, like many others, that the power gained in the program often isn't enough to bridge that frightening chasm back to the family. This is when many people have had what the program calls a "spiritual experience" or a "spiritual awakening."

Millions of 12-Step people, many of whom had no religious background before coming into the program, have discovered the crucial secret that spirituality culminates in an ever-deepening intimacy with God and with other people.

The power and security we need to risk living and relating intimately as free Persons comes from an intimate relationship with God. For us, only God is present in the inner citadel of the soul to guide and strengthen us when we go alone to risk intimacy with those who have frightened or hurt us in the past, or who threaten to hurt us now.

This brings us to the doorway to Tournier's third movement in the process of becoming a functional Person—that of entering a Person-dialogue with God.

We can begin to call on God in the face of the taunting shame voices. We become able to confront them with God present and tell them to be quiet, that we and God are in control of our lives now and together we are stronger than our parents, the introjected abuse of society and anyone else they want to try to intimidate us with.

We learn to know God more intimately in Step 11 through prayer and meditation. In the 12-Step context of intimacy, prayer is speaking to God and meditation is listening to God. By practicing such sharing and listening, and by reading things that reveal God's personality, purposes and power, we can receive an amazing sense of power and worth in our Person. As we grow more confident that God loves us and is for us, we can begin to see that many of our old fears are illusory and our old self-defeating habits are no match for God—particularly since we have learned steps to take to get back in relationship with God and people when we fail. This gradual transition takes place as we give God the central place in our lives and become conscious that God is present—loving us, strengthening us and encouraging our Persons to risk becoming all we were meant to be.

Although the inner battle will no doubt flare occasionally all our lives, should we drop away from God and the principles we have learned, we now know that the power of the Person-dialogue with God is available to us if and when we recognize our powerlessness, surrender to God and do the Steps.

The inner battle has been won in one sense, but the Big Book tells us that the continuance of the victory in the practical arena of our lives is contingent on our spiritual condition.

In order to maintain this spiritual condition, many of us have been advised to go to our own religious heritages in order to find ways to improve our conscious contact with God and express our gratitude. As people who have worked the Steps begin to read about God from their own heritage, they often discover that the secret of all spiritual growth (including what they have discovered through the 12 Steps) is that if they want to *keep* intimacy with God and other people, if they want to keep "the faith," they *must give away* what they are finding. In other words, the program's experience, along with the spiritual wisdom of the ages, indicates that intimacy will dissolve and disappear—and the controlling shame-based compulsions will reappear in our lives—if we don't continue to share our reality with new people. We must seek out those who do not have intimacy with people, God and themselves and are in desperate need of it. And so the founders formulated Step 12.

Step 12:
Having had a spiritual awakening as a result of these Steps, we sought to carry this message to others and to practice these principles in all our affairs.

Earlier we discussed how spirituality has to do with reality and intimacy. Spiritual people are in touch with reality—their own reality, the reality of other people and Ultimate Reality, or God. So whatever else it is, a spiritual awakening is an awakening to and grasp of the realities in which one lives.

Spiritual awakening may seem sudden, but, as Step 12 indicates, it is a result of the one-step-at-a-time approach. Here's how the steps to a spiritual awakening break down in terms of the 12-Step process:

- We discovered our powerlessness and unmanageability in Step 1.
- We saw the insanity of our lives in Step 2.
- We grasped the ultimate wisdom of offering our lives, our will and our future to God in Step 3, and decided to do so.
- We took a searching moral inventory of our lives in Step 4 and got the past out into the present.
- Then we intimately shared that "hidden, shameful" reality with another human being, with God and with ourselves, in Step 5.
- We asked God to expand this healing into all of our lives in Steps 6 and 7.
- We went back to past relationships and offered to do our part to rebuild the bridges of intimacy in Steps 8 and 9.
- We began to keep the channels of intimacy open as a daily way of life in Step 10.
- We sought ways to share this same intimate life *with God* on the road to ultimate recovery in Step 11.
- Finally, as we realized our lives had changed, been re-centered and all the doors and windows opened to let life in, we saw that this *entire* 12-Step journey had been a spiritual awakening. We began to understand the "happy, joyous and free" meaning of life for us and that life is an intimate, loving journey with other people and with God.

One of the marks of shame-based people is that we experience life as a closed system, like a house with all the shades drawn. Because of our fear of the shaming voices and our low self-esteem (even if it's buried under an arrogant, confident exterior), we often have trouble believing we are loved and that we are going to be truly happy. But as we open the shutters of our experience through the program, we find that different areas of our lives are opening up and getting fresh air and light—as if the windows had been opened in formerly closed rooms in our house. A spiritual awakening causes our lives to be more confident and open-ended—the opposite of the closed, secretive and "safe" directions our shaming voices urged us to take.

This change, sooner or later, has led many of us to feel that we are stronger and less afraid of failing. A spiritual awakening gives us a new set of supporting inner voices—the voices of our friends in the program, our sponsors and the sense of God's voice in our inner experience. Together these voices are stronger than our inner shame voices. As we open the windows in more and more rooms in our houses, we are not afraid of people close to us seeing inside our lives. We invite them in to visit with our inner Person through our offers of intimacy.

The founders saw that the "control" of life, of large material possessions and other people, was not the name of the game of living. They saw that the sharing of life, love and this intimate journey with God and other people was what it was all about. This change of awareness in whole or in part, is what people in the program have called "a spiritual awakening."

Those who experience a spiritual awakening have humility. They have no illusions about their own self-centeredness and sinfulness, and yet they are equally aware of their preciousness in the eyes of God and the fact that God is, with mercy and generosity, making them not just well but "weller than well" by putting them on this journey of "happiness in the midst of problems." Often their joy comes from a conviction that they are discovering what for them is the meaning of life. This gives them a great impetus to want to go out and find other people who are suffering from the same controlling and addictive diseases they were—not to "fix" them, not to try to "change" or control them, but simply to share with them their experience, strength and hope, their reality. They simply want to offer intimacy and a possible personal contact with God in the 12-Step community—nothing more. Those fellow sufferers take the 12-Steppers' offered hand and walk with them into meetings and into the spiritual family of those who understand about love, about a serene way of living, about the intimate sharing of reality.

... we sought to carry this message to others ...

By this time it becomes apparent to most people that the 12-Step program expresses itself largely in the truth of paradox: To *find* the power to defeat the controlling shame-based diseases, one must *admit to being powerless*. To receive sanity, one must admit to being insane. To *capture* the power to heal one's life, one must *surrender one's power*, life and will to God.

Here, in the middle of Step 12, we find yet another paradox regarding the continuance of the healing life we've found: To *keep* the sane, reality-oriented intimate life with people, God and one's precious inner Person, we must *give this life away to others*. We must share our experience, strength and hope with other sufferers.

This means we must tell our "shameful" story of control, addiction, surrender, and finding freedom from the compulsions to hide in the inner shame closet and to control others from our inner isolation. As we retell this story to those trapped in addictions and the compulsion to control, we *experience again* the power of the program and of God. That has the effect of letting our shame voices know in a continuing way that they are no longer our Higher Power and can no longer control our lives and silence our authentic Person. As we do this sharing, self-esteem and the renewed freedom to be real and intimate can follow.

... and to practice these principles in all our affairs.

Finally, in the last part of Step 12, the authors of the program realized that they could use the principles they had discovered in doing the Steps on the new issues that came up after they had gone through the whole 12-Step process. They saw that using these principles regularly keeps the reality channels clear and brings them back to sanity, self-esteem and intimacy again and again. They saw that these spiritual principles were not just applicable to their alcoholism or their other addictions or their attempts to control in certain areas of their lives, but that these principles could be practiced effectively in *every area of their lives.* All of life was meant to be an intimate, sharing, loving experience touched by the reality of the caring Higher Power, which they had discovered through the tragedy of their failure and attempts to replace God.

The amazing paradox was that a group of people, who had been bound by the need to control life and who had failed miserably, discovered not only freedom from their addictions but an entirely new way of living. They found the spiritual principles that made it work through a process that from beginning to end was based on the simple belief that if they shared their reality nonjudgmentally with others, God would lead them into love, into community and into an unselfish giving of themselves—all through the phenomenon of intimacy.

The principles of intimacy have been found to be a difficult but possible road to happiness for alcoholics, addicts and other people who have the compulsion to control. Moreover, there is a direct relationship between the experience of recovery we have been describing and the recovery of intimacy in families and romantic relationships.

PART THREE

The Recovery of Intimacy in Close Relationships

13
Phase One
Getting Reparented:
An Individual
Journey in Community

One of the hypotheses of this book is that it is not possible for a couple to reestablish authentic long-term intimacy in a close love relationship just by working together on their relationship with a counselor, regardless of how good the counseling may be.

When couples only work with each other to "patch up" their relationship, and do not work on their *own* issues, what usually results is just that—a patched-up relationship. One or both partners decide that being together is *the* important thing. As a result, they make growth-inhibiting accommodations that often limit their ability to face their own inner shame battle—and may even be a surrender to the shame voices and a denial of the potential of the inner Person of one or the other. But since the alternative seems to be divorce in the case of married couples, or total separation in the case of parent-child, friend-friend, etc., the parties make whatever accommodations are necessary to stay together, with one partner submitting to a lopsided negotiated truce or surrendering to the other party. They may feel great relief after months or even years of hostility and distance. And this may be the best arrangement many people can make. Unfortunately, such an accommodation can lead to two people living isolated lives within one home. They may share certain duties and privileges, and even a name, but the two partners are not developing together intimately or spiritually.

My experience indicates that only when *both* parties in an intimate relationship have been trained (or parented) to have some grasp of the five characteristics of a mature adult (see chapter 5) can the relationship reflect a mature intimate sharing.

Authentic intimacy takes place when two people are sharing their reality with each other. Each gives the other equal status without judgment or controlling so that one can't reparent the other. Intimacy assumes the following: (1) that each person is consciously aware of his own reality, and (2) that each has the freedom to share freely (or not share) his thoughts and feelings. Since these two assumptions are not true in the case of people who were abused as children, then before authentic intimacy can be recovered, each person must: (1) come out from denial and become aware of his own reality and (2) deal with the inner issues of abusive, shaming parent voices that say the only safe way to live is to keep secret one's painful, fearful and shameful reality.

Both parties coming out of denial and dealing again with parent messages constitute an individual journey for each party, though it can be taken while still in a relationship. I can build a bridge of intimacy only part way, and only from my side. One of my control issues is that I have tried to be the "project engineer," controlling my loved ones' reality and trying to build the bridge from their side as well as from mine. But in recovery I've learned to discover and deal with my own issues with the faith that whether or not the relationship grows back together is God's responsibility and not mine. My job is to face my *own* abusive, dysfunctional behavior and deal with it (in my case) through the principles found in the 12-Step way of recovery.

One of the hardest things for me to face was that I had to give up the outcome of my efforts to relate successfully to those close to me. My part is to get in touch with my own reality, the reality of God and God's will, and to try to do what I perceive to be God's will for me. But I have to listen to and watch my beloved as she communicates with me if I am to perceive her reality. I've had to be prepared for the fact that my loved one may *not* want to continue a close relationship with me. At that point I've had to commit my life to my Higher Power so deeply that I trusted God with that outcome, too. If I couldn't do that, I knew that my wife, not God, *was* my Higher Power.

Reparenting

Since trying to control healthy people drives them away, our best shot at having a healthy, intimate relationship is to put its outcome in God's hands. But this is not easy! Where do we go to relearn living?

I suppose the dream of every caring counselor is that she can locate with her clients a functional loving family somewhere with healthy boundaries to which to send each abused client. This healing family would provide a safe place where the recovering Person could express openly his painful and joyful reality and practice the behaviors he needed to learn without being judged, blamed, discounted, ridiculed, condemned or fixed. In such an atmosphere of acceptance, the client's inner Person could be renurtured as a child, this time in a functional way. The Person could be "reparented" and grow up as an intimate, spiritual adult in a non-abusive family.

For me, several 12-Step groups and sponsors have provided such a "family," with this incredible healing atmosphere and support.[1]

I learned in the 12-Step program that this individual journey of recovery in a love relationship requires that I begin getting "reparented" in my own life so I can develop the characteristics of the mature adult I missed in my childhood. Then eventually, God and I can stand together in the center of my soul and say firmly to my abusive inner voices, "You are *not* in control of my life any more. I choose to claim my reality, which is that I am a precious child of God, a precious Person who wants to share and love and find out how to live."

How does this reparenting take place so that we do not feel overwhelmed or controlled by internal or external shame voices? To get an idea of how this reparenting works, I'd like to go back and look at the five basic characteristics of a child as described in Pia Mellody's work. In almost all of us, these nascent characteristics have been abused to some extent, setting up our adult co-dependent behavior and shame-based personalities. How does the 12-Step program reparent us with regard to the five characteristics of a child growing toward maturity so that we can be intimate?[2]

Every Child Is by Nature Valuable

Our parents' or caregivers' parenting often did not make us aware of our inherent value. We introjected their shame and felt less-than and fearful about not being accepted. When we were not perfect, we had shame attacks. Finally we built an unreal personality out of "personages," people-pleasing or people-manipulating mini-personalities that we adopted to gain approval or status, first from our families and later from the world outside. For example, I knew my mother was very lonely, so as a little boy I listened to her by the hour, even when I'd rather have been out playing. It wasn't that the listening was bad, but the fact that I was listening to earn love. I didn't develop an internal sense of self-esteem, so I wound up as an adult having to earn my sense of self-worth through things outside myself, such as accomplishments and helping other people. Since my sense of self-worth never got inside, I felt shame and inadequacy most of the time behind a personage of confidence and success.

In recovery, as we come out of denial and face the realities of our lives and relationships, we see our unreal self-defeating and abusive personages a little at a time. As we *claim* our powerlessness and our "insanity," we begin to sense approval from our sponsors and from other people in the program—approval for being *what we actually are*, not for faking it. This approval of our emerging honest child somehow gets to our inner Person and strengthens it, along with the approval from God. In the recovering community we may have, perhaps for the first time, a sense of approval and value from a family for the Person we really are. This constitutes a kind of reparenting in which we are affirmed for having integrity and for being and becoming the Person we were evidently made to be. As this happens we can begin to experience our own self-esteem.

When I go back into an intimate love relationship now, I can feel okay. I'm not a second-class person; I'm a lover or husband, parent or friend. I have a real Person to bring to the relationship, and I often feel good about myself. My wants, needs and abilities are worth consideration.

Every Child Is by Nature Vulnerable

We human beings are not born with a shell to protect us. Part of functional parenting is to help a child develop adequate boundaries. An adult who does not have functional boundaries may wind up being either a perpetual victim or else an offender of other people. Without boundaries, I cannot stop the shaming voices from controlling me. If someone calls and asks me to be secretary of the P.T.A., I can't say no for fear I'll feel shame and dislike myself or that they will think I'm not a good person. This reaction may take place even though I have a full traveling schedule in my business and have sworn to myself that I won't—can't—take on a single other commitment. Or I may be able to turn down the P.T.A. easily but not some other person, an authority figure or possible customer, making a similar request.

As I develop boundaries through the program, however, my intimate relationships also begin to change. I no longer have to accept invitations to do things that leave me overcommitted and frantic. I don't have to charge into your space when you are busy and introject my agenda onto yours, until my life absorbs yours. I can learn to hear you without either immediately dropping my agenda and going with yours to avoid being put down or shamed, or throwing up a wall of anger and blame, and shaming you for interrupting me and not being what I need you to be.

Using functional boundaries, facing things and sharing them openly, has allowed many of us to discover that the shame voices have subsided and in some instances disappeared altogether. In this process we are being reparented about our lack of boundaries.

Every Child Is by Nature Imperfect

When parents criticize and shame children for making mistakes, the children must hide their "true" reality from people and from God to avoid the shaming internal voices. As adults, such children may have trouble even owning their true reality. One party's denying things that are obviously true is an automatic block to intimacy, and leads to constant misunderstandings and anger in close relationships.

Through attending meetings, talking to sponsors and working the Steps, some of us are learning to share the painful mistakes we have made. At first this was frightening, and we sometimes had shame attacks for making ourselves so vulnerable in front of other people. But gradually, as it sank in that making mistakes is how *everyone learns about life*, we began to accept our imperfect natures and deal with our mistakes as soon as possible. This keeps the hidden mistakes from causing festering "shame boils" and helps the recovering person learn how to avoid making the same mistakes again. This reparenting process begins as newcomers hear others share their own experience with handling the same issues.

As this habit of openness slips into one's intimate relationships, a wonderful change can take place. For example, I have always had an overwhelming need to be right. When I'd be accused of having "blown it" or "done it wrong," my mind would instantly manufacture several justifications for my mistake, my "sin." After I had been in the program for about a year, my denial about this self-protective process cracked open. I couldn't believe the lengths to which I had gone to keep from admitting I'd been wrong (and thus avoiding being shamed by my inner voices).

At first I couldn't see my massive self-justification apparatus. But after hearing many people in meetings describe their own awful need to be right, I started admitting my self-justification in meetings. Then one day at home I was right in the middle of justifying myself for working on a Sunday when I'd promised to take the time off to go somewhere with my wife. Just as I was burying her with the nobility of my sacrifice of working on a Sunday and subtly twisting her act of reminding me of my promise into the interruption of a shameful, carping wife, I suddenly saw what I was doing. I stopped, looked at her and thought about what I'd just said. Then I said, "Honey, I'm sorry. This is all about me and my fear of being wrong and not enough. You were right. I did promise not to work, and I want to make amends for my abusive attack of you. I hope you can forgive me." Then we spent some time together. This was a significant breakthrough for me, and my inner Person felt wonderful! Sometimes I still can't see my self-justifying, or I can see it but I can't stop it at the time. But now, in many instances, I can go back and make amends, usually after sharing in a meeting or with a sponsor.

I never learned growing up that making mistakes is a natural part of growing, but I have been fortunate enough to have a chance to get reparented in this most important area of living. This is allowing me to be in touch with my reality more, so when I share in my closest relationships, I am more likely to do so without falsely vindicating myself and blowing the possibility for intimacy.

One of the remarkable side effects of this change has been the awareness of another one of my major character defects, which has sabotaged intimacy in my life since I was a child. When people close to me fail to be perfect about something they said they were going to do for their own life, such as going on a diet or an exercise program, I have always been compelled to note their failures for them—just in case they might have missed them. I noticed how angry and silent or rageful they got, but I couldn't understand why they were so upset; I was "just trying to help" them. But when I saw to what extent I would go to avoid others' accusations of *my* not being perfect, I realized why I point out others' mistakes and omissions. I now see that I tell them about their mistakes as a way of controlling them, bolstering my own weak self-esteem and suppressing my fear of not being adequate. After all, if they make lots of mistakes, I'll look better—less likely to be judged inadequate by comparison. I now realize that this is an example of the insane thinking to which Step 2 refers. My friends don't feel better when I remind them of their failure to do what they set out to do, and they will probably shame me when an opportunity comes. Except for a momentary pleasure in saying, "Gotcha!" I don't feel better either.

Lately I've been catching myself in this deadly control game that slams the door on intimacy and brings pain and anger to those close to me. If my wife goes on a diet or has an exercise program and fails to keep her regimen, it is *none of my business*. She is a grown woman. I now know that no one will take care of himself or herself until the pain of not doing so gets greater than the pain of the discipline. After a lifetime of fixing other people, it is very hard for me not to "fix" her. But now we can discuss the difficulties we are each having with our disciplines, if we want to, because we are not so afraid of being fixed. Before, when I was into this kind of controlling, we both withdrew and were more angry and distant. Intimacy disappeared, sometimes for days.

Although I have a long way to go in this subtle control temptation, things are much better than they were because of the reparenting we are receiving in the program. We are no longer enemies of each other's Persons as we were when we unwittingly became allies of the other's shame voices.

Every Child Is by Nature Dependent, Needing and Wanting

Abused children are not taught healthy attitudes about being interdependent and asking for help appropriately. They grow up not knowing how to meet their own needs and wants in healthy ways. As a result, many of their intimate relationships are sabotaged. This happens because it is not okay for one or both parties to share their needs and ask the other directly for what they want.

For example, my father evidently did not believe it was "manly" to need or ask for help. He once told me, "Keep your mouth shut, son, and they'll always overestimate you." There is a sense in which this is true in the short term in business. But when I got married, this attitude caused a lot of problems for me. I had legitimate wants and needs that I couldn't meet by myself and that my wife could help with. In my family of origin, each family member was supposed to guess what the other people needed and give it to them. When my wife didn't guess my needs and meet them (after I had given her my family's subtle, indirect signals), I got very upset. I felt shame. I wasn't worth having my needs met. Then I'd get very angry and attack my wife for being insensitive. She was surprised, hurt and angry that I hadn't told her directly what I needed or wanted.

I'd heard people say in meetings that they were learning to ask for what they wanted and needed. I remember my sponsor suggesting that maybe I could ask my wife for what I wanted. I said, "What if she won't give it to me? I'll be filled with shame and anger and I'll think she is controlling me."

He laughed and said, "Well, you're not getting what you want now, are you? And she has a right to say no, but no is not necessarily about you."

I saw that he was right and began to ask for time to talk, special times to be intimate and sexual, and even hugs when I felt lonely and like a lost little boy. At first when the answer was no, I felt shame as I had as a child. But as I shared those feelings with my sponsor—and later with my wife—I realized that there was nothing to be ashamed about. This reparenting by my sponsor and others in the program has helped us in our marriage to be in touch with and share our physical, mental and sexual realities in all kinds of new happiness-producing ways.

I realized recently that I have almost no shame feelings when I ask for something and am told no because of my wife's conflicting needs and wants. This has been a direct result of learning to talk about what we are feeling in meetings. Sometimes even a refusal can be an occasion for closeness and intimacy, as each realizes what a breakthrough a healthy boundary decision by the other represents.

Every Child Is by Nature Immature

When children are not allowed to be immature—to operate at their own age level—often they will learn to hide their imperfect natural reality and try to act perfect to avoid being shamed. Conversely, if children are allowed to operate at a much younger age level, they may grow up to be chaotic and childish "on purpose," to avoid the shaming of not knowing how to "act mature."

Coming into recovery, many 12-Step people fall into one of these extremes—either being perfectionists or out-of-control children. They listen in meetings as others like themselves face openly their perfectionism and childish, outlandish behavior and the harm these have done. As these old-timers become intimate about their own pain of not being enough, the new people begin to listen and do the Steps.

Often in amazement, perfectionists and controlling co-dependents see themselves relaxing and becoming more honest, childlike and detached. As they learn to trust God and their inner child Person, they begin to make more appropriate and less rigid decisions, and are thus reparented about their perfectionism and immaturity. At the same time, chaotic alcoholics, food addicts and irresponsible co-dependents begin to take responsibility for their lives and become more dependable and "present" in their relationships, all of which tends to foster sanity, reality and intimacy.

In some ways I had the worst of both worlds. I was a super-responsible perfectionist-religious work addict on one hand, but my personal organizational habits were chaotic. This meant that I was always looking for something that was lost, *had* to get things in on time, but had to expend enormous energy getting them together to send in. In recovery I am learning to take time off every week to play. I have also asked my wife and my secretary, who are both well organized, to teach me how to get my personal life and files organized so I don't spend so much time looking for things I need, or badgering *them* to look for them. This all happened as I heard others in my 12-Step family share their experiences about issues that were also mine—like having difficulty asking for help and direction. So in a non-shaming way, I began to get reparented in order to be a more happy, comfortable and mature adult.

This reparenting has helped me with regard to intimacy in that my personal disorganization used to fill me constantly with a sense of inadequacy and shame. My inner voices shamed me severely when I couldn't find something I needed or was about to turn in something late. Unfortunately, when I am feeling inadequate, I tend to look for ways to blame other people—especially those closest to me—which unfortunately sabotaged intimacy every time. Although I have much more to do to become both mature and childlike in healthy ways, the reparenting I've received in doing the 12 Steps has made me feel like a new person more of the time.

Let's say that you have begun the recovery process and are beginning to get in touch with your reality, and have started the reparenting meetings with others in recovery. You are beginning to feel better about yourself and have developed a personal and intimate relationship with God. Now you want to take what you are learning into your intimate love relationship. How do you handle the nitty-gritty hidden issues that come up when you are alone with your loved one, with no sponsor or fellow recovering person present? This is Phase Two of the journey.

14
Phase Two

Re-approaching Your
Loved One

I f you have not had a miracle in your life, chances are you will think it is impossible for you and your spouse, (or other person in a relationship of long standing) to have a safe, authentic and loving intimate relationship of the kind I've been describing—especially after years of painful and frustrating interactions and misunderstandings. But if you have been in a 12-Step program, seen your whole emotional and personal worlds turned right side up, and found sobriety, serenity and happiness after years of anxiety, resentment and depression, you may be ready to try again in your marriage (or if your marriage has ended, in another close relationship). Indeed, my own experience would indicate that the new eyes and ears that can come from the 12-Step experience (or something like it) are essential for establishing authentic intimacy.

If you have made up your mind that you are going to make your intimate relationships work "come hell or high water," I think I can promise you both hell and high water—*without* your relationship becoming a safe and growth-producing "place." I have already suggested that to recover intimacy in your close relationship, you may have to lay aside the question of trying to fix the relationship—which, any way you cut it, seems to get into controlling—and start working on your own controlling behaviors in an appropriate recovery program.

Another reason for concentrating on your own issues is that one of the primary components of authentic intimacy is *emotional equality.* Many of us coming into the program are so co-dependent that we have no boundaries and cannot take care of ourselves, or we have to control our partner's reality to feel secure and adequate. Even if our partners change and become open and vulnerable, we do not have the tools to keep from being manipulative and dishonest. We learn the remedies for these things in doing the 12 Steps.

What If Your Loved One Is Not in Recovery?

In most cases, both parties in a relationship must be on their own individual journey toward wholeness in order for the couple to have authentic intimacy. If only one party is in touch with his reality and is aware of denial and the compulsion to control, it can be very difficult to communicate with the other. In some cases, if the recovering person is enough in recovery to be free to share openly, the other party may become free to share by experiencing the honest, nonabusive communication. But until *both* parties see their self-deception and their deep and often denied passive-aggressive needs to control, it is extremely difficult to have authentic intimacy. It is especially difficult for the recovering person to stay open to the inevitable judgment, misunderstandings and control games of the partner who is not in recovery.

It is also true that if your mate chose you because in your co-dependence you were easy to control, he may not be happy with your changing into a precious child of God who deserves—and expects—emotional equality. The fact that you expect the freedom to become the Person you were "designed" to be may not warm your mate's heart. So you will very likely need the support of meetings, a sponsor and the tools of the Steps to protect yourself against the expectations of your unrecovered mate.

This statement may seem harsh and judgmental, but I am speaking out of the experience of many hundreds of people.

Different Views of Pain

I am not saying that those not in recovery are "bad," "dumb" or "vicious"—only that the compulsion to control is so insidious and so powerful that a person in recovery has to have *excellent* boundaries in order to remain open in a relationship with one who is not in a recovery process. Since people not in the program can rarely see their denial and control issues, or face the pain these things cause them, they almost certainly *will* continue to use them on you.

The problem seems to be pain. People who have not been through the 12 Steps or another recovery process often see pain only as "the enemy" and flee from it in any way possible—even over the bodies of their loved ones. But many of us have learned in recovery that pain is the doorway to intimacy and wisdom. Later many of us learn that pain is not only the "way in" the program but the "way on"—down the road of recovery. I was told that a mature person will not run from necessary emotional pain, but will stand in it and ask what its message is. Many of us feel that pain virtually always has a message from God about something we need to learn or attend to in our lives. A person with this belief will have a very different attitude toward the pain in an intimate relationship than one who is trying to escape pain at any cost. A wise person uses pain as a farmer uses organic fertilizer, to support increased growth.

As we work the 12-Step process, we become increasingly aware that it is not our responsibility to "accomplish" the re-establishment of the intimate relationship. But the benefits we are gaining through facing our own reality and learning to make amends will spill over into the relationship simply because they are a natural by-product of working the Steps.

When my denial began to crack open and I got to Step 4, I started to become aware of the specific ways I have controlled and hurt people around me. This awareness included many ways that I have tried to control my wife and her reality and change her to get her to meet my needs and expectations. In Step 9 I had to go to her and make amends. I didn't do this (as I had in the past) in order to get her to like me or to heal our relationship so that I could get my needs met again. I made amends because the program told me that the only way to get well and find any peace in my life was to work the Steps, concentrating on changing my own character defects.

As I began to share my own reality, I noticed a strange effect. At first people close to me were suspicious. Was this yet another of my almost invisible control devices? Had I really changed? But since I was *not* trying to convince anyone or change their reality this time, they finally appeared to relax more around me.

As I began to work my program and share within our marriage, without demanding that my wife change or even accept my changes, the climate began to change to one of reality and intimacy. This does not always happen. Sometimes a mate will get angry, rage or try to get you back into the fighting and control mode—it's familiar and more comfortable than the detachment that you are exercising in order to get well. But I discovered that if I do not slip back into my old manipulative fighting pattern, but instead continue to learn to be more direct and honest about my communication, my thinking becomes much clearer. Since I know that I can make amends when I have done something wrong (instead of trying to keep score about who is right or wrong in our relationship and who is doing the most or the least), I do not feel so compelled to "win" or to "be right" so often in our conversations and encounters during each day and night.

Sometimes I wake up feeling insecure and blow a whole day with my picking, judgmental, competitive self-justification. But now I have the principles of a daily inventory and surrendering my need to be perfect (and my will) to God leading me back to sanity and intimacy. I am working a program to clean up *my own* life so I can be the creative, loving Person God made me to be. That's my focus now most of the time, rather than "making my marriage right" or "helping" (controlling) my wife's thinking so we can relate better.

So if you are in recovery and your mate is not, you can offer intimacy and often have a greatly improved relationship. You can also practice keeping your boundaries in place so you won't get clobbered or straightened out too painfully. When I got in recovery, several people close to me quit wanting to be around me because I didn't drink anymore. They thought I'd be preaching at them to quit drinking. They thought I'd made a mistake quitting in the first place. This was painful. But because I have developed good emotional and intellectual boundaries, I can usually be around these old friends, hear them and share my reality without judging them or feeling rejected and put down. Besides the support of my wife and my sponsor, I have a good relationship with God and a "family" in several 12-Step groups to whom I can go for support, reality checks and continuing growth.

Our Relationship with God Comes First

Needless to say, it is *much* harder to stick with the recovery process when your marriage partner or lover feels alienated by your new life. But to become a whole person capable of an authentic long-term loving relationship, I believe you must put your recovery and relationship with God *first*—before the relationship with the other person. If you don't, you will wind up hiding those parts of reality that you feel are too threatening to the relationship—and you will have made your spouse your resident Higher Power. I now believe that intimacy is a by-product of the overflowing of love and reality of two people, each on a journey toward becoming a whole Person doing God's will.

If as a recovering person you put God first, then you can have an amazing sense of security in the relationship. If you are rejected and deserted when being yourself, God will be there to pick you up and support the next steps you need to take to get on with life. Experience indicates that without God, a recovery program and meetings, it is almost certain that we will consciously or unconsciously sell out our integrity, lie, or hide those parts of reality that could bring spiritual growth and joy in an intimate relationship. This is not an accusation, just an example of how denial seems to work.

The bottom line is that if you get in recovery and your loved one does not, you can learn and practice intimate sharing in meetings, with your sponsor, and with individuals you meet in recovery groups. In the meantime, it is often disastrous to try to control your partner into recovering and "sharing."

I have a friend who discovered in counseling that she and her husband needed to share more in order to have intimacy. "My husband just wouldn't share his feelings. I was always trying to share and he never would." She badgered him until finally one day he said, "Okay, here goes. I think you are ruining our son's life the way you smother him and demand that he check with you about every decision he makes." She was furious. Instead of hearing his reality and sharing hers, she attacked him and tried to defend herself for several hours. He never opened up again.

You can, however, develop a functional boundary, learn to detach from trying to change your mate and be as thoughtful, kind and loving as possible in your daily relationship—without either controlling your mate or letting your mate control you.

As I began to try to look honestly at my responsibilities as a person rather than at who was "winning," I began to try to do my part more in the marriage. Sometimes I now do things to help my wife without having to call her attention to the fact that I've done them—though not as often as I'd like, since I still seem to have an addiction to praise. But I have learned from others that doing our share as fairly as we can is one of the conditions that allows intimacy to take place. In other words, if I am being unfair and not doing my part and not taking responsibility for my own actions, this assures that intimacy is blocked. Whereas if I reverse that process in my own life and begin to share honestly, take responsibility for my actions, do my part in the marriage and with the children (or the animals, the chores and so on), I am rebuilding the bridge of intimacy from my own side.

Your mate may not be able to accept this, may not even want a healthy relationship like the kind you are becoming capable of having. When you are working the program with the support of a sponsor and recovering friends, your partner may not be able to control you. As I've suggested, your mate may not want a marriage in which he cannot control you. But I have learned that others' decisions about how to respond to my recovery are not my responsibility. I can hear their anger if it comes, and understand it, but I can't change them.

You can keep your part of the relationship going, but experience indicates strongly that it's probably *not* wise to read a book or go to a couple of meetings and run back to your significant other, attempting to be intimate and to share all your newly found wisdom (it will probably sound like a new attempt to control). But if your life really changes as you work the program, chances are that your new honesty and humility, and the cessation of some of your previous control behaviors will begin to reach your partner in positive ways. In some cases (though not all, of course) the other partner will get into a recovery program on her own. But getting into recovery in order to get your partner to change is usually doomed to failure. It is just another co-dependent manipulation that most mates can smell.

When Only One Partner Is in Recovery

When your partner is not in recovery, and your new way of living is direct and detached from carrying other people's feelings, and you are being responsible only for your own behavior, you will really need your boundaries. Most of us in recovery have discovered that our new behavior can be perceived by our families as lacking in love and caring, as self-centered and "not doing our part." Why? Because if you have been doing 80 percent of the instigating in the relationship—or caretaking, or trying to make things right—and cut back to 50 percent, it may seem to your partner that you are no longer doing your part, that you are guilty of emotional desertion because you keep your boundaries up and do not participate in abusive arguments.

Several things can happen if you decide to put your life, your will, and your mate in God's hands and work a good program, but your mate has not decided to do the same. Some of these consequences can lead to the establishment of authentic intimacy in a marriage.

1. Your mate may feel enough pain to recognize that he has to do something to relieve it. If you have been caring and honest, your mate may come to you and ask for help, or may be open to help in a wholly new way. In our marriage, my wife and I both got into recovery at about the same time. We had to work our programs separately until we got far enough along not to try to control each other's recovery.

2. On the other hand, your mate may accelerate his compulsion, addiction and angry resentful feelings and get into real trouble. (An alcoholic husband, for example, can accelerate drinking to the point that he loses his job or is picked up by the police for public drunkenness.) In any situation in which your mate is getting out of control, you may need to contact a treatment center and find out how to do an intervention. You can have an intervention on a co-dependent (as well as on an alcoholic) who is being very abusive.

   An intervention can result in getting someone directly into treatment. *It is essential to get professional help to conduct the intervention* so that you and your family have a safe way to confront the addict or co-dependent. In the intervention, the addict is told that unless he goes to treatment, you (or the addict, depending on the circumstances) will have to leave because the behavior is becoming very harmful and dangerous to you or your children. This may sound terrible and like unloving desertion—and likely it *will* sound that way to your mate—but sometimes it is the only kind of tough love that works for people who are truly out of control.[1]

3. When one party is learning how to be intimate, the other party may slowly begin to feel safe. Your partner's denial may begin to crack open a little in the face of your sensitive, intimate sharing. Your mate may not feel as much need for self-protection and may see his own problems becoming visible in your changes. Your mate may start sharing with you. Genuine intimacy can be started in a quiet, almost unconscious way as a result of the authentic intimacy of the recovering partner. When this happens, the other party will sometimes voluntarily join a 12-Step group, get a sponsor and get into the program, or go to a counselor. This has often happened in the 12-Step programs of which I have been a part.

4. The confronted partner may become so enraged, or his life may become so unmanageable, that he leaves the relationship or becomes so abusing to you or your children that you may be forced to separate for your own safety and the continuation of your own recovery.

A great number of people have reported that as they begin to work the program, to get some self-worth and to be intimate people who deal with their own issues, suddenly the "crisis" nature of their living with people close to them subsides. They realize they are not God and they *can't* fix everybody, or indeed, anybody. They realize that they have to let people live or die by their own choice—even their husband or wife, since it is a fact that they can't keep people from ruining their lives. (Many addicts and co-dependents have the tenacious delusion that they can save the other party by their own commitment and hard work. More often, by trying to fix the situation, they enable the disease to continue and help the other person hold onto the delusion that they can take care of their own problems.) Of course, if the partner not in recovery gets out of control in ways that have serious negative consequences for you (e.g., irresponsibly spending the family into great debt, or physically or sexually abusing you or your children), it is wise to get professional personal or financial counseling at once.

But what if your partner does want to get into recovery? How do you negotiate the specific differences and conflicts that come up as you both try to be intimate with each other? Phase Three explains these questions.

15
Phase Three
Relearning to Communicate

E ven when both parties are in recovery programs, their ability to relate in a loving, intimate way does not follow automatically. Perhaps the most difficult aspect of spiritual growth is translating into our closest relationships what we are learning while doing the 12 Steps.

We learned our secretive, manipulative and controlling ways in our earliest significant family relationships. Those behaviors seem like wagon ruts that we are stuck in when we try to bring our new insights and behaviors back into our adult intimate relationship. We are amazed that our loved one can't understand us, and we are angry that he continues to misinterpret what we think we are saying so clearly. One of the most difficult delusions to get over is the assumption that intelligent people of good will should have no difficulty communicating in their intimate relationships. Virtually every couple periodically has difficulty with communication as they grow. In most *functional* relationships, there are miscommunications of some kind virtually every day, however trivial they may be. Realizing this has allowed me to relax and learn much faster about communicating with my wife and family.

Relearning to Communicate

Although I am a professional communicator with many years of experience in helping other people communicate, sometimes I am helpless to make myself understood at home—even after years in recovery. The amazing thing is that in my professional life I have been affirmed for presenting my ideas clearly. But at home the audience has different ears. On reflection, though, it's not so amazing. Most of us did not learn how to communicate clearly as children, so it's not surprising that we also have trouble communicating in our most intimate relationships as adults. The big passageways into each other's arms and hearts are often blocked by closed doors that are stuck on very small hinges.

In this section I want to deal with some of the crucial areas where I believe change must take place if authentic intimacy is going to flourish. When describing conflict in these examples, there is no way I can capture on paper the intense fear and anger that can be generated by the most trivial differences in intimate encounters. The fear of being put down or shamed is just below the surface for many of us, ready to send us into an irrational rage at our loved one.

I remember one couple telling me that soon after they were married, they invited friends over for a dinner party. She set the table, putting the napkins in some inexpensive napkin rings. He had been raised to think that napkin rings were "tacky." These were "important" friends, so he reset the table *without* the rings. She told me that she was so enraged at that moment, she wanted to kill him. He couldn't understand why she was so upset over his removing the napkin rings. But he had shamed her by saying with his actions that she didn't know how to be a proper wife. At this stage in her marriage, her shame voices were telling her the same thing. The rage occurred to cover the fear that she wasn't going to be good enough to make it in this new part of her life. The man was surprised, but his fear was that he would be shamed when the guests came and saw the napkin rings. The fight was intense and very serious.

Skunks and Turtles

We come into relationships with communicating styles that we have adopted from our families of origin. Unfortunately, there are usually great differences in these styles. If partners do not understand these differences, much frustration will result. In our communicating styles, we seem to be divided roughly into "skunks" and "turtles." Skunks are people who like to solve problems and express their feelings by talking them out. They spew out words as a skunk spews out odor. They have been taught that talking *is* intimacy. The only trouble is that such people sometimes are not in touch with their own reality, and in any case do not share their honest inner feelings (of shame, guilt, pain, anger, sadness, fear and joy).

The other basic style of communication in close relationships is that of the turtles. They do not like to talk. They come home, get in their shells by picking up a book or turning on TV, and do not often share their inner thoughts or feelings at all. They are present but don't want to talk. The problem is that skunks and turtles often marry or get into close relationships. At first, skunks secretly admire turtles' ability to keep their own counsel. Besides, turtles are quiet and therefore appear to be good listeners—and skunks love to talk. Turtles, for their part, think they have found someone who will talk to people for them.

After the wedding, however, the skunk is often furious that the turtle won't talk, or won't work out problems verbally.

When confronted with this, turtles seem to draw their heads back into their shells and disappear emotionally, taking some reading material, work or TV with them. Turtles find that when the skunk's barrage of words is focused on them, it is often anxiety-provoking. It sets up angry feelings, sometimes fearful and lonely ones.

This week a friend who is a skunk told me that he has at last had it with his wife of 21 years. She is a super turtle, an intellectual whose passive resistance makes Gandhi look like General Schwarzkopf. My friend is just getting into recovery and sees some of his denial. But he can't get his wife to talk about their issues, so he has decided to clam up and get her to make the first move for once.

I wanted to wish him good luck, but the chance that his clamming up will solve their marriage problems seems extremely remote. When turtles feel threatened, they often begin digging themselves into safer turf—underground. I felt sad and wanted to tell him that the only hope I saw to save his marriage was to begin working the program himself and learn how to be intimate in a functional way.

I have found it very helpful to realize that because of different child abuse issues, we all have different ways of hiding from intimacy. It may be very difficult for skunks to learn to be still, and to allow God to show them how to listen and give and receive love in ways their partners can relate to. It may also be difficult for turtles to learn the necessity of sharing feelings in order to get well, stay sane and sober, and have intimate communication with those who are different from themselves.

Of course, there are many other such differences in styles of being intimate. My wife and I, like many people coming into the program, had to listen with both ears to hear the Person in each other.

Roger and Sue: Relearning to Communicate

Roger and Sue have been active in 12-Step programs for a year now. They are aware that before coming into recovery programs, they had long ago lost any semblance of what they now know to be intimacy and spirituality in their marriage. Now they are trying to learn to communicate in a direct, straightforward way and are amazed at how difficult it is to hear each other through the old dysfunctional communication habits they learned at their parents' knees.

Mind Reading

The "mind reading" Roger and Sue had engaged in to interpret the tone of the other's voice had led to paranoia with regard to what the other party meant by almost any comment. Many of these suspicions of abusive controlling had turned out to be true in the prerecovery past. These old preconceptions are very hard to break out of. When the new intimacy began, the interaction soon started to slip back into their old wagon ruts of expectations. It was very difficult to get back on solid ground.

> For example, one morning Sue said, "Roger, would you like to go downtown today?" Roger felt anger and a tightness in his stomach. Often in the past if he'd say "Yes," thinking she wanted to be with him, she would hand him a list and ask him to pick up a few things for her while he was out. In recovery, Roger saw that he was reading Sue's mind and becoming angry before he even knew why she was asking him.
> He'd learned in the program to check out his thoughts and feelings, and he shared them with her now. When he did this, she was floored and angry—she had not been aware of the manipulative game she'd unconsciously played for years. Now when she thought about her motives, she realized that she *did* want him to pick up some things for her, and although it was difficult, she told him so. As it turned out, she went with him and they both relaxed and had a good day.

As time went on, they had to face a lot of their preconceptions, their tendency to read each other's minds without checking. They had to face their manipulative control games honestly to begin to have trust in their communications.

Unless this checking of feelings goes on, suspicions that one is being manipulated can lead to immediate defensive reactions that can be manipulative or overtly abusive.

Communication Skills

Roger and Sue have had to learn some new communication skills. Many of these skills they learned in 12-Step meetings, but it may take marriage counseling for them to learn how not to become trapped by their own past. They have had many failures, but some wonderful changes are taking place, too.

Roger had to learn how to test reality by saying, "When you say what you just said, I think you mean such and such. Is that in fact what you mean?" This gives Sue a chance to clarify what has just been said because she may have meant something entirely different from what Roger "heard."

For example, one weekend Roger and Sue had overnight guests. At the end of the weekend, the guests were in the car, ready to have Roger and Sue drive them to the airport. But on the way out the door, a very tired Sue whispered to an equally tired Roger, "Do you mind if I stay home and clean up the kitchen? I'm frantic to get some quiet."

Roger felt a little angry at this surprise change of plans. He had to make the long drive to the airport, and suddenly he wanted her to suffer, too. But being in recovery, he stopped, thought a minute and replied, "Okay, honey. I know you're exhausted. I'll take them myself." He smiled and kissed her and as he turned to leave, she added, "Here, take the movie back to the video store on your way home."

Now suddenly Roger felt rage. Here he had been thoughtful and offered to let her stay home as a conscious decision to do something nice, and now she was trying to use him. Before he actually flew into a rage, as he would have done a year ago, he checked himself by saying, "I feel angry, as if you are controlling me and ordering me to take the video back. I'm very tired, too, you know."

"No! I wasn't doing that!" Sue shot back. Then she thought a second and said, "Oh, gosh, I can see how it would sound like that and I guess you're right. I'm sorry. In my mind I meant to ask you if you would please take it back now so we wouldn't have to go out again tonight. I was so tired I slipped back into my old controlling voice. I've heard it a million times coming from my mother. I did say that in a controlling way and I'm sorry. I hope you can forgive me." Roger couldn't believe that she would admit that—she never had before. He felt much better and decided that he would take the video back. But now he had *made a decision* to take it back, not merely responded to an order.

This situation may sound trivial—unless you are married and trying to recover from the control disease.

This is a retraining process, in which each party begins to see and hear more clearly the reality of the other as they both get in touch with their own reality and share it. In recovery, each person quits twisting what's happening and using it to manipulate the other. But until a couple is ready to begin this process of withholding a reaction until each has checked with the other, it is very difficult for authentic intimacy to take place. Many of these same principles apply, of course, to dealing with broken relationships between children or parents.

A description of the type of therapy that can bring couples back into an intimate, growing relationship is beyond the scope of this book. But many people can get the training they need to be intimate Persons in the context of a 12-Step program if they have the willingness to practice sharing with each other.[1]

Finally, as Roger and Sue discovered more of their control techniques and confessed them in meetings and to their sponsors, they were able to share them with each other. They had come a long way toward re-establishing intimacy in their marriage.

Stating a Loaded Feeling Can Defuse It

When my wife and I began to share feelings that might threaten each other, it was a frightening experience for me. I have always been terribly afraid that if people really knew my inner reality, they would not be able to accept me, and particularly

some of the hostility, resentment and controlling habits that
have always lurked around the edges of my mind. I have
denied much of this because I was "too good a person" to have
such "negative reality" (really too afraid of rejection to express
it). But I learned through the 12 Steps that expressing a real
thought, fear or anger is very different from acting these feelings out in an abusive way.

For example, for years I was afraid to express any anger
toward my wife for fear that it would trigger rage in her, or that
I would be rejected and punished for expressing my anger. I
was also afraid that if I truly let my anger out, it would be too
big for me to handle. I might hit someone or hurt someone with
it. Both of these turned out to be delusions that were fostered in
my own family of origin and that I had always believed. In
recovery, I began simply to state my anger, saying, for instance,
"When you say that I feel angry," or "I am angry this morning. I
don't know exactly why, but I have feelings of anger and I just
want to share them with you. I don't think they are about you,
but I don't want to hurt you the way I will if I stuff them."

I found that just saying those things out loud in a nonabusive way drained off some of their energy and also informed my
wife that this anger, which was apparent to her, was something
I was not focusing on her. Even in cases where the anger *was*
focused on her, I was aware that there was a component of it
that had to do with my own fear rather than her actions. But at
first, such sharing may be more than either can handle.

Couples have to begin to share at whatever level they can,
just to break the sound barrier of being honest about their feelings. Years ago a man who was trying to learn to be honest with
his wife reported waking up one morning very angry.
Determined to be honest, he turned to her and said, "I'm angry.
I'm angry at you!" She looked crushed by his statement. Then
he said, "I'm angry at everyone! But if I start liking anyone
again, you'll be first." A little humor can be very helpful—*if* it is
directed at *your own* foibles and not your partner's.

As this retraining goes on and both parties have shared hith-
erto hidden feelings, many of us have discovered that the fact

that the other person is angry at us isn't going to kill us. Since we too have anger, we find that just by sharing it and trying not to hurt each other, we are able to deal with the feelings that cause our anger: the shame, fears and lack of worth that prod us toward retribution when our often unrealistic expectations are not met.

As I worked the program and felt more loved and accepted by other recovering people and by God, the intimacy in my own marriage began to be reestablished, however raggedly, and with many jump starts. Now a sense of rest and serenity has entered our relationship much of the time. I am not on edge, afraid my wife is going to blow up and I'll be shamed or deserted. If she or I do have such thoughts and get angry or want to leave, we are committed to "talk about it." Both of us will likely be helped by the experience of sharing. Now I am not afraid that I am going to have an uncontrollable rage attack when I get angry. I am not afraid as I was for years that my expression of true feelings will destroy our relationship.

This openness has led to a greater security in our intimate life and a greater sense of being accepted and loved, for which I have always longed. When I express my true reality in a non-judgmental, nonpunishing, nonmanipulative way, and I am accepted—even if my wife does not like the feelings expressed—then it means that the *real* I, the precious wounded but maturing Person inside, is accepted. This sense of being accepted for what I am—warts and all—affects almost every-thing in a positive way. The walks we take together, our vacations, the way we handle money, our intimate love life.

Living the principles of the program at home is not easy, but because each of us has a support system in meetings, in our spon-sors and working the program, the likelihood of our knowing how to share in a vulnerable, nonabusive way is greatly increased.

Learning to Express Scary "Negative" Feelings

For a couple to begin to be intimate and free with each other, sooner or later this sharing must begin—even if feelings are dif-ficult to express because of your partner's childhood abuse or your own. This can be especially complicated because each partner's experiences (and prohibitions) were different.[2]

For example, in the family Sue grew up in, it was not okay to express certain "negative" feelings like anger or resentment. It was also not appropriate to express fear, sadness or even loving feelings.

In Roger's family however, it was natural to share feelings of love, sadness or fear, but not anger. So it's hard for Roger to understand why Sue has trouble expressing love to him and their children. Until he heard many people in meetings talk about their fear of expressing certain feelings like love, he had assumed that Sue's lack of expression meant that she didn't love him as he loved her.

In recovery, when Roger or Sue feel angry, they realize that anger is a healthy, normal feeling and a signal to tell them something about themselves. They know now that their feelings of anger are more likely to come from their own fears rather than the other's "hostile intentions."

> One morning Roger chuckled and pointed out that Sue's slacks were too tight when she was bending over to pick up a shoe. Sue felt a rush of anger. But she's discovered that underlying that sort of anger is the fear that Roger "won't love me if I am fat." After she blasted him verbally and calmed down, she told him about her fear.

Confessing those fears is very threatening, but I don't know of any other way to get them out in the open and to stop the cycle of damage the angry response causes. I used to feel that any admission of "weakness" or fear by me would destroy my wife's confidence in me as a strong male. But instead she often feels a great sense of relief, as I do when she tells me the truth about what is going on with her.

I remember the night I told her that I have been afraid most of my life. I always had been so out of touch with my feelings that I thought I was just intense or excited. But I was afraid of failure, big time. We'd reached the point at which I wanted to share this with her. I told her I wasn't crazy or having a break-down but just wanted to share my fear so I could get over it. I thought she might want to leave. But she was quiet and then thanked me and told me she felt closer to me because she'd been afraid, too, and felt as if she needed to look capable. It was a very loving breakthrough for me. In dysfunctional families people seldom share their feelings, except when they are so swollen as to be dangerous or filled with self-pity and blame. My uncertainty about what my wife might be thinking caused me to fill in the blanks with my own deepest fears, angers and shame.

After Roger and Sue discussed her angry response to his comment and her fear about it, they could then put the strong feelings aside, making sure that they both had a chance to recover from their reactions to the revealed feelings. There may be some basis for Sue's fear—Roger may indeed be turned off by fat women. But as intimacy develops, even that can be discussed. Often by getting the reality of such feelings out, people can learn to accept and affirm each other in spite of expectations and imperfections, as they both become starkly aware that neither is perfect.

Several years ago, when I was single, I was jealous of a cer-tain man. The woman I was having a relationship with was very friendly with men at social occasions. I was angry when I saw the way she looked at the man I was jealous of, but then I real-ized my fear and owned it. The woman began to think about what I had said, and suddenly she realized she really did have strong feelings of attraction for the man in question. I panicked. In the past she would have denied her feelings, saying, "Oh no, no, I don't have strong feelings of affection for this guy." But in the safety of an honest relationship, she was able to be very open and say, "Yeah, I really do have these feelings."

If she'd just moved on and left me hanging there, I'd have been gone. But when she realized she was attracted to this man, she communicated to me the fact that she also realized she had no intention of doing anything about the feelings. In fact, she felt very relieved to be in touch with what had been going on, so she wouldn't get trapped into doing something that could destroy our relationship. She said that she cared a great deal for me. After my initial shock, I felt that our relationship was even stronger.

I remembered that I had sometimes been attracted to another woman, but I had no intention of moving closer to that person in any way that might have threatened my present relationship. If we had not been able to own and share our true feelings, that kind of situation could have destroyed the relationship. For one thing, I would have felt sure at some level that she *was* attracted to him, and I might have been panicky with fear and lack of trust because she wouldn't admit her "obvious feelings."

Since being in recovery, I have realized that feelings of attraction are universal; I hadn't been allowing her humanity to have any space. But once I allowed it, I was able to face not only her situation, but my own in relating to other women.

Sharing Intimate Feelings on a Regular Basis

Another skill that is helpful in maintaining intimacy is for both parties to communicate how things are when there is no crisis. Sometimes I just say, "Hey, I'm really glad to know you. Have I told you lately that I love you? Well, I really love you a lot." This is not a technique; it is just something I do occasionally when there's nothing wrong.

If she laughs or says, "Why?" I'll be specific. "I really think you have a neat mind" (or "a neat body," or "I like the way you laugh"). To communicate what someone means to you when there isn't a crisis is very different from saying affirming things when you are in trouble or want something from that person. I used to be afraid to say good things about how special my wife was because I was afraid she might want to leave me. (I felt so unspecial inside.) But in recovery I feel better about myself as a man, and I know that even if she left me I would survive—though I would hate it and be very miserable about her leaving.

Confronting Your Mate

It is very difficult to confront an intimate partner when something needs to be changed in the relationship to meet important needs in your life. But in recovery, successfully confronting sensitive issues is possible.

My wife has always been an enormous help to me in my work. She is also a writer and works full time with several clients. After she got into recovery, she came to me and said, "I'm sorry, but I realize that it's not in my best interest to continue to do certain things I have been doing with regard to your work. I don't have time to do my own work now if I do those things. This is not about you; it's about my time crunch, and I wanted to talk to you about it." This was an enormous breakthrough for her, since she had always done her job and the jobs of many people around her. At first I was shocked, disappointed and angry. I had become used to her taking care of my overload as being "part of her job." Because of the way she presented it, however, I could see it was true that she had a full load of her own and that, although it irritated me, I had to make some changes and give her additional space.

It was hard for her to say, "I am afraid when you make demands on me that I can't fulfill them and still get my own work done. I've felt this way before but not wanting to hurt your feelings, I never said anything. But now I need to back off some when you get overcommitted instead of coming in and rescuing you." When she said this, I suddenly realized that I have *always* overcommitted and then expected people around me to bail me out. Consequently, I have had to reexamine my commitments and cancel some—something I should have done years ago. This was very painful, but it is enormously helpful to my peace of mind now.

Confronting your partner with your needs is a real step toward maturity, as your Person begins to claim her own life and the right to be a safe, free individual. But it's been helpful to my wife and me to discuss such confrontations separately beforehand with sponsors or counselors.

Many people have told me that when they tried setting such boundaries by confronting their mates, the mates went into treatment because of the sudden realization of the enormous change that had taken place, as they saw their loved ones setting functional boundaries for the first time in their lives. Other people have elicited very negative responses from their mates when trying to set legitimate boundaries. Sometimes such a response is about the partner, but sometimes it is because boundaries are set in a blaming or defensive manner. Counselors and groups can help one deal with those kinds of responses. My own experience inclines me to support people in beginning to get well at whatever speed they can, to try to be sensitive, even if their healthy behavior triggers all kinds of strong feelings in them and the people around them.

16
Making It Real

Dealing with Your Unacceptable Strong Feelings and Thoughts in a Close Relationship

In some ways, recovery from addictions and the compulsion to control is like turning our less than functional personal worlds upside down. Instead of trying to fake it to look adequate, we are to admit our powerlessness. Instead of running from pain into alcohol, food, tranquilizers or controlling behaviors, we are to stand in our pain, face it and listen to what God is telling us about our denied reality. Instead of trying to "win" and to control other people in our close relationships, we learn that true strength and intimacy are discovered in the humility to share our weakness.

Even after going through the Steps, many of us recovering people still need to know how to unmask the delusions we've been living under in our close relationships. My wife and I have discovered a number of delusionary unexamined preconceptions.

Letting the Feelings of Love and Hate Ebb and Flow Without Panic

When we were first married, one of our delusions was that if we worked hard at relating and loved each other, we would always have loving feelings. But in recovery, I have come to realize that the feeling of love in an intimate relationship is always an ebb-and-flow matter. We need not panic if our romantic feelings are not always receiving high-voltage expression. Sometimes emotion must build slowly. It's like gathering a bouquet of flowers. The flowers don't seem very important alone, but when you gather enough of them, they can be very beautiful.

This is evidently the way of sexual rhythms, and I have found that it's also the emotional rhythm of intimacy. It's like kissing your mate good-bye at the front door in the mornings on the way to work. If you had a big rush of feeling every time, you'd never make it to work. But each of those small touches of affection without charged feelings is somehow stored in your life. When the occasion for loving does come, it can be greatly enhanced because of these prosaic bits of affection at the door.

As M. Scott Peck has pointed out, it's normal to have less than exciting feelings part of the time, even in the best of intimate relationships.[1] I have found that although it is scary to talk about, it is comforting to know that everyone has blah feelings sometimes—accompanied by the assumption that the relationship is "failing." When this first happened in my life, I felt lost and wanted to run away and say, "We've lost it." But as Peck says, that is the point at which true love can begin in earnest.

The Terror of Losing the Feelings of Love

After Andrea and I had been married for a little less than a year (during which I had been very much in love with her), I woke up one morning and realized I felt dry—as if I had no "deep emotional feelings" for her. I liked her and thought she was a fine person, but the strong, highly charged feeling was gone. I panicked and said to myself, "Oh, no, maybe our romantic love is over!" And I began to get very tense. I even avoided talking to her for a day or two.

But in our relationship, we have been committed to being very open about our feelings, whatever they are. We feel that in a truly intimate relationship, God can (eventually) help the partners handle any truth.

I would certainly *not* advise couples who have not been in recovery a long time, or who have not been meeting with a therapist or marriage counselor regularly, to just "start being honest." The pain stored inside us, the powerful shaming voices and the compulsion to control are often *very* strong, and can place an unconscious or blaming emotional overload on any sort of unaccustomed communication. So just starting to "be honest" could have harmful effects and destroy more than it healed.

But it is almost impossible—even with God's help—to resolve a difficulty that is hidden or about which we are being dishonest. We'd had a number of frightening but revealing experiences of working through some threatening personal revelations. But this was a real test of our commitment to openness.

Although I was afraid it might ruin our relationship, I finally said, "Andrea, I love you. As a matter of fact, I love you more than I ever have and I don't understand this. But I don't have the same exciting, stimulating feelings I've had since we started going together."

I asked her, "Have you ever had any 'dead feelings' like this?" After a few seconds she breathed a sigh of relief and said, "Whew! Yes, and it scared me to death. I've been having them this week and I was trying to figure out how to tell you."

We decided to walk hand in hand through that experience, to see what would happen to us. We had never known anybody who spoke frankly about these "dead feelings"—even though we know now that most couples go through them. Sooner or later, everybody who falls in love evidently has an experience of losing the glow similar to the one I have described.

After we had put our fearful feelings out in the open and assured each other of our love and that we were glad to be married, we both relaxed and felt a great wave of relief. During the days that followed, as we walked through this time together, we felt much closer. To our delight and surprise, the strong feelings of love came back (although we've discovered that we have to face these times of arid feelings periodically).

Talking about such a dry spell is a very scary thing to do. What if the other person responded to your confession by saying, "Well, no, I still have the great feelings of love all the time"? It takes a lot of understanding to receive this kind of communication. I'm not advising anyone else to do this. But it was helpful to us.

It was a great relief to me to know that deep, intimate relationships don't depend on the feelings always being "electric." As a matter of fact, I've learned that there are times in every honest, intimate relationship when the partners don't like each other and would really like to be out of the relationship. But far from being a sign that the relationship has gone bad, it can be a sign that the partners are in recovery enough to be in touch with their true feelings. I have counseled with people whose actions toward each other almost shout the fact that they heartily dislike each other, yet who continually assure one and all that this not true and that they have always been intensely in love. It has been a relief to realize that many such continual "required" feelings are not necessary to a functional intimate relationship. So if you're experiencing this deadness in a marriage, don't just assume that intimacy and love are gone.

For a shame-based controller, the fear of losing the "in love" feelings is actually often the tip of a much deeper iceberg of fear: the fear of rejection and desertion. For this reason I would advise talking to a counselor about such dead feelings if they frighten you. Bringing them up to your mate could be disastrous.

Sooner or later in an intimate love relationship, the strong initial feelings must change. The bad news is that it's a scary thing to face. The good news is that the relationship can move to a deeper, more comfortable level . . . and the warm feelings will probably come back.

The Fear of Rejection and Desertion

Rejection or desertion is the ultimate lack of control. When either happens, the other person is gone, so there is no way to manipulate them into staying. Therefore, any conflict that might bring on rejection or desertion becomes a matter of great fear for the shame-based person. Because of this fear many controllers use the *threat* of rejection or desertion to manipulate their partners into doing what they desire. This is hardly intimacy, but when many couples get into recovery, it is the situation they encounter because of their history.

If your relationship was deteriorating before you got into recovery, you may have been somewhere on the following scale of deterioration with your attempts to keep the relationship together:

1. Winsomeness—trying to please the other to get him to love you and not reject you.
2. Manipulation—trying to use pressure to avoid desertion (for example, talking about the kids and how they need both a mom *and* dad).
3. Anger and the threat of consequences (for example, if your mate even thinks about leaving, you'll tell about his affairs and ruin his business opportunities).
4. Pleading as the other is on the way out the door, and promising to change if your partner will stay.
5. Beating your mate to the punch either by leaving first or sabotaging the relationship (as with an affair), so that even if he leaves, you will still have been "in control" by *having caused* him or her to go.

All these are symptoms of the control disease and are almost never effective. But without a sponsor (or counselor) and a 12-Step program to deal with your own shame voices, the fear of failing and being shamed seems almost inevitably to drive people into abusing others or becoming a helpless victim to try to keep from being rejected or deserted, and thus more greatly shamed.

There are some important things a couple can do early on to allow room for differences in needs and wants. For example, I believe everyone needs some emotional space in which to withdraw to consider what's happening when things are difficult—and private space in which to grow spiritually.

The Problem of Space:
The Honeymoon Box—A Shrinking Paradise

Another delusion I brought into marriage was that if people *really* loved each other, they would do everything together. But in recovery, I was told that healthy people need separate spaces in which to grow spiritually and emotionally. This led me to the whole issue of how two people in a close relationship can share a joint emotional "space" and yet carve out private space in which to develop into the creative *Person* he was meant to be. The problems arising from this often unrecognized need for private space can start right after the honeymoon.

When the closeness that happens in a romantic relationship gets very intense, both parties may find themselves wanting to be together all the time—even though one or both may sense flaws in the other that were not apparent earlier. They call each other during working hours, write notes, meet or talk on the telephone every free moment. But sooner or later, one or the other may feel that his freedom and identity as a *Person* are threatened, or that neither will be able to get any work done. It feels as if there is a gentle and yet very strong control-cage being built around one's life by the other. The urge rises to run away, and it may be almost overpowering, *even though one is still in love.*

It's very hard to understand this paradox—being in love yet fearing that your partner will box you in and control you. This is especially painful in love-addicted relationships in which the love addict *wants* too much closeness or enmeshment (having been emotionally abandoned by a parent in childhood) and the other partner is terrified of it (having been enmeshed as a child by a parent).

The only way I've found to deal with this (when love addiction is not involved) is to confess those fears of losing personal freedom using "I" statements and giving specific data. "Yesterday you called me five times at work. I loved hearing your voice, but I'm afraid that I'm not going to be able to get my work done. It feels as if I am not in control of my time any more. I love you very much, but I need to talk about these feelings so I won't sabotage our relationship to alleviate my fears."

It is very sane and healthy to negotiate separate space for each other. I once heard my friend Richard Grant express the healthy kind of emotional space a couple needs by equating each person's boundary with a Hula Hoop. In an enmeshed relationship, both parties are locked into the *same* space by encircling themselves with both hoops together. In an emotionally healthy intimate relationship, both parties stay in their own hoops, always keeping space that the other cannot enter. Each partner stands in his separate hoop next to the other. The two can be very close physically and share a great deal, but they *do not reside in* the other's private space. Sometimes the hoops can almost completely overlap when you're together and no one's around, yet there's space that is separate for each partner. At other times the hoops barely seem to be touching.

To learn to share our lives without making our boundaries enmeshed or coterminous is sometimes difficult for people from dysfunctional families. They may feel a strong urge simply to "merge" with someone, allowing neither to have individual space. Without healthy boundaries and private emotional space, the deceit and manipulation of the control disease tend to dominate the relationship as each tries to control the joint space. A kind of pseudo-intimacy may develop in which the parties claim to have intimacy but instead have an unspoken agreement to suppress (or repress) any feelings that might threaten the enmeshed relationship. Spiritual growth can virtually stop in such a relationship. To have authentic intimacy, a couple must leave emotional/spiritual space for each other to have time apart.

Sabotage as a Way Out

The destructive acts that constitute "sabotage" are usually about issues unrelated to the real problem (such as the need for growth-space), leaving both parties bewildered and hurt. Sometimes couples have a strong need to negotiate some space, or to talk about "dead times" or the ebb and flow of loving feelings, but they can't do it. In their families of origin, they did not learn to express any feelings that "might cause trouble." If one partner feels a need for personal space and becomes lonely, frustrated and wants out (because there seems to be no direct solution that he can instigate), that partner may choose a dysfunctional and even dangerous act to destroy the relationship without ever confronting the real issues that need attention. This "sabotaging" often succeeds in burning the bridges to intimacy.

For instance, let's say that I want more freedom but don't want to tell you, my significant other, because the desire for freedom might look like a rejection of you. Instead of facing the fact that what I really want is more space or personal freedom, I may begin to pick at you about being late or being messy, starting a fight to destroy the relationship over one of those smaller issues. If picking fights won't break us up, I may create a stronger issue by having a "careless" affair and getting caught.

If I would face openly my need for more private space, it might be threatening to us both, but the pressure would be less. We could talk it out and maybe I could have some of the freedom I need within the relationship. The truth is that the other person often wants some space too (or whatever the hidden issue is about). But when couples do not ask for what they want, either party may break up the relationship because of the fear of being submerged into somebody else's life. Since it doesn't occur to people raised with "family secrets" that it's logical to ask for what we want, sabotaging often seems to include irrational thinking, feelings and acts that are self-defeating. Unfortunately, some element of sabotage is almost always a part of the breakup of long-term intimate relationships. What seems to happen in most cases is that sabotaging the relationship *causes* the breakup by putting the focus outside the relationship or on the other party, rather than on the real fears or difficulties inside our own lives.

Adjusting to Each Other's "Timing": A Hard Negotiation for a Compulsive Controller to Swallow

Another valuable tool to maintain intimacy is for each partner to learn to take into account the other's "timing." For example, some people wake up in the morning talking, while others wake up silent and don't want to talk until they have had some coffee or washed their face. To learn to listen to each other and discuss each other's comfort zones is harder than it may seem. Because of the control disease, each party tends to want the *other* to adjust.

I wake up talking. I felt rejected when my wife didn't respond to my early-morning questions or comments. As a matter of fact, they seemed to make her angry. Finally, after we had been in the program awhile, she was able to tell me the pain and irritation she felt at my insisting on talking to her early in the morning. She asked why we couldn't talk late at night—when she's wide awake. I shared my feelings of disappointment and irritation about that, and the fact that I'm tired late at night. I could understand how she might feel, but I'm so selfish I wanted to talk to her anyway and share all the "wonderful ideas" I wake up with.

After some painful arguments, we decided to negotiate the timing problem. Finally we developed a plan whereby on work days we don't talk much when we wake up, but on weekends and times when we sleep late, we spend some time visiting before getting up. When she has a special need to discuss something at night, we try to talk earlier in the evening while I can still hear, unless she is under a great deal of pressure. Then she will ask and I am generally willing to stay up. This arrangement feels good to both of us. Couples have to learn when to talk and when to be still. It may be different at different times for the same person.

Other timing adjustments include when one party likes to go to bed early and the other prefers to stay up late and read, watch TV or work. Let's say your partner wants to go to bed early and you decide to start staying up late and studying. If the two of you haven't discussed such changes, your partner may start feeling very paranoid and angry, or frightened and distant. It can be very helpful for you as the one staying up to tell your early-to-bed partner that you love her—but that late at night is when you are most creative, and staying up is what you've always liked to do. If it turns out that your partner feels terrible staying up late, each party is subject to feeling controlled, shamed or unloved by the other unless the matter is negotiated.

In our marriage we have found that talking about what we need and want in our relationship, and what's going on with us inside, has helped each of us see that having different times to go to bed and get up doesn't mean the end of the relationship. We negotiate times when we want to be together that may call for some temporary change in our usual negotiated routine. We may need to adjust traditional times for getting exercise and making love. But contrary to the stereotyped expectations of what a loving relationship should be like, we find that in many ways we can both be comfortable and happy by negotiating our timing differences.

Boundaries—A Necessary Key to Intimacy

Earlier I pointed out that boundaries are those invisible fences that mark off the physical, sexual, emotional, intellectual and spiritual "space" that is designated to you. No one has a right to come inside your boundaries without your permission—and that includes your mate.[3] You will probably have certain areas of physical closeness that you agree are comfortable for both without specific permission. But there are other areas that may have to be renegotiated after you have been together awhile.

If you are a co-dependent with no boundaries or with damaged boundaries, you may not be able to say no to your partner's needs and wants (sexual requests, for example—even if you are sick and feeling terrible). When you are approached but know you will not enjoy it (because of a painful back or upset stomach), your inner shame voices may say, "If you were any kind of spouse, you'd try to be sexual." So to avoid the fear of being shamed, you don't say no to your spouse, even when you should because of sickness or physical discomfort. Your partner may use your lack of boundaries and your readiness to be shamed as a control device to get what he wants. After a few years this situation can lead to a great deal of resentment.

Before I understood about boundaries, I used to walk up and hug people at meetings. But one day a woman friend said, "Please don't do that anymore. I really care about you but it frightens me." This was a good friend. But she told me she had been raped as a child and nobody knew it. Now, she said, "I just go into an experience of terror when a man gives me a surprise hug." A lot of people have been abused in ways that those around them don't know about. Now that I know hugging can be abusive to some people, when I see someone I want to give a welcome hug to, I say, "May I give you a hug?" Sometimes people respond, "No, I don't feel comfortable with that." Whatever their reason, I no longer feel shame or rejection.

I am also very sensitive about asking people to do something to help me. So that I won't use them in a manipulative way, I try to say something like, "This is what needs to be done. I would like for you to do it if you can." I won't "take care" of them, but I try to state the request in a way that allows them to look at it without a lot of emotional pressure. This is very difficult for me as a compulsive controller. I like to manipulate and sell to get what I want accomplished. It's especially difficult to be straight about my requests when dealing with my wife.

In the program, many of us have learned that we have not only the right to our own space but an obligation to our inner Person to maintain our space. It is within these boundaries that growth of the Person and a spiritual life can take place. To meditate or pray, you must have "space" without the people around you abusing you and tramping about in your requested privacy, destroying those fragile new beginnings. Of course, the situation is complicated when there are small children, but the way you handle this can be an occasion to teach them the use of healthy boundaries.

Learning to Set Boundaries

The way we learn to set functional boundaries is to experiment with setting them. When we are going to be in the presence of people who have been able to manipulate us or control our thinking, we practice putting on our boundary before we meet them. When one particular person in my life comes to see me, I put on my boundary immediately; otherwise, that person will be controlling me and I'll be angry when we part.

It takes time to learn when to set boundaries, but it is very important to have good boundaries if we hope to have authentic intimacy. We need to keep our boundaries on when talking to our kids, parents, mate, friends or business associates so that they won't dump feelings on us—and we won't dump feelings on them. Putting our boundaries on symbolically can stop incoming requests, or whining and shaming looks. This gives us time to listen to what people are really saying and watch what they are doing before we respond. That split second to think about what we are being asked to do, for instance, and our existing commitments, can change our life. But we have to practice if we want to learn to set healthy boundaries.

At first I had to consciously put my boundaries on every time I visited certain members of my family and friends. But now it has become a habit to set boundaries in any close relationship. Sometimes I get caught without my boundaries up and I go into shame or feelings of inadequacy. But putting on our boundaries can often keep us from shame attacks. Without boundaries, shame can jump on us before we even think about it. Setting boundaries is a skill like any therapeutic skill. We have to learn to do it over a period of time if we want peace in our closer relationships. There is no easy way I know to get these things in your life.

I was one of those who used to think that true intimacy meant no boundaries; but that's true co-dependence, and it will destroy the kind of equal and authentic sharing we've been talking about. As I said in the section on "space," both parties must have an emotional place which they can go to when they need to get away from the relationship. This can only occur when they learn to set and maintain good boundaries.

If you are a co-dependent or a shame-based person, you may have to retrain yourself to believe you have a *right* to have boundaries. You can tell yourself every morning, "I have a right to my space." This is very therapeutic for a co-dependent. I was told to put on my boundary when I got up every morning and say, "I have a right to my physical, sexual, emotional and intellectual space, to my own thinking and feelings, and I have a right to protect them from abuse."

When you are around people with whom it is hard to set boundaries, try backing off physically until you get comfortable. You can do this very slowly and imperceptibly in most cases. If someone calls when you're in the middle of doing something you need to get done, you can learn to say, "I'm sorry I can't talk to you right now. I'm doing something I really need to do. I'll call you back as soon as I'm finished, probably in about an hour." I have had to experiment with this, but pretty soon I began to feel safe and not shameful about setting boundaries.

My feedback from others after many years is that I have excellent boundaries. I didn't have good boundaries at all before I got into recovery. In fact, I had to quit my profession as a public speaker at one point. Because of overcommitment, my inability to say a healthy no had led to my having serious heart trouble. Now I have time for an excellent fitness program, I sleep better and feel much sharper than I was because I have this space that has been given to me by healthy boundaries. I still commit to a lot of things, but most of the time I'm choosing what I do, rather than being swept along by it. Having functional boundaries is an enormous relief.

For example, let's say your friend, George, keeps getting into your space by standing too close. He gets too close to other people as well. You can't do anything about what he does with other people because that's telling him how to run his life. But when he comes too close to you, you can learn to put your hand up in front of your chest, palm out, and without touching him, step back and say something like, "I don't feel comfortable standing that close to people." You are not blaming him; you are saying that *your* action has to do with *your* feelings and *your* comfort zone, not that he is doing something "bad." If you say, "You're standing too close," that's about him and implies he's "not doing it right"—which can be shaming and anger-producing. But if you're stating that *your reality* is that it's too close *for you*, then that is part of an intimate exchange. Some of us are beginning to learn to make statements that are about us, our feelings and our reality. We are becoming much more comfortable in social situations that used to produce anxiety because we felt helpless.

Someone may become angry and not honor your feelings and requests for space. If you are dealing with such an offender, then you may need walls. You may need to get up and leave the room and have a wall of distance. Or you may need a wall of anger if you think someone is about to rape or attack you physically. Being nice and letting the person abuse you without mentioning it, so as not to hurt the person's feelings, is not appropriate. An offender will not pay any attention to your niceness. A wall of anger stops some people who will not pay any attention to arguments. A wall is appropriate in the face of an offender. But you have to practice these things. If you can't learn how to get space through the program you're in, you can learn this in counseling and therapy groups, where the therapists are familiar with boundary setting.[3]

Since functional boundaries are also to keep you from offending others, you may have to learn how to exercise them with certain behaviors of your own that offend other people because they transgress their boundaries.

17
Lifelong Relationship Killers

Handling Destructive Attitudes
That Can Clobber Your Partner—
and Your Serenity

M any couples run into serious communication difficulties because of unconscious dysfunctional mental habits picked up early in life. These attitudes are like invisible currents that suck us down into deep, angry water in our intimate relationships before we know what has happened.

Self-Justification

Because of the shrillness of the inner shaming voices—and often the caustic or subtle shaming voices of their families of origin—many children develop a horror of being wrong and thus caught in shame. In their powerlessness to change their giant-seeming parents by argument or force, or to defend themselves against the weight of their judgment, children and grown co-dependents develop to a fine art the skill of self-justification and diverting shame as they build their personages. The trouble is that this skill, in its various manifestations, often includes shaming those with whom one is in intimate relationships. Thus it becomes one of the major forces in the destruction of intimacy.

By the time I was eight years old, I was so afraid of failure and criticism that I had an excuse for everything I did that wasn't perfect. When criticized or even questioned about my behavior, I could justify anything I did or said instantly. I remember my mother laughingly saying to me as I was coming home late one day, "Well, here comes Alibi Ike." I was shocked at the time, and I still remember the shame I felt when she said it because I had no idea that I made more excuses than anyone else.

When I got married, my habit of self-justification was neither cute nor joked about. I still wasn't aware that I *had* to be right and would "argue with a post" (another statement I *just this moment* remember my mother saying about me). But the abusing thing about self-justification in my case has been that if I have to be right, then *someone else* usually has to be wrong. Until I got into recovery, I didn't know that sometimes being "right" or "wrong" is not relevant to an intimate exchange about something that has happened. But I now know that self-justification in my life is a major destroyer of intimacy. If my "perfection" is at stake and others try to share their differing reality, I will discount it, twist it or dismiss it as being unimportant. This can happen even in the face of solid evidence that I've made a mistake. I feel very sad as I'm writing this, since I have been in touch with just how much misery my self-justification has caused in my intimate male-female relationships and with my adult children.

This habit seems absolutely normal to many co-dependents and other controllers. After all, we want "the truth" to come out (and the truth is that I'm right and innocent and that we all should agree on that). If you point out my faults or mistakes, I have an instant interior reaction: "That's not right! You don't understand. Here's what really happened." My immediate reaction is to claim that your perception is not accurate. I blurt out, "I did *not* say that! What I said was . . ." I unconsciously correct my previous statement to say what I *meant*, or what I wish I'd said (but in reality did not say clearly).

Self-justification is a major character defect that destroys intimacy because self-justifiers *have* to be right or they start an argument to support their delusion of being perfect. In many cases, they feel sincerely that they are right. To those doing the self-justifying, it seems as if all they are doing is straightening the record. In the program, many of us had to learn that healing and growth don't happen until we face our denial, lies and delusions of perfection, admit them, make amends and change the behavior of justifying ourselves.

I have a talented, brilliant and very capable friend who was once late to an important business meeting. When he came in everyone was braced for his smooth excuse. But all he said when he sat down was, "I'm sorry I'm late. I blew it." Period. Suddenly we all saw ourselves. The truth is that when we are late, it *is* usually our fault. We have started too late, tried to handle too many things before coming, or did not have good boundaries and let someone "important" derail us. This positive, no-excuse change regarding self-justification often happens to people in recovery.

It has been *very* difficult for me to face my own self-justification with my close loved ones. But if we want a life of love and intimacy, I believe it is essential that we try.

Blame

When we are practicing self-justification, blame is not far behind. Blame is another attempt to avert the shaming voices in the inner warfare for self-esteem. If I can blame someone else for what has gone wrong or been done imperfectly, I will not be shamed. Even if I can shift part of the blame onto my wife so that we are both responsible for something that went wrong, the sense of failing does not seem to be as bad.

Blame almost always triggers anger and defensive control behaviors in our mates, which is a method of self-defense against internal shame attacks on the Person for being wrong. Blame never helps. For "scorekeepers," our blaming them is like a resentment in the bank that they can withdraw to justify an abuse of us later.

Some people use blame as a way to justify an attack on their partner. If I am angry at my loved one, to just walk up and hurt her with a nasty comment is too dastardly for a good-guy perfectionist like me who needs to be right. But if I, as Mr. Righteous, can blame my loved one for a wrong I perceive she has done, then it is amazing how justified I can feel in this cheap-shot way of "getting her back."

Pointing Out Faults

Just pointing out a loved one's faults or mistakes without specific "blaming" is another common shaming control device— even if you are correct about the fault or mistake. The fact that you "caught them" often triggers the shame they felt as children when their parents (who at least had a teaching responsibility) pointed out their faults and mistakes. This control habit puts you in a parental role and usually turns off the desire for intimacy in your partner. Who wants to share her reality with someone who's going to point out both what's wrong with his reality and with the person sharing in the process?

Blaming and pointing out the faults of people around us are parts of a very unpleasant aspect of the control disease called "judgment."

When I put myself in the center of my life and the lives of those around me, I think I know better than they do how our lives should be lived. That puts me in the position of God and judge above them—and in my case, those close to me have all resented this deeply.

Judgment

In my own fear of not being enough, I have spent a lot of my life judging the people around me—although I sometimes thought I was only helping them. But in recovery, I have seen that a lot of my basic motivation for judging people I love has been the unconscious notion that if I find them imperfect or inferior in any way, then I will feel better about my own shameful self. I can focus on their faults (the ones that are not the same as mine, of course) and say, "Well, at least I don't do that." This has not usually been conscious, but I now realize that judgment has been a real part of my compulsion to control.

Judging loved ones is a powerful control device and an almost guaranteed intimacy killer. When I judge the behavior of others, I am not only setting myself above them, I am also shaming them, since I am pointing out their failure to be enough (by my standards). It was very difficult for me to see that it is not my business to judge my loved ones about their behavior. They are adults under God. Just because I am spouse, parent (of adult children) or lover does not mean that I have been automatically appointed to correct them and shame them into their full potential.

I have a dear friend who is in love. The woman he loves is beautiful, kind, loving, talented, wealthy . . . and 25 pounds overweight. He is a body-builder who is very conscious of health, diet and fitness. His question is, "How can I get this woman to change her behavior without judging and controlling her?"

The program's answer is that unless she decides that she wants to change because of the pain of being like she is and of the health threats she is facing, she won't do it anyway. Oh, he might threaten not to marry her and get her to go on a diet. But unless the decision to change is her decision, then at some point after the honeymoon, the chances of her giving up her diet when they are safely married are enormous.

All the man can do is share his experience regarding what it means to him to work out and follow healthy eating habits. To judge others and badger them to change is to control them and reject them as they are. This seldom works to bring about long-term change. Many times I have counseled people who are angry at their wife or husband because they quit smoking while they were dating and promised they would not smoke any more. Then after the wedding, they started smoking and would not quit.

When we try to judge people and control them to change in accordance with our judgment, intimacy sneaks out the back door. Our delusion, as controllers, is that we can get them straightened out and they will be grateful to us for doing it. In only a very few cases has this been true in my experience. I'm not talking about a formal intervention here or helping people who have come and asked for your advice. I'm talking about the picking, badgering sort of correcting that seems to go on when we are in our most intimate relationships, without anyone else around.

One of the miracles of the program for me was that when my wife got into recovery and quit monitoring what I was eating and reminding me of my dietary decisions, some strange and unexpected things began to happen. At first I was a little hurt and angry, even though I had resented her reminders. The thought crossed my mind that maybe she didn't love me any more and didn't care if I let my cholesterol get too high and died of a heart attack. But then I realized that she wasn't going to remind me any more because she'd learned that it was my job to take care of myself. I realized that my cholesterol *might* get too high and I *might* die of a heart attack. I got on a food plan and exercise program, which I have no trouble keeping and actually enjoy! Before, I hated the diet because I felt controlled. This may not be true for anyone else, but it has been for me. If she hadn't quit judging that I was too forgetful to take care of myself and decided to let me live or die as an adult, I might never have grown up and taken responsibility for my physical health. This may sound strange and very abhorrent to some of you, but only when we quit trying to control each other do we give (and get) the chance to grow up and be responsible for our lives.

People have said to me, "But what if you *hadn't* changed and decided to take care of yourself?" Well, that would have been my decision. Even though I might be dead by now, it would have been my choice. Recently my wife told me that she had to accept that possibility when she made her decision and it was agonizing for her. Making a healthy break from controlling others can involve serious risks, but spirituality and authentic intimacy demand that neither party control the other and take away his choice. This kind of intimacy is the toughest life and love I've ever known. But because I have tried to live this way, I like myself more than I ever have, have more self-esteem and self-respect, and am closer to my wife than I ever have been. It hasn't been easy for me to give up my lifelong habit of getting people to take care of me, and judging them and caretaking them rather than letting them be responsible for their own lives. It has been especially difficult to quit judging my grown children.

Expectations

Once we unconsciously start judging people "so that we can help them," we start using our own criteria for what they should be like. These (usually unconscious) standards against which we judge them are our introjected expectations, often from childhood, of what they should be like and should be doing.

Our expectations can become a powerful control force in our intimate relationships. These expectations are often received by those we are focused on as "judgment" and "condemnation." When I expect my wife to want to talk early in the morning because I wake up filled with ideas I am eager to share, but she is silent and grim looking, I judge her as being angry and selfish. Or if a woman's expectation coming into a relationship is that lovers should make love every day, then she feels rejected and unloved if her partner doesn't always respond to her daily mating call.

The person with the expectation makes a "negative" judgment about the other's feelings and behaviors, based on the unmet expectations. Such expectations soon become onerous and one's beloved wants to escape, even if he really loves the person with the preconceived scenarios. Even if such expectations are not expressed verbally and specifically, they can be communicated by disappointed looks or body language. When that happens, the other partner may feel as if he is being controlled and shamed in an invisible and uncomfortable way. Intimacy often dissolves when the expectations are standing there staring at you with an unaccepting or disappointed face. It's too fearsome to risk sharing your reality, which often seems prosaic to you, with someone who appears to have such high expectations of you. The risk of being shamed is too great.

Discounting Others' Reality

People have very different styles of perceiving and organizing reality. Some very intelligent people take everything literally and can't make the kinds of cognitive poetic jumps that are often involved in certain kinds of innocent jokes. For other people it is necessary only to have shorthand symbols to grasp a situation or what someone else is trying to communicate. Such people may be very intelligent also, but they sometimes think that those who don't understand what they say instantly, or see life the way they see it, are slow or dumb. They discount the reality and intelligence of the more literalist person as being inferior.

This opinion is often a delusion that nevertheless makes one party feel superior and angry when the other can't understand half-told directions and the like. This is a subtle form of controlling.

Roger and Sue have this kind of difference. Roger comes from a family of kidders. They could make a joke out of anything. When Sue first visited Roger's parents' home at Christmas, she was bewildered by how fast the conversation went and how much joking went on. She kept thinking people were being serious. When she responded with serious answers to their jokes, they all laughed uproariously. Sue blushed and felt shame, but they were very loving and reassuring, telling her everyone knew the Carsons were crazy. She felt reassured. Roger was a little embarrassed that Sue didn't seem to catch on as fast as he'd thought she should. But she was so pretty and fresh with her honesty that he was very proud of her. And besides, he knew she was almost a straight-A student and was plenty smart (and had told the family that).

But after the honeymoon, Roger kidded Sue one day, saying she was so beautiful that she had him hot all the time, and he wanted to keep the thermostat on 50 degrees all day. That night when he came home, the house was freezing. He asked her, "What in the hell are you doing? The air-conditioning bill is going to be $1,000 a month!" Sue cried and was very embarrassed, and Roger couldn't believe she didn't know he had been kidding.

In recovery Sue was able to tell Roger her pain about his kidding so much. When she was a little girl, everyone in her family had spoken very precisely about what they wanted to say. If anything was not clear, the kids were told to ask about it because they would be expected to act upon what they heard or be punished. Roger finally realized that she was serious. In doing the Steps, he had been confronted by his sponsor about using humor as a way to hide from his feelings. He shared with Sue that when someone tried to get serious in his family, his father would make a joke out of it so that everyone learned to hide their feelings through humor.

As Sue and Roger shared their feelings and pain around this issue of having one's reality discounted, they agreed to stop and check with each other when one of them was in pain or in doubt about the other's communication or expectations, or when one suspected that the other was discounting her or his way of being.

There are many other ways in which people discount the reality of a loved one. This can cause great pain and shame and destroy intimacy without either party knowing what has happened. Although it may seem tedious to have to stop and do these "feeling checks," they can add a great deal of happiness and security in an intimate relationship.

Another form this discounting of reality takes is when one party expresses a feeling, such as sadness or loneliness, and the other party discounts that reality by saying, "You shouldn't feel that way." This attempt to fix the other party is a form of discounting their reality of loneliness or sadness, and it destroys intimacy. Who wants to share and be instantly discounted and fixed, even if it's done in the name of loving? This is a shaming and subtle, if unconscious, jab at the other's self-esteem.

Teasing

When the purpose of "kidding" is to get the other party to blush or feel stupid, it is often called "teasing." Whereas kidding or joking can just be a play on words or telling a funny story designed to make people laugh, teasing, even when it seems very innocent or innocuous, is about shaming people and controlling them by being better than (sharper than) they are. There is no way to tell how much agony teasing causes in close relationships every day. Teasers would be shocked to hear that what they are doing is emotional abuse, leading to feelings of shame and being less-than.

Although teasing is a favorite American pastime in family and love relationships, it can be a strong control device and used as a subtle way of judging and discounting the reality of the loved one. Teasing can destroy intimacy and be especially shaming to shame-filled people. People who have been raised in families in which everyone was teased sometimes treat teasing as a game and develop strong boundaries in teasing situations. Such people, when entering a new intimate relationship, often hurt their loved one deeply and never know it, tending to say, "What's the matter? Can't you take a joke?"

When they were first married, Roger almost lost Sue over a teasing incident and didn't know it for years. He had always thought Sue had a very attractive figure—great legs, slender waist and small but shapely breasts. One evening Roger teased Sue about the small size of her breasts in front of his father, saying that she could pass for a boy to get into men's night at a local club where he and his dad were going. His dad was embarrassed for Sue, but he laughed, not knowing what else to do. Roger thought his teasing was funny and had no idea he'd hurt Sue . . . although she was cool to him when he came home that night. Recently, Sue was able to share that pain with Roger and how she has been embarrassed for him to touch her breasts since then. Ordinarily Roger would have defended himself. But this time, after several years in recovery, he listened and was not defensive. Then he made amends, telling Sue how sorry he was for being so insensitive. As they talked, they both understood how much that one evening of teasing had affected their love for *years*.

I don't want to overdramatize this point, but much intimacy is destroyed by thoughtless, "innocent" teasing.

In my own years of experience and counseling with other people, I have noticed that even teasers can be deeply hurt when they get in intimate situations. To keep this from happening, they often tease their lover, keeping him off balance and thus staying "in control."

Teasing children is abusive and almost always makes them feel less-than or worthless. To compensate and avoid being caught and revealed as inadequate, many such children grow up and become teasers themselves, not realizing that they have been trained to be shaming offenders to people who have not been taught how to defend themselves.

I was trained to tease. My brother teased me continuously and mercilessly. I was absolutely miserable, but I really learned how to tease. When I grew up, I was attracted to women who liked to joke but who were not always trained in the rapier-like art of teasing. Without exception, I hurt and shamed them and never knew it until I got into a 12-Step program, where I finally learned not to tease. I think the fact that they knew I might suddenly tease them had a very negative effect on the depth of intimacy they were willing to risk. In the past few years, I have learned about shame and different kinds of abuse, and I have seen my own use of various control devices—including teasing—as a way to avoid being shamed and to maintain my fragile self-esteem. Teasing is a powerful if subtle control device and a very effective way to avoid intimacy.

Facing fears and other uncomfortable feelings and beginning to see dysfunctional and self-defeating mental habits can help prepare a couple for dealing with the specific nitty-gritty issues of life. But couples must still learn to deal with these issues on a daily basis. For instance, how does an intimate couple learn to deal with each of the big three: money, child-raising and sex? The next chapter will take a look at sex in an intimate relationship.

18
An Outward Sign of Intimacy

Expressing Your Sexuality and Recovery in Intimate Relationships

In this book I have tried to show, with specific illustrations, how the compulsion to control insinuates itself into every area of life, particularly every aspect of an intimate relationship. We have seen how controlling or being controlled impedes the Person's battle for self-esteem, freedom and integrity. So far we have examined the way intimate sharing can create an atmosphere in which very painful specific issues involving conflict can be negotiated and resolved.

One of the most valued aspects of marriage, and yet one of the most difficult and potentially painful specific areas of conflict in intimate relationships, is sex. How can recovery from the compulsion to

control lead to different strategies in dealing with the loneliness, pain, resentment, fear, jealousy and shame that are often
hidden from the world in the privacy of intimate sexual
relationships?

Sexual Issues in an Intimate Relationship

At an emotional level, sex is one of the biggest mysteries of
the human experience. I have already suggested that, ideally,
sex is a sacrament of intimacy, an outward and visible sign of
that inner sharing of reality between a man and a woman in the
ambience of loving. Because it is a basic drive, sex is very powerful. Of all the basic drives, it is the only one that we have
some choice about. If we do not respond to the drive for food
and water, we die. But people can choose to abstain from sex,
even though it is a strong basic need.

Although the major biblical religions see sex as part of God's
creation and call it "good" (see Genesis 1:31), many people
following so-called biblical faiths have had a strong anti-sexual
bias—making sex shameful and a sort of necessary evil. The
effect of such thinking has been that children are often repri-
manded or shamed when they ask about sex or when they
experiment with natural childhood sexual behaviors. Parents
who don't know how to teach children about sexuality often
avoid the subject, piling more shame on the children's sexual
thoughts, feelings and questions by their omission in the child's
teaching. This, of course, is the abuse of not teaching children
how to meet their own needs and wants or how to be men or
women.

So when two adults get into an intimate relationship in our
society, it is often very difficult for them to share their sexual
feelings and desires in a straightforward and uninhibited way.
Even in cases where the partners have had some sexual education and experience, they must work out their own particular
wants and needs with each other through intimate sharing. The
following are some of the issues that may come up in an intimate relationship in which sex is involved.

Frequency, and Communicating Needs and Wants

At first the question of frequency of sexual intercourse may not be an issue, since couples newly in love seem to have an added infusion of sexual hormones. But after the honeymoon period, this issue can be a cause of much pain and frustration. Because no one has told most of us what is "normal" sexually, we don't know how often sexual intercourse is appropriate. This wouldn't be a problem except that people have very different needs, wants and expectations when it comes to the frequency with which they want to be sexual. If couples do not face this issue and talk about their feelings openly, then they will almost surely trigger the control disease as each partner tries to establish her or his own frequency desires as normative for the couple's sex life.

This may sound obvious, but it has been sobering for me to listen to rational, intelligent people who have lived in a state of resentment or rage for years because they kept waiting for their partners to be sensitive to the point of guessing what they wanted and making sure that happened for them.

It is very important to learn your own and your partner's preferred frequency of sexual intercourse, and to be able to express sexual needs in ways that are straightforward and nonabusive. This is really hard to talk about sometimes. Experience with the control disease often causes one party to feel that the other uses the withholding of sex as a control device; or the withholding partner may feel that the first is over-sexed and obsessed with making love. Unless the couple learns to talk about sexual wants and needs without shaming or blaming statements and to negotiate these needs, the buried resentment in the lives of one or both parties can poison the possibility of authentic intimacy.

I once heard Dr. Jonas Salk say in a lecture that the Golden Rule—do unto others as you would have them do unto you— simply doesn't work in close personal relationships. He told of a time when he came home from work at five o'clock and drove around to the back of his house and parked his car in the garage. His wife came home from work at five o'clock and drove up to the front of the house and walked in the front door. They met in the middle of the house. As I recall, she had been working all day on some files that were in the bottom drawer of the filing cabinet, and her lower back was very sore. He had been working on an experiment that required him to lift some things up high and look through them, and his upper back was very sore and tender. They met in the house and applied the Golden Rule: He rubbed her upper back and she rubbed his lower back. Unfortunately neither one of them got what they needed.

The point of this story was that if the Golden Rule is going to work, you first have to listen to the other party and discover what his need is so that you can negotiate how to meet that need. That, it seems to me, is "doing unto the other as you would have the other do unto you," not guessing, reading their mind and then doing what you would like to do for them. In sexual relationships it is very important not to try to make your partner read your mind all the time, but to communicate what is positive and negative to you about the sexual lovemaking. Often we have a lot of hidden fear about sex, based on childhood shaming and feelings of not being desirable or attractive, which can make this sort of disclosure especially difficult.

Sexual Performance

If either party cannot perform sexually to the other's expectations—or the perceived expectations of the partner—that person may block sexually and not be able to have orgasms for a time.[1] Men and women often blame their failures on each other. But in an authentic intimate relationship, each party can express his own fears and talk about things that the other does that inhibit sexual response—without blaming or putting down the other. Experience would indicate that such conversations are best held for most couples *away* from the bed and not at a time when approaching sexual contact.

It is difficult to emphasize adequately how threatening this sort of intimate dialogue is because of the shaming or secrecy often attached to enjoying sex that is communicated in American child-rearing practices.

The Self-Putdown

We co-dependents of the "overfeeler" variety often tend initially to blame ourselves when things don't go right. Our inner Person thinks, "If I'd only been more sensitive or done it better, things would have worked out right." We may listen as our shame voices bombard us with the old familiar abusive words about how inadequate we are. But as I suggested, when we go through the 12 Steps and begin to get a sense that our sponsor, our friends in the program and even God may be on our side against the shame voices, we can tell them, "Shut up! I'm a precious child of God who is perfectly imperfect. I don't have to be perfect. I can change what I don't like about what I'm doing, but there is no way I can make my partner happy by trying to control her reality!" At this point many of us quit focusing so much on "how we were doing" and begin to be intimate by sharing our thoughts and feelings about sex, and to negotiate trying new ways to brighten this part of our lives.

The Attempt to Bury Our Feelings

When things don't go as we had hoped sexually or our partner hurts our feelings with some flippant comment or selfish neglect, many of us try to shrug it off as our inner voices say to us, "This isn't important. Why would you get upset over a little thing like this?" But when we are still tossing sleeplessly in our bed at 4:30 A.M., it might be worth asking ourselves, "If this is such an insignificant thing, how come I'm still awake and thrashing around with a tight stomach?" This may be a clue that we are in denial and that we are not facing our hurt, anger or fear.

In recovery I have learned to say to myself at such times, "I can see that I am angry and hurt." Then I do Steps 1 through 3: "I admit that I am powerless over these feelings, and that here at 4:30 A.M. my life is unmanageable. But I believe you can restore me to sanity, God. I hereby offer my life and my will and these hurt, angry feelings to you." Then I say the serenity prayer, often falling asleep before I get through it. If this doesn't work, I may take an inventory of the relationship, focusing on what I may have done to hurt the other party. Often I see how my behavior set up my partner's hurtful jab at me. Or I may get up and read the Big Book, a devotional book, the Bible or a novel. The next day I call my sponsor or someone else in the program and go to a meeting. Just knowing that I have these tools available often keeps me from sabotaging my intimate relationship until I can get some perspective on what happened—and sometimes see my part in it. But even if my partner has abused me and we cannot talk, my inner Person can come out intact and aware of being a precious child of God as I share my reality intimately in the program or with a therapist, and I am accepted.

We Learn by Trial and Error

It's important to know that we learn about things like sex and play in intimate relations by trial and error and honest sharing. You can't "memorize" the approach to sex your partner wants once and for all. For one thing, some people's wants and needs vary at different times. And trying to concentrate totally on pleasing the other person without getting your own needs met is co-dependent. Sooner or later it may lead one to resentment, just as concentrating only on your own needs is selfish, and sooner or later will cause resentment in your partner.

Authentic intimacy is characterized by a communication of feelings and a willingness to listen without fixing or being defensive. You can't control other people's responses in an intimate relationship, but you can express your wants and needs and negotiate them with your significant other, realizing that there will necessarily be some give and take. We may change during a week or month. If we are in touch with our feelings, sometimes we will want different things. Some individuals or couples enjoy a rough-and-tumble sex life, while others like a gentle, slow approach. And some want the same things the same way every time they meet sexually (saying, "If it works, don't fix it"). It can be very helpful (and will certainly be appreciated) to remember what brings pleasure to your partner in sexual loving.

As recovery progresses, many people become aware of their own sexual feelings and desires in a whole new way. As they feel better about themselves, they feel more secure and that they deserve to have good feelings. They may want to play more at being sexual. This change may be threatening to a partner and it may be necessary to get counseling to negotiate the change, but it can lead to a whole new level of intimacy.

As we seek to be intimate, we must continually communicate, realizing that, even with regard to sex, our remembered behavior may not always work in the same way for both partners. This is why learning to share current reality is so important for the intimacy to grow. The payoff can be an increased sense of freedom, spontaneity and joy in the relationship.

A helpful awareness often develops in recovery that sometimes, even under the best conditions, things just don't always work out sexually on any given occasion. But it is also true that such a failure to have "perfect sex" does not have to be a tragedy or an occasion for blame or shame. The partners can learn to smile about those inevitable imperfect times and accept and love each other when one or both are disappointed at their performance. But unless people face the fact that it is normal for both men and women to have times when they cannot perform sexually, the shame voices may make the "failing" partner avoid sexual contact.

The same principle is as true here as when a couple is negotiating when to read, when to separate and go away for some space, or when to take a walk alone. When the question of control subsides, we begin to hear what our partners are really saying and what their feelings are without thinking any change in them is a negative statement about us.

For example, when I was first married, if it were suggested that something I was doing in our intimate life (especially if it involved sex) might be changed, I didn't know how to respond. I often felt as if a personal inadequacy were being singled out.

Sometimes I felt hurt, frightened and angry and thought that perhaps the relationship was failing. Now, because of what I've learned in co-dependence recovery, when my wife needs to be alone or has some other request, I do not take that as being about what an inadequate companion I am. Before, I felt it was my job to "make her happy" (control her reality). Now that I realize this is a sign of my co-dependence, I am more likely to hear her needs. The miracle is that I can also state *my* needs regarding sex and even regarding privacy (which for years I didn't think I had a right to as a good husband, if my wife wanted me to be with her).

The Double Back-Off and Other Games

People can fall into some tricky and self-defeating control games concerning sex that are baffling and confusing. For example, after Roger and Sue had fallen into a routine about sex, a strange thing sometimes happened.

> Before supper one evening, Sue indicated that she would like "to make love tonight." Roger had some work he hoped to do, but agreed with her. Later Sue called from the bedroom, "Honey, it's 10 o'clock."
>
> Roger said, "Okay, just a minute," and kept working. In a few minutes Sue, all dressed up in a pretty nightgown in bed, began to feel shamed and angry and started feeling resentful. Sometime later Roger realized how long it had been since Sue called. He jumped up and hurried to the bedroom with a big smile on his face. Sue held back her unhappiness till he crawled in beside her, feeling very romantic by this time.
>
> Turning her back to him she mumbled, "It's too late now. I'm half asleep." Now both parties were angry; both felt resentful and both were shamed.

Roger and Sue played variations of this game for years. One of them would make a tentative sexual signal to the other. But if the other didn't catch the signal or realize how important the response was, the signaler would unaccountably switch to a hostile or critical stance.

Recently, several years into recovery, Sue said to Roger when he got into bed after one of these episodes, "Could we go in the breakfast room? I have some feelings I need to share." He agreed. When they got there, she continued, "I feel like I did as a hurt little four-year-old girl when my dad promised to take me places and didn't remember. I used to be so angry and resentful I wanted to kill him, but really I was hurt because I felt he didn't love me. I got those same feelings tonight when after we'd agreed to make love, I called and you didn't come."

Roger felt the old urge to defend himself rising. But this time he listened and said (as he might have in a meeting), "That sounds painful, Sue. I'm sorry."

Sue said, "This has happened a lot and I know that sometimes I'm the one who doesn't come. Sometimes I'm hoping to sabotage the lovemaking so I can finish reading a novel. I'm ashamed to tell you that, but I want you to know I realize it's not just you. I'd like to negotiate some kind of change with you, since the pain of those childhood memories leads to such anger that the last thing I want to do is make love when you finally get to bed. I miss you and," she smiled and continued, "I want more time to love your gorgeous body."

As they both shared their hurt feelings and confessed their part of the games, they were able to commit to setting a time when they would start for bed and both agreed to give it priority. Although there have been some tense moments, this negotiation has been very healing and helped them both to feel closer and not so threatened about possible rejection.

Some people are turned off at the idea of negotiating or asking for what they want regarding anything, particularly about sexual needs. Co-dependent "magical thinking" makes such people believe their partners *know* what they want and just won't do it. But the truth is that the partner is usually not aware. At first it is hard for any co-dependent or shame-based person to express intimate needs. My own experience and that of thousands of recovering people is that this airing of wants, needs and feelings in a nonabusive and nonblaming way is a big doorway to a more loving intimacy and a better sex life.

Some Blocks to Intimacy Often Related to Sex

In its universal loneliness, the inner Person is apparently "programmed" in some sense with a need for intimacy with people and a Higher Power. When we get into an intimate relationship that includes sex, it is as if our lifelong dreams are all going to be met by this person we have fallen in love with. For a while we may make our loved one not only confidante and lover but also our Higher Power, as we invest him with exaggerated positive traits and the almost total focus of our lives. These projected traits often come from our childhood expectations of the heroine or hero who was supposed to come and save us from our loneliness and shameful feelings of being unworthy. Any hint of a threat that our mate might desert us can cause a great inner crisis of fear and anger. Two of the primary examples of the cause of this sort of crisis are jealousy and the fear of being deserted.

Jealousy and the Fear of Being Deserted

Jealousy is an experience that combines strong fear and anger. A jealous person experiences an acute fear that a loved one is going to leave or be disloyal. If the jealous person is in recovery and the partner is engaged in disloyal behavior, the jealous one will realize that the behavior is about the partner, but will still have a "normal" jealousy or fear of loss.

But there is a kind of jealousy that is as different from "normal" as rage is from anger. A person who has been neglected or physically deserted as a child, or whose parent emotionally deserted him for another child, may have a paralyzing kind of jealousy: a combination of transrational fear and anger that can lead to an obsessive frantic state of panic or rage, and possibly to violence.

Jealousy can be a serious threat to intimacy in a relationship. Although most jealousy and the fear of desertion may come from childhood abuse, the emotions feel very painful and are often focused totally on behavior in the current relationship.

Instead of facing the fact that the root cause of the present experience of jealousy is in one's self, the tendency is to slip into the control disease and try to change the behavior of the "misbehaving" loved one, often leading to unconscious acceleration of the jealousy-producing behavior. The other party feels controlled by the jealous partner, who denies being controlling and gives example after example of the partner's improper jealousy-producing behavior. In many cases there is a jealousy-provoking behavior that one or both parties may consider improper. This no-win cycle can cause endless haggling, accusations and exquisite pain.

This problem is often enlarged by the fact that the parties have different ideas about what is appropriate with regard to personal relations with people outside of the committed relationship. What one party considers innocent fun, the other may see as almost adulterous.

Negotiating the Parameters of Outside Relationships

The most successful way I have found to deal with this issue directly is for both parties to face the fact that jealousy and the fear of desertion are childhood abuse issues, and yet they are current and very painful experiences focused on the behavior, or perceived behavior, of a loved one in the here and now.

When potential partners first approach the place where a commitment (or a recommitment) is going to be made, it is very helpful if they can discuss what their commitment to each other includes, and what in fact they consider appropriate behavior with people outside the relationship.[2] By doing this, they can often avoid some of the sabotaging kinds of behavior later. In other words, if it's a dating relationship, is this dating relationship exclusive? If a marriage is contemplated, under what conditions can each feel comfortable about the partner seeing people of the opposite sex?

Sexually involved intimate relationships seem almost always to call for an exclusive, or at least a clearly number-one priority commitment to that relationship. When we have given up the controlling and dishonest behaviors learned as a defense against early shame and abuse, we are in a deeply vulnerable position, particularly after sharing our deepest hopes and dreams with a partner in a committed way.

Let's say that I'm jealous of you as my partner. You have several courses you can follow. Either you can deny any cause for jealousy and call me unreasonable, which will just drive me up the wall and increase my fears that you don't realize the seriousness of what you are doing. Or you can understand the irrational nature of jealousy and how it's tied to my basic insecurity and fear of desertion as a child (or actual experience of desertion in favor of someone else). You can help me by not inciting jealousy through flirting behaviors, not being secretive and not hinting subtly or openly how people of the opposite sex find you attractive by telling me "hero stories" when we meet after you have been away from me.

All this may sound clear-cut and rational, but it is complicated by the fact that the non-jealous partner often has strong needs for approval from the opposite sex. Experiencing feelings of jealousy coming from a mate can be fearful and anger-producing. This may be true because the jealous partner is hyper-jealous and controlling. But it is sometimes true because the need in many of us to get attention from the opposite sex is often unconscious. In addition, the subtle "attraction" signals we may send out to other people are largely unconscious. Because we need the gender affirmation that people outside the relationship bring to us, we strongly resist attempts to break our denial or change our behaviors in this area.

What we may have then in a "jealous situation" is a combination of two of the following:

1. An insecure person who has always been jealous and afraid of desertion because of childhood neglect or abuse.
2. A "normal" partner who sees her or his mate engaged in disloyal behavior.
3. A partner who has a strong need for approval from members of the opposite sex even after marriage—usually

stemming from child abuse and learned co-dependent behaviors or lack of boundaries.

4. Or number 1 above and a normal mate who is relating in a normal, appropriate way to members of the opposite sex.

Let's say that we have an intimate sharing relationship, and both of us are in recovery. Suddenly I, as an insecure person (1, above), become extremely jealous. I will likely tell you my feelings of fear about whomever I am jealous of in a nonjudgmental way, talking about me and my fears. If you are a "normal person who is relating in a normal way to people of the opposite sex" (4, above), you can listen to my feelings, realizing that they are about me and my history. You may want to reassure me that you love me. Then you may decide to be aware of my feelings when you are with the person who is the object of my jealousy and not incite my jealous feelings by careless or intentional jealousy-provoking behaviors. I should probably get some counseling about my family of origin, if possible, as I continue to improve my self-esteem by working the steps.

If, however, I become intensely jealous (whether I am number 1 or 2, above), and you are a partner who has a strong need for approval from members of the opposite sex, even after marriage (number 3, above), the problem is much more complex. When I tell you about my fears concerning the person I'm jealous of, you may be angry and irritated with me for "accusing you"—even if I stick to my feelings and do not blame you. This anger can be a clue that you are possibly in denial and need to take a hard look at your relationships with members of the opposite sex. It may be helpful for you to go to a counselor to take a look at your family-of-origin issues, which might allow you to see the source of your need for so much attention from members of the opposite sex.

When trying to live out one of the above scenarios as a jealous person or as the partner of a jealous mate, things can get very complex and painful in a hurry, as one or both parties snap like rubber bands back into their childhood fears of shame, desertion or being controlled. They may also reactivate their childish and exaggerated dysfunctional childhood responses. This can lead to a personal warfare in which honest and caring intimate sharing is long gone.

The underlying situation seems to be that inside each partner is a fragile little boy or girl, a Person struggling (consciously or unconsciously) with strong shame voices saying that he is not okay, not enough. It doesn't matter if the woman is gorgeous and smart or if the man looks like Arnold Schwarzenegger and is brilliant. One or both Persons may be afraid of hearing the inner voices say, "You are *not* enough to deserve, to attract, to keep your mate!"

"You Can't Catch Me!"—A Dangerous Game

I've counseled many people whose conscious intention is to be totally faithful to their husbands or wives, or to their principles, only to be horrified when someone makes a pass at them or even tries to seduce them. Such experiences are often the result of a chance encounter with a sick offender. But if it happens again, it may be the result of an unconscious psychological game, which is very common. And yet the repetitive nature of the experience seems to be taken by the victim as resulting from her attractiveness or from random chance. These people (falling in the 3 classification, above) almost always deny the possibility that they could be playing such a dysfunctional but unconscious game, and ask me to describe what a game is.

I tell them that a game, in psychologist Eric Berne's usage, is a way of avoiding authentic intimacy yet still getting close contact with another person.[3] Games constitute a way of hooking people, grappling them to you, without being honest. You have the feeling of closeness, which is the nearest thing to intimacy, without intimacy itself. But both parties usually wind up being hurt. A woman may have as her conscious intention only having casual and social relations—dinners, movies, talking with the men around her. But she finds that contrary to her wishes, almost all the men she spends any time with "practically turn into animals," as she says. She stiff-arms them in horror, and the men are embarrassed and frustrated. Both parties wind up being hurt, bewildered and often angry.

But what has happened in many cases is something other than her conscious intentions. A woman I once knew helped clarify my own tendency to "flirt innocently" by explaining her analysis of her behavior and that of others she knew. She said that although her conscious intention was not to seduce the man, she unconsciously gave him encouraging glances, or laughed and kidded in such a way that he felt increasingly that she wanted him to come closer and closer. Finally, when he felt her encouragement was very real, he moved in physically—or tried to. But since my friend was not conscious that she had sent any "come hither" signals, she was surprised and offended at his approach. In recovery, she discovered this dishonest game and the way it has hurt her chances for intimacy with her husband. As she spoke, I was shocked to realize that I had done that as a man who wanted to be moral but had enormous needs for affirmation.

When men and women are not aware that they are sending out "come hither" signals, they may have a great deal of trouble being sensitive to an intimate partner with problems of jealousy and the fear of rejection. A man with a jealous wife, for instance, may reason that other women are simply attracted to him. Can he help it? Of course, the answer is yes. He can help getting involved with women by not playing games. But the tragedy is that many intimate relationships are destroyed by jealousy and attention-getting games. The problem is made much more complex by the fact that the world is filled with very needy people who may take almost any signal, even an innocent one, as a serious invitation to intimacy or sex.

If two parties in recovery are committed to having a loving and authentic relationship, they will be willing to share their feelings about what is happening to them, not to manipulate the other into changing, but to begin a Person-dialogue that can lead to increased security and growth for them both. Out of these discussions, one or both can get outside help in the program or through counseling.

Good recovery programs have, as a by-product, relieved thousands of people from lifelong fears of desertion and jealousy. As the inner Person begins to experience value and self-esteem through acceptance of other recovering people, then the power and presence of God become real through the changes brought about in working the Steps. The resulting deeper levels of trust and peace can lead one beyond the irrational fear of jealousy and desertion to a whole new way of life filled with meaning and purpose.

19
Learning to Live

Experiencing Intimacy
and Spirituality

In the beginning of this book, I observed that the compulsion to control others is primarily a spiritual problem of low self-esteem, of being out of touch with reality. It is the result of the pain and fear of shame, of being revealed as inadequate, and of being out of control in the inner battle for the soul. As the internal struggle between our childlike inner Person and the introjected shaming voices heightened, we tried to block out the pain we were experiencing as we feared being revealed. This pain and fear led us to try to control our lives and relationships. To stop the resulting pain we used compulsive and addictive behaviors, including the acceleration of the compulsion to control the people around us. In this process, we were in denial and lost touch with our own thoughts and feelings, with our physical and sexual reality, with other people's reality and with Ultimate Reality or God.

This control disease kept us from being spiritual, since a spiritual person has experienced some self-esteem. And a spiritual person is in touch with many aspects of emotional reality and can share them in a loving, nonjudgmental way.

But when I started out on this spiritual journey myself by hitting bottom in my personal life, I just wanted out of my pain. I had no idea that I was about to learn to *live*—to gain a sense of being okay and a growing hunger for reality and intimacy with people and God.

As I came to this last chapter, I wondered how I might show you a picture of how spirituality now looks to me "on the hoof," walking around. Then I remembered that I'd begun this book with a description of a fight between Roger and Sue. The changes in the couple they represent, since they became involved in 12-Step programs, are profound. Yet from the outside it would appear to most people that nothing has changed.

Recently I saw Roger and he told me the following story:

> Sue had finished her master's thesis after two years of hard and almost constant work on her degree. Roger had supported her in every way he could, although it was a very busy time for him too. But he washed lots of dishes and fixed breakfast and cooked numerous other meals so Sue could keep working on her thesis. Then Sue had finished, and Roger had taken her out to dinner to celebrate.
>
> The next morning Roger had a report to write. Sue came into his study, put her arms around his neck from behind and whispered in his ear, "I love you." Roger smiled up at her as she continued, "And I'm going to fix you a wonderful candlelight dinner tonight!" Roger felt warm all over. Later that morning they were having a glass of iced tea together, and Roger said in his little-boy voice, "Are you going to fix me a special dinner tonight?" Sue frowned and didn't answer.
>
> Roger saw something was wrong and asked, "What's the matter?"

Sue said in an irritated voice, "Roger, I *told* you I was going to fix you a special dinner this morning. Don't you *remember* what I said? You do this a lot, you know."

Roger was crestfallen. He had just been playing, a little boy wanting to hear about his surprise again. He couldn't believe she didn't understand. He blurted out, "Well, I guess you've felt irritated like this during the whole 20 years of our married life and just haven't wanted to hurt my feelings!"

Sue nodded. "That's right!"

Roger was furious. He felt shamed and very angry. Sue's family didn't play, and he and Sue did. But now it seemed that it had all been a sham to her and that she'd thought he was silly the whole time. He became a turtle and said nothing for a couple hours.

Sue was amazed at the turn of events. She felt rejected and misunderstood, but decided to be big about it to get things back to a peaceful place. "I guess," she said quietly, "I've been pretty hard to live with during these past two years."

Roger was angry and hurt by now. "Yes," he said, "you have." (This really wasn't true, but Roger had been building a case against her in his silence.) He continued, "You've been picking at me and correcting half the things that I've said, as if you were editing my conversation for publication. I attributed it to your work, but in fact it was irritating and you *were* hard to live with."

Sue started crying and said, "I knew you didn't want me to get my master's and make something out of myself. You've been harboring all this anger for two years, haven't you?"

Roger hit the ceiling. At last he had something absolutely absurd to attack—since in fact he *wanted* her to get her master's so she could make more money and be happier. He said, "That's a bunch of *garbage!* For God's sake, you're doing your old thing of changing the whole subject because you can't face what we're talking about!"

After about an hour of going their separate ways around the house, they met in the hall. While apart they had both remembered the program, and Roger had done the first four Steps on his part of the problem. He saw that he had been dishonest about Sue's having been hard to live with. In fact, he had remembered that the whole two years she had continued to do at least her share around the house and had not complained about it. So Roger made amends for what he'd said.

Sue had done a Fourth Step and seen that she had tried to hurt Roger because she was again a literalist and had been ashamed that she had not caught the fact that Roger had been playing when he'd asked again about dinner.

Roger, in turn, admitted that when Sue had opened the door by saying, "I guess I've been pretty hard to live with the past two years," he had wheeled in a baggage cart of complaints and started unloading them on her in order to hurt her in return.

As they each confessed and made amends, they saw more things they had done to hurt each other—and laughed as they realized that most of their techniques were right out of their parents' arsenals, and a shade dishonest.

When they finished the discussion, they still felt a residue of pain and irritation about what had been said, but by supper time it was all gone. As they looked at each other across the candlelit table, they were very grateful for the gift of intimacy.

Roger said to me, "I guess I thought that having intimacy was a way to stop having fights and misunderstandings. But now I realize that what we've been given is better. It's a way to deal directly with all our dysfunctional stuff with God's help, and to walk through the pain into understanding and a deeper love for each other.

"Hey," he concluded, "maybe *that's* what intimacy is all about!"

In my own life, I am beginning to get in touch with my child-like inner Person. Through the 12-Step program and community and a deepening relationship with God, I have been able to stand with my inner Person in the lonely battle against the voices of shame that have so often defeated me and held me back.

As a result of beginning to reside consciously inside my life and not desert myself in compulsive activities, my sense of who I am and what I want to do has cleared more in the past 10 years than I would have dreamed possible. I feel as if my lonely inner child has at last found a family of other lonely people in recovery, and we are learning to surrender our frantic compulsion to control as we commit our stress-filled, over-accelerated lives and our wills to God as our Higher Power.

For me, this has meant a freedom to attempt new things I've always been afraid to try for fear of failing. I can do this because my shame voices are gone almost all the time now. I'm writing songs and novels at 70 years old!

Recently I was on a radio talk show for two hours in Pittsburgh. On that show the host played, for the first time, several songs about recovery for which I had written the lyrics.[1] I wept with happiness. My inner child couldn't believe that this was happening to me!

I realized that at 64 I was exactly the same age at which both my father and mother died over 35 years ago. But because of this journey toward recovery and reality, I feel like a young Person in the first pages of a new chapter in my life, on a journey with a new family—which includes some of my old one. Many of us have been humbled by our failures to be able to control our addictions and/or the people in our lives and the worlds we live in. Some of us have been broken like crazy wild horses from our compulsions to control. But in the discovery of our "weakness" we have found a strange new strength in our Higher Power.

As I look around at these loving gentle giants I meet with in the program, I see tough, realistic, spiritual Persons with self-esteem who are growing carriers of a profoundly simple medicine: a social and personal remedy for much of the stress, pain, fear and isolation of our time. I have begun to believe that those who are in recovery from the compulsion to control are somehow carriers of self-esteem, and of the intimacy and love of God.

At least they have been for me.

APPENDIX A
BOUNDARIES

The Boundary System

There are two parts to a boundary system: the external and internal boundaries.[1] External boundaries protect us physically and sexually outside our skin. Internal boundaries protect us intellectually, emotionally and spiritually inside ourselves.

These invisible fences mark off a space around us that no one else has a right to come into without our permission. With healthy boundaries, we can protect ourselves from people who would abuse or control us—everybody from strangers to friends, parents, mates or children. We may still hear people's harsh or controlling words, insinuations and criticism, and see and hear them expressing emotions apparently aimed at controlling us, but we are able to protect ourselves from the manipulative impact of these control devices. We can stop their words and demands at our boundaries and consider them. When we can stop such control attempts from entering our emotional space, we are not compelled to act, think or feel in ways we do not choose.

A boundary is something we are *supposed* to have. Exercising healthy boundaries is not "keeping people out" so that we don't relate to or interact with them. A boundary system is a symbolic membrane that gives us protection from being controlled by others and from controlling them, but through which we can have healthy, intimate relationships.

The symbolic membrane is like an invisible field of energy. A healthy *external* boundary can be imaged in our minds as a Mason jar large enough to fit comfortably over our head and tall enough to stand inside. We can see through it and breathe through it; but unlike a glass jar, it is very tough yet flexible, so we can make it smaller or larger. We can hear through it, but it's sturdy enough to stop the emotional impact of most things that are coming at us from someone else: their words, insinuations, demands, criticisms and emotions (see figure A.1).

A helpful image for a healthy *internal* boundary is a tough, invisible bullet-proof vest with tiny doors that open only from inside.

This image may not work for everyone. Sometimes people come up with other images for the boundaries they use to protect themselves. Someone who heard me describe boundaries said that a glass jar was not permeable to her; it was too much like a wall. She imagined healthy boundaries as being like the Force in the movie *Star Wars,* a force field of energy that is impenetrable, tough and flexible, but you can see through it and adjust its size around you. The important thing is to develop *some* kind of image to represent your boundary system and learn to use it.

A person with healthy boundaries has them in place all the time. But when we first become aware of this concept, we often don't know we have a boundary. As I began to learn about this, I had to consciously put the Mason jar over my head and button up my bullet-proof vest when I came into the presence of someone I had allowed to control me in the past (or whom I had controlled, since my boundaries are also to keep me from crashing into others' space and attempting to control them). So I still consciously "put my boundary on" when I come into a potential control situation, even though having my boundaries in

Figure A.1. Boundaries*

Nonexistent Boundaries

No Protection

Damaged Boundary System

Partial Protection

Walls Instead of Boundaries

Anger Fear Silence Words

Complete Protection but No Intimacy

Moving from Nonexistent Boundaries to Walls and Back Again

Intact Boundary System

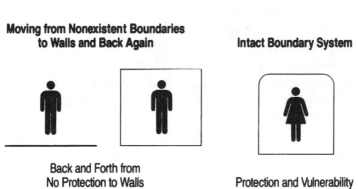

Back and Forth from
No Protection to Walls

Protection and Vulnerability

* From *Facing Co-dependence: What It Is, Where It Comes From, How It Sabotages Our Lives.*
© 1989 Pia Mellody, Andrea Wells Miller and J. Keith Miller.

place has become a habit in many relationships. For example, if we want to hug somebody, we don't take off our boundary. We ask permission for a hug and pull our boundary in close to us and hug that person. A healthy person never lets anyone inside her boundary. Even God, evidently, won't come in unless we ask.

Many of us were not taught as children that we have the right to establish boundaries for our own bodies, physically or sexually, particularly with a parent and later with a spouse. But it is appropriate to keep your sexual boundaries on even in bed because you can often get hurt there. If you want to make love, you pull your boundary in very close to you, skin-tight. I used to think that if you really loved somebody, you could take off your boundaries altogether, but I have learned that having no boundaries makes you so vulnerable that you're likely to get injured—or to thoughtlessly transgress your partner's boundaries. Paradoxically, you can love with more abandon with boundaries because fear is reduced.

With healthy boundaries you can choose whether you will say yes or no to other people, including requests from your children, your wife or husband, and people outside your family. You can also use your boundaries to give you time to choose what interpretation to give certain data coming at you, regardless of the interpretation of others. By being in control of your own thinking, you can influence your emotions so that you don't have to feel unnecessary guilt, anger, pain, fear or shame.

If we do *not* have healthy internal boundaries, we find ourselves continually getting overcommitted because we can't say no to people, particularly certain authority figures, when they ask us to do things, even though we may already be feeling stressed by too many commitments.

The Same Incident Experienced Without and With Boundaries

Imagine, for instance, that you are going home to your mother's for her birthday dinner. (She has insisted on cooking, which she loves to do.) Granted, the following is an exaggerated illustration, but, tragically, not very exaggerated for some people. She asks you to be there at 2:00 P.M. You and your family get up early because you have a long drive, and you get your four little boys in your station wagon all dressed in their Sunday best. Since you are going to drive back late that night, you don't pack extra clothes for them. Just before you leave, a rainstorm hits. It follows you all the way to Grandma's.

About 30 minutes before you are to arrive, a pickup truck driven by a drunk driver lurches out of a side road and hits you broadside. Your station wagon ends up on its side in a very wet, muddy ditch. It has been raining hard for the past hour. After making sure that no one is hurt, you exchange information with the pickup driver and the police officer who has arrived on the scene. Meanwhile, your kids climb out of the car and gleefully jump into the muddy water, getting their clothes and skin covered with black, oily mud. A wrecker comes, your car is righted and you finally pull up to Grandma's house two hours late. Everyone is muddy and exhausted, but you are grateful they are all alive. However, you remember how your mother hates people to be late for dinner.

Now let's say you are a person with no boundaries. When you start up the front walk, you are an adult, tall and proud. But as you anticipate the encounter with your mother, you start shrinking; by the time you reach the door, you are about three years old. You know that she hates it when people are late to dinner, and she does not like the kids to be dirty when they visit. By this time you practically have to reach up to the door to knock. When your mother opens the door, she has an angry look on her face, a combination of self-pity, rejection, anger and hurt as she says, "It's four o'clock. Dinner's cold. It's my birthday. Don't you care?"

Those words go straight into you, and you automatically feel shame and guilt. You start excusing yourself and apologizing. "What a rat I am," you may say to yourself. You can't seem to stop yourself—although you know it's stupid and unnecessary to feel guilt and shame when *you were hit by a drunk driver and are lucky to be alive!*

Now let's say that you are the same person, only this time

you have learned about boundaries. This time, before you start up the walk, you put on your Mason jar boundary and your bullet-proof vest. Now you are still an adult as you knock.

Your mother comes to the door and makes the same shaming statements. But this time you stop the words at your boundary and ask yourself if her accusation that you don't care about her is true for you, or if it is just her interpretation of events. When you do this, you realize that her criticisms about your lateness are not realistic from your point of view. After all, you had a wreck and you are fortunate to be alive. You conclude that your being late does not mean you do not care about your mother. So you do not respond to her shaming words as if they were true; you do not let them inside your boundary. Thus you can choose not to have shameful feelings about being late. Without the powerful feeling of shame driving your behavior, you are able to refrain from groveling to placate her.

When she realizes that her control attempt has failed to get an embarrassed response from you, she may get angry and intensify her attack or change direction and say, "And your kids are filthy. How did you know I wouldn't have my friends here, too?"

Again you stop her words at your boundary before you let them in and have your feelings about them. In that split second you can decide whether her shaming words are about you and your behavior, or about her and her anger and shame. Your resulting feelings can be very different than they would have been without boundaries. This is roughly the way boundaries can keep you from being controlled by other people's verbal control attempts.

If the situation had been different, and you were late because you watched a football game and delayed leaving your house for two hours, you would stop her accusations at your boundary to consider them as before. But this time you would determine that you *were* at fault and you could let her words in, feel the guilt and make amends. Again, this is a very different thing from having a baffling and exaggerated automatic shame attack the moment her accusations were spoken. Healthy boundaries allow you to respond intimately as a mature adult. The second scenario had at least the makings of an intimate encounter, since you were dealing with your own experienced reality instead of her feelings resulting from her skewed perception of it.

If the mother continued and increased her shaming abuse of him and his children after the son explained what happened and told her about the wreck, the son may have had to leave— use a wall of distance. This would be a very difficult call if one were just starting to learn about boundaries.

Impaired Boundaries

Many people have not been taught how to have healthy boundaries. Instead, they may (1) have no boundaries at all, (2) have functional boundaries only part of the time or only with certain people, or (3) use walls instead of boundaries. (See figure A.1, which also includes a picture of healthy boundaries.)

Often, people who have no boundaries feel compelled to do everything that is requested of them. They may expect others to read their thoughts and do what they want them to do in return. They may become very angry when people around them don't read their minds (or take their hints) and do what they want.

Some people find that they have very healthy boundaries most of the time and can say no or resist attempts at manipulation by others, but with particular people they have no boundaries at all. (For example, it may be that one of your children can get through your boundaries and talk you into almost anything most of the time, whereas you have good boundaries with your other children and can say no appropriately.) Some people find that at certain times, such as when hungry, tired, angry, lonely or sick, their boundaries fail to protect them from being controlled or from controlling others.

Walls

People who do not have functional boundaries to protect themselves sometimes use walls. Walls are usually made up of strong emotions such as anger or fear, designed to keep people and their control attempts away. A wall is emotionally solid, impenetrable and rigid, and nothing (with the exception of a major offender) can get through it (neither manipulating people *nor loving* ones).

For example, someone using a wall of anger often rages at the people around him or her in a very threatening way. Let's say that an authority figure such as a school principal or minister calls a woman with no boundaries to bake a thousand cookies for a parents' meeting. This woman had baked a thousand cookies for the same person just a week before. Her two children have typhoid fever, and she has diarrhea. But because she has no boundaries, she starts to say yes. Then something snaps inside her. Instead of yes, she screams into the phone in a total rage. "Don't you *ever* ask me to bake cookies *again!* I'm sick of baking cookies and doing things for you! Don't ever call me again. Got it?" That's a wall of anger, and the caller probably won't ask her again.

Another person might not scream aloud but instead emit a sinister, nonverbal message indicating that he might soon burst into a formidable rage, even though the person isn't raging at the moment. People keep away from him for fear of triggering the anger. This is another example of a wall of anger.

A wall of fear might be in effect when a person withdraws and isolates, emitting a nonverbal message of fear. The sense is that if someone approached that person, he would be overcome with fear and perhaps fall apart or flee. Such a person may stay in social contact but lurk silently around the edges of the group, withdraw all social energy or disappear from the group's awareness. Other people use walls of silence. They just won't talk about issues. Still others use walls of words, continuous monologues about things that are meaningless to the person one is talking to, an apparently bottomless sack of words. The person with a wall of words often wasn't listened to as a child and thinks that talking is reaching out for intimacy. But since the words are not a sharing of the Person's inner reality, they wind up *blocking* the very intimacy sought. The only trouble with walls is that, although they can protect us and keep people out, they also keep intimacy out. And the person behind a wall often gets very lonely.

Healthy Boundaries Can Protect Us from Compulsive Behavior

Many people who have an alcohol, drug or control addiction, or a problem with compulsive behavior, describe how they decided to drink or use drugs again by saying something like, "Well, the situation came up and I just could not say no." They had no boundaries, no defense against drinking, using drugs or whatever the compulsion was.

Healthy boundaries provide that split second between a temptation-event and your emotional response in which you *can* stop the incoming invitation at the boundary, think about it and decide whether to say no to the emotional chaos that would result from giving in to your addiction.

For instance, if someone keeps offering a recovering alcoholic with no boundaries a drink, sooner or later he may uncritically accept it and get back into his addiction. With good boundaries, one can stop the invitation at the boundary and realize that the invitation to drink is an invitation to go back into chaos, failure and insanity. That realization makes it much easier to say no and not let in the invitation to drink and have "craving feelings" about it. This split second to consider what's coming at us, which a healthy boundary provides, is the space in which recovery can occur and the space that can protect us from being controlled by others or controlling them.

For most people in recovery, it is necessary to do the Steps in order to get the power of God to make these decisions. Working out changes and character defects in one's personality involves this sort of boundary-setting at critical times. The development or recovery of authentic intimate relationships can hardly be accomplished without the security provided by boundaries or their equivalent.

Boundaries Protect Us, Except Against a Major Offender

Healthy boundaries will work when you have learned to use them, unless you are dealing with a major offender, someone who attacks you with great power. The attack could be physical, sexual, verbal, emotional or psychological. Someone who is more powerful than you and who is bent on offending you can usually get through normal, healthy boundaries. Pia Mellody recommends that you use walls when you are confronted with such a major offender.[2]

First use a wall of fear or distance and disappear if you can—get yourself out of the offender's presence. If that doesn't work, use a wall of anger to make it clear to the person in no uncertain terms that you do not welcome his advance. This wall of anger will sometimes give you the strength and energy to take care of yourself when this is possible. Each person must decide when and how to use boundaries or walls when facing a major offender.

It is easy to see that healthy boundaries are essential to leading a mature life in which we can choose to enter intimate relationships with the knowledge that we can protect our inner Person and not abuse or control others.

APPENDIX B
A BRIEF FORAY INTO THE LITERATURE ON CONTROL AND INTIMACY: 1955-1991

In 1513 Niccolo Machiavelli startled the world when he produced *The Prince* and *The Discourses,* self-help manuals to guide his young Borgia prince toward success in complex interactions through the clever use of tactical deception, acumen and manipulation. He advised:

> It is good to appear clement, trustworthy, humane, religious, honest and also to be so. But always with the mind so disposed that, when the occasion arises not to be so, you can become the opposite.

Therefore, it is not too surprising that four centuries later noted psychologists at the Center for Advanced Studies in the Behavioral Sciences turned to Machiavelli for guidance when they wanted to study interpersonal power, and in true Machiavellian fashion purloined selected statements from his work. These statements became the basis of a Machiavellian scale that launched a series of studies on the characteristics of people who endorse manipulative interpersonal tactics and a skeptical view of human nature, while seeming to support some of the attitudes of traditional morality.

Christie, Geis and others discovered that there is very little relationship between Machiavellianism and socioeconomic status, education, religion or the Machiavellianism of the person's parents. Machiavellians arise from all arenas, but younger people and males obtain higher scores on the scale.

Generally, researchers found that high "Machs" tend to be cool and detached in interpersonal dealings, cognitively motivated toward self-defined goals and tasks. They operate well in ambiguous situations and are unlikely to take chances if the odds appear against them. Otherwise they initiate and control structure, exploit and accumulate resources. Suspicious and resistant to influence by others, they have an unflattering view of people as a whole and support few of the socially accepted mores embraced readily by low Machs.

Low Machs, who are socially and emotionally oriented, are more susceptible to influence by others, accept structure well and recognize implicit limits. They enjoy encounters with people, work conscientiously "within the lines" and tend to be carried away in interaction processes. They are thus less likely to win in situations against high Machs.

A study by Abramson in 1973 revealed that counselors using Machiavellian tactics were significantly less empathic than those who did not. Steininger and Eisenberg (1976) determined that contrary to expectation, high-Mach college students tend to be significantly more dogmatic in their interpersonal dealings than do low Machs. Interestingly, the authors suggest that women may actually be at least as Machiavellian as men, or even more so, despite the fact that their scores usually suggest the opposite.

Simultaneously, in the late 1960s and 1970s, David C. McClelland and his followers were investigating the way in which power-oriented men and women develop emotionally and socially, describing male and female styles of expressing the power motive. In McClelland's *Power: the Inner Experience,* published in 1975, he proposes that there are four stages of development that people may pass through, each with a different thrust. The people may express one type of power (e.g., competitive striving) in one setting, while selflessly sharing for a good cause in another.

According to McClelland, men with a high power need seem to be more tense, argumentative and emotional than reasonable, appearing to be readying themselves to push ahead and make an impact on the world. He reports that women with a strong power drive "are focused more on themselves, particularly on their bodies, thinking in terms of having resources to share" (p. 75). He notes also that the consumption of liquor increases power thoughts in men. Not surprisingly, researchers such as Glass, Strube and Werner, who are studying the Type A personality, confirm that these tense, impatient, driven, highly activated males (who fit the picture of the McClelland male with a high need for power) have an overwhelming need to control their partners in intimate relationships—a pattern that appears to come from a deep fear of women.

During the same period, Shostrum (1967) began examining the manipulations of people whom he saw as losing spontaneity, the capacity to feel and the ability to express themselves directly and creatively. He described in *Man the Manipulator* that the manipulator is

> all of us, consciously, subconsciously or unconsciously employing all the phony tricks we absorb between the cradle and grave to conceal the actual vital nature of ourselves and in the process, reducing ourselves and our fellow man into things to be controlled (pp. xi, xii).

Shostrum proposes the "actualizor" as the opposite of the manipulator. He describes the actualizor as a person who can appreciate self and others as people with unique potentials who are able to express their actual selves. Since he considers each person to be a blend of both—actualizor and manipulator—his thrust is to present the alternative to manipulation and to encourage people to be the selves they really are in order to learn how to feel alive and enjoy life again.

He agrees with Fritz Perls that a basic cause for manipulating to control others lies in the eternal conflict between self-support and the need to be supported by others. Shostrum notes that the actualizor is able to fight with another creatively and to grow from the experience:

> A person can never have a true and lasting relationship with another until he is able to fight with him. When we're able to show we *are* angry, that we *are* afraid, that we *can* be hurt and *can* trust—then we can love. When we can really level with each other, telling each other how we feel and getting all our feelings out in the open, only then do we begin to feel this closeness (pp. 42-43).

Eric Fromm suggests that people may manipulate for another reason. In his 1957 article "Man Is Not a Thing," he argues that love is knowing another person as that person actually is, but loving the "ultimate essence." Since love is the ultimate relationship between people, Fromm postulates that we try to be flawless in order to be loved more. Because love is difficult to achieve, the manipulator then chooses a desperate alternative. We try to gain complete control over the other in order to make the person do, think, feel what we want, thereby making the other person into our *thing*. In contrast, Shostrum describes the actualizor as having concern and respect for the "thou" of the other.

Eric Berne and William Glasser propose that people engage in manipulation in order to avoid intimacy or involvement. In *Games People Play* (1964), Berne states that people engage in games in order to regulate their emotions and avoid intimacy. R.D. Laing puts it another way in his book *Knots,* (1970) describing the intricate bargain people make:

> They are playing a game. They are playing at not playing a game. If I show them I see they are, I will break the rules and they will punish me. I must play their game, of not seeing their game.

Glasser indicates that one of the basic fears is the fear of involvement (1984). According to these theories, the manipulator relates to significant others in various ritualistic controlling ways in an effort to avoid intimacy.

Shostrum concludes his chapters on the manipulator by reporting that the

> basic philosophy of the active manipulator is to maintain control at all costs; of the passive manipulator, never to offend; of the competitive manipulator, to win at all costs; and of the indifferent manipulator, to deny caring (p. 20).

As such, the manipulator cannot relax and enjoy himself because he is always playing a role.

Shostrum and Kavanaugh contend in *Between Man and Woman* (1972) that love should be a kind of rhythmic interdependence that carries people beyond their own boundaries and creates a new reality, that effortlessly lifts each to a new level that cannot be reached by self alone. Instead of acting in rigid institutionalized roles, two people keenly alive are able to relate in "mini and maxi swings" of strength and weakness, anger and love.

> Instead of going nowhere . . . the rhythmic relationship is a dynamic ever-changing process of growth . . . a duet in which each alternates as soloist and accompanist, but together creating all the sounds and varieties of feeling which make the living of every day a creative symphony (p. 195).

Claude Steiner, one of the Transactional Analysis authors, delineates types of power plays a person uses to make others do something that the power player thinks they will not do voluntarily. In his 1972 *Scripts People Live,* he gives reasons for the difficulty men and women have giving each other the things they want most: strokes from a good mutual working situation, and strokes from intimacy. He remarks that since women are not allowed to use their Adults in a working situation, women and men find it very hard to work together. On the other hand, intimacy, which is heavily based on the capacity to be intuitive and nurturing simultaneously, is strongly scripted out of them.

Consequently, lacking the two most rewarding forms of strokes, people turn to power plays to get what they want.

In *Take Effective Control of Your Life* (1984), William Glasser, a Reality therapist, takes a somewhat different point of view. He agrees that most "serious conflicts evolve from our attempts to control others who will not accept our control, because what we want does not satisfy them" (p. 147). However, he states that we, as other living organisms, function as *control systems:* he does not consider control a need but rather as the way we must function in order to fulfill our needs. Therefore we are in a continual struggle with each other, since we are all acting in the same manner.

> And, though each of us wants to be in control, no one of us wants to be controlled. The task then becomes a struggle to gain control in order to fulfill our own needs without depriving others, especially those close to us, of satisfying theirs (pp. 43-44).

Researchers Abigail Stewart and Zick Rubin (1976) examine the power motive in a dating couple to determine its relationship to the couple's anticipation of problems, their satisfaction with their interactions and the longitudinal stability of their dating experience. Men with high Hope of Power were dissatisfied with the relationship and anticipated problems concerned with impulsivity and interpersonal conflict. Couples with males being high in Hope of Power were more likely to break up than to marry. However, Hope of Power in the female partner was not related to these issues.

From his perusal of the psychodynamics of violence-prone marriages, Martin (1978) found two types of violent marriages. The first comes from the characteristics of the husband, with violence entering the situation at an early stage in the marriage. The second comes from conflicts in the marriage relationship that trigger violent reactions and appear to emanate from a failure to communicate. These conflicts center on issues of power, intimacy and boundaries, with the behavior of one partner seeming to threaten the psychological defenses of the other.

Mason and Blankenship (1987) studied power and affiliation motivation, stress and abuse in intimate relationships, and decided that the need for power was significantly associated with the infliction of physical abuse on their partners by men. Highly stressed women with high needs for affiliation and low activity inhibition were the most likely to inflict abuse (although high needs for affiliation with activity inhibition generally moderated the effect stress has on inflicting abuse). For women, but not for men, infliction of abuse was correlated with receiving abuse. Apparently women who strike out are liable to be struck back.

An article by McAdams and Powers (1981) looks at the connections between intimacy motivation and interpersonal behaviors and communication. Results support McClelland's contentions that need for power and need for affiliation are negatively related and, when equally strong, are in conflict with each other. Subjects in this study, who were high in intimacy motivation, engaged in behaviors that are contrary to those used in studies with high need for power. They emphasized inclusiveness, surrendered manipulative control, took pleasure in mutual delights and placed themselves in proximity to others. They also referred to the group as "we" and "us" and gave few commands. Other group members saw these people as warm, natural, sincere, likeable and loving. They were seldom seen as dominant.

In 1982, Hermanowicz studied the effect of "authenticity" and Machiavellian attitudes on styles of communication, which she defined as being partnership or non-partnership. As she expected, she found that "authentic" people communicated in a partnership style *if* their level of Machiavellianism was low, supporting Shostrum's contrasting behaviors between actualizor and manipulator.

Stephen Thayer (1988) conducted research on different categories of touch based on people's roles and relationships, emphasizing the power of touch intimacy. He concluded that touch had symbolic meaning as a powerful communication channel to convey and receive affection, inclusion and control.

On the other hand, Judith Siegel (1990) sees the giving and receiving of money as the medium through which couples express the core dynamics of power, mutual respect and trust. She postulates that couples' conflicts over money will persist until underlying issues of esteem, commitment, control, identity, closeness and affection are resolved. Goldberg (1982) discusses the dynamics of marital interactions and marital conflict as emerging from control struggles that develop because each spouse is afraid of being controlled. He suggests that problems of intimacy might be resolved if there were a better balance between privacy and intimacy.

In the 1980s interest in three separate but closely related movements resulted in a proliferation of popular psychology/ self-help books on bookstore shelves. The men's movement, the women's movement and the Adult Children of Alcoholics and co-dependence literature became immensely popular. Everyone was pronounced traumatized and/or addicted and/or co-dependent. Authors rushed to the press with books describing what was wrong with men, women and relationships. Kiley (1983) described men who have never grown up to face the responsibilities and challenges of intimacy in *The Peter Pan Syndrome*. Harriet Lerner produced *The Dance of Anger: A Woman's Guide to the Patterns of Intimate Relationships* (1985) in an attempt to help women move toward healthy and fulfilling interactions.

Robin Norwood took up the female cudgel with *Women Who Love Too Much: When You Keep Wishing and Hoping He'll Change* (1986), in which she indicated that drama and chaos in childhood lead women to seek a similar challenge by engaging in chaotic and distracting interactions with unhealthy men. This keeps them from feeling the depression and pain beneath the surface of their lives.

> In this way, a cruel, indifferent, dishonest or otherwise difficult partner becomes for these women the equivalent of a drug, creating a means of avoiding their own feelings—just as alcohol and other mood-altering substances create for drug-addicted persons a temporary avenue of escape and one from which they are not to be separated (p. 61).

Norwood notes also that soap operas and romance novels immerse us in the false glamour of unrewarding immature relationships, which are glorified to the point that we accept the notion that suffering is an integral part of true love. She remarks that there are few models of people relating in mature, honest, open, nonmanipulative and nonexploitive ways, and suggests that we need to work consciously at developing a more mature way of relating so that we can trade chaos for a deeper intimacy.

In their book *Men Who Hate Women and the Women Who Love Them* (1986), Dr. Susan Forward and Joan Torres explain the destructive behavior of the abusive male as a cover-up for his tremendous anxiety about women. He is described as being in conflict between his need for the woman's love and his deep-seated fear of abandonment. If he strips this woman of her power and self-confidence, she will become dependent upon him and he will not need to fear losing her. The authors suggest that women who marry misogynists tend to come from backgrounds with a controlling, tyrannical father and a passive, dependent mother. If there is abuse as well, the child sees herself as dirty and worthless. She disowns her feelings of anger, which return disguised as illnesses, since she does not know how to express anger. A return to health requires that women let go of the self-denying behaviors that have not served them well and hold on to the strengths of intuition, comfort with feelings and strong emotions, and the ability to nurture, since the most wonderful gift to self or one's partner is a sense of self-worth and an expectation of love and good treatment.

Dr. Kevin Leman's book, *The Pleasers: Women Who Can't Say No and the Men Who Control Them* (1988), discusses the characteristics of the controller including the need to have his way and to win, the use of put-down humor, an inability to laugh at himself, flaw-picking, rough treatment, visible hostility and disrespect toward women. This man has an overwhelming need to control, and his weapons are words and moods. Although he may physically abuse his wife, he is more likely to engage in psychological battery. Leman encourages pleasers to run from the controller and, if already married to him, to take positive action for therapy and to pull the rug out from under the controller instead of descending into the swamp of despair, discouragement and guilt.

John Bradshaw, author of *Healing the Shame That Binds You* (1988), sees "control as one of [the] major strategies of cover-up for shame, all the layers of cover-up are attempts to control the outside so that the inside will not be exposed" (p. 99). Like Norwood, Forward and Torres, Bradshaw postulates that manipulative and self-destructive behaviors serve to cover the pain and shame so that the person does not have to feel or acknowledge the painful blackness within. He adds,

> With toxic shame, you are either more than human (super-achieving) or less than human (underachieving). It's all or nothing. You either have total control (compulsivity) or you have no control (addiction). They are interconnected and set each other up (p. 100).

Winning by Letting Go by Elizabeth Brenner (1983) takes a somewhat different stance. Brenner remarks: "Most of us have dispossessed ourselves of much of our capacity for self-control—we have buried it" (p. 9). What covers it? Often, an unwillingness to confront the paradox that we are both completely in and completely out of control. Similarly, we may fear surrender, "believing that letting go or giving in will be the end of us" (p. 9). Since control and surrender are already prominent parts of our lives, we need to clarify our choices in order to profitably channel our drive to control and to give up our self-imposed limitations.

These books are only a sample of the many volumes of the 1980s dealing with intimate relationships, issues of control and techniques for restoring health to self and to the relationship with a partner. Some provocative thoughts come also from research into the lives and behaviors of the chimpanzees of Gombe. In Jane Goodall's book, *Through a Window* (1990), she notes that the chimpanzee is more like us than any other living creature, possessing 99 percent of the DNA structure of humans, and with minds that are "uncannily like our own." It was proved experimentally "that chimpanzees could recognize themselves in mirrors—that they had, therefore, some kind of self-concept" (p. 21).

The possession of power for the male chimpanzee is of great importance, since he can maintain all but exclusive mating rights over any female who attracts him. Power is good for the community, too, since conflicts between other members of the community are kept to a minimum under the control of a powerful male. The goal of the consorting male is to keep the female away from rival males during the time she is likely to conceive. If the male is powerful, he can summon the female and take her away from the community on a private consortship for the period of her fertility. If the female is unwilling or reluctant, the male becomes aggressive and bullying until he achieves his goal. At that time he becomes benign and tolerant, willing to adapt his behavior to her wishes. She becomes calm and responsive. Generally, this pattern ensures that the powerful male's genes are passed on to the community. Thus, the rhythmic alternation of power/control and intimacy are beneficial both to the individuals and to the community. Goodall remarks that,

> This whole set up—the prolonged period of the exclusive relationship, the calm and relaxed atmosphere that prevails and the unusual sexual interactions—suggests that chimpanzees have a latent capacity for the development of more permanent heterosexual pair bonding; a relationship more similar to the pattern of monogamy—or at least serial monogamy—that has become the cultural tradition in much of the Western World (pp. 95-96).

And finally, there is an article by James Shreeve, "Machiavellian Monkeys" (1991), which describes work from the journal of two psychologists at the University of St. Andrews in Scotland. Richard Byrne and Andrew Whiten catalogued the deceptions, betrayals and machinations of monkeys and apes as witnessed by primatologists around the world. Shreeve considers the work a "testament to the evolutionary importance of

what Byrne and Whiten call Machiavellian intelligence," the
ultimate how-to guide for prevailing in a complex society
through the judicious application of deliberate tactics by the
animal. The two psychologists gathered information on
episodes of deceptive behaviors employed by primates to distract another animal, to conceal a choice bit of food from
another, to hide their own intent from a peer, to kidnap a willing female from a more dominant male or even to trick a peer
into revealing the source of a treat. After looking at the data,
Byrne and Whiten reasoned that,

> If primates other than humans deceived one another on a
> regular basis . . . then it raised the extremely provocative possi-
> bility that the primate brain, and ultimately the human brain, is
> an instrument crafted for social manipulation. Humans evolved
> from the same evolutionary stock as apes and if tactical decep-
> tion was an important part of the lives of our evolutionary
> ancestors, then the sneakiness and subterfuge that human
> beings are so manifestly capable of might not be simply a result
> of our great intelligence and oversized brain, but a driving force
> behind their development (p. 70).

If so, the findings add weight to the theory of English psychologist Nicholas Humphrey, who suggests that the evolution
of primate intelligence might have arisen from the complex
cognitive demands of living with one's own companions.
Chimpanzees have proved themselves to be natural psychologists in dealing with their own kind.

According to Shreeve, it is certainly suggestive that our closest living relatives, the great apes, seem capable of deceit based
on reading the thoughts or intent of their peers. Not that chimpanzees are necessarily more intelligent than other primates,
but they spend their lives in "a shifting swirl of friends and relations, where small groups constantly form and break apart, and
reform with new members (p. 72.)"

Primates or early hominids who could comprehend the sub-
jective impressions of others and manipulate them to their own
ends would have a distinct advantage over their peers, perhaps

in access to food and mating opportunities. In a setting where the targets of manipulation were constantly trying to outwit the manipulator, a hominid species might well evolve a brain bigger than it "should" and be capable of far more than deceiving others.

Humphrey thinks that the adjective "Machiavellian" is too negative and suggests that the ability to attribute intentions to peers could have been an enormous building block for many human achievements. Higher intelligence can function to keep the social unit together and to exploit the environment successfully. Intelligence could be seen as driven by the need for cooperation and compassion as well. In response, Byrne and Whiten note that cooperation itself is an excellent Machiavellian strategy—sometimes (p. 71).

Whether the development of human intelligence is driven by a need to deceive and control, or a need for compassion and cooperation, it is apparent from the brief review of the literature that a need to control others is prominent in our lives as well as in those of our primate relatives. The solution appears to be to learn to live freely and authentically with one another in the rhythmic interdependence described by Shostrum, so that we are free to be who we actually are, and together, to be more than each of us can be alone.

NOTES

INTRODUCTION

1. Mythologist Joseph Campbell has pointed out clearly that we in the Western world have often put our minds in charge of our lives, thinking that we are controlling life by understanding it. But, in fact, we are separating ourselves from the deepest and most reality-oriented part of us: our feelings and the unconscious reality we experience through our bodies.

This concept—that we are totally rational beings who, with a little more discipline, will be able to handle all our problems—is widely held among intellectuals of all kinds and even a large number of therapists. While it's true that intellectual understanding is a crucial component to human growth and that many of us could certainly use more discipline in the conduct of our life and work, my own experience and that of people I've counseled indicate that it is a delusion that "enough intellectual discipline" would allow us to solve all our problems.

2. *Sin: Overcoming The Ultimate Deadly Addiction* (San Francisco: Harper & Row, 1987)—retitled in the paperback edition *Hope in the Fast Lane: A New Look at Faith in a Compulsive World; A Hunger for Healing: The 12 Steps as a Classic Model for Christian Spiritual Growth* (San Francisco: Harper & Row, 1991). With Pia Mellody and my wife, Andrea Wells

Miller, *Facing Co-dependence: What It Is, Where It Comes From, How It Sabotages Our Lives* (San Francisco: Harper & Row, 1989), to help co-dependents work through their abuse issues in recovery. Also with Pia Mellody and Andrea Wells Miller, *Facing Love Addiction* (San Francisco: Harper & Row, 1992).

CHAPTER 1: *Falling Out of the Speedboat*

1. As with all the cases cited in this book, Roger and Sue are composites of people I have known and worked with, myself included.

2. Appendix B describes some of the literature relating to the major issues in this book.

3. Carl Rogers, *On Becoming a Person* (Boston: Houghton Mifflin Company, 1972), 128.

CHAPTER 2: *What Is Controlling All About?*

1. Although the Diagnostic & Statistic Manual III does not identify anything called the control disease, the compulsion to control "acts like" a disease most of the time. It has discernible symptoms that are predictable, progressive and debilitating. I want to make it clear I am *not* proposing a new "disease" to the American Medical Association, but using the language here hypothetically because it makes more sense out of the data than any other word I can think of.

2. See John Bradshaw *Healing the Shame that Binds You* (Deerfield Beach, Fla.: Health Communications, 1988).

3. See Mellody, Wells Miller, and Miller, *Facing Co-dependence.*

4. For more information, see Mellody, Wells Miller, and Miller, *Facing Love Addiction.*

5. *Alcoholics Anonymous,* 3d ed. (New York: Alcoholics Anonymous World Services, 1976), 60-61.

6. Mellody, Wells Miller, and Miller, *Facing Love Addiction.*

CHAPTER 3: *Additional Factors in the Control Disease*

1. Mike Barnicle, "All Robert Redford Wants Is to Be Paul Newman," *Esquire,* March 1988: 114-124.

2. The reader may be disturbed by the implication that most parents are abusive, but we will look at the nature of the parental behavior I am calling abusive in chapter 5.

3. This will be merely a preliminary definition of intimacy. A more in-depth description of intimacy and the way it seems to work is spelled out in Part Three.

CHAPTER 4: *The Child's Journey*

1. When I was almost 50 years old and a professional speaker, I took the Birkman Inventory. On the introvert/extrovert scale, a "0" score would indicate a total introvert and a 100 would indicate a total extrovert. To everyone's amazement, I scored a "1." But to gain love and approval and be what my mother needed me to be, I was functioning as a public-person extrovert. Now I try to speak as an introvert from my inner Person and feel peaceful about that.

2. In the United States, the Medicine of the Person Group maintains an active network among physicians who strive to combine scientific excellence and faith through the dialogue of the Person. Some of the concepts in this book relating to the development of the Person can be found in Paul Tournier's *Secrets* (Richmond, Va.: John Knox Press, 1965) and *The Meaning of Persons* (New York: Harper & Row, 1957). Some of the material in this chapter appeared in a chapter I contributed to *The Reality and the Vision* (Waco, Tex.: Word Books, 1990).

3. The topic of "personages" is now being researched extensively and is falling into the category of dissociative disorders. This continuum has multiple personality on one end and normal dissociations, such as thinking while driving, on the other. The specific place on the continuum that I am writing about refers to Ego State Disorders (ESDs.)

James Bloch says in his book *Assessment and Treatment of Multiple Personality and Dissociative Disorders* (Sarasota, Fla.: Professional Resource Press, 1991), "Although MPD [multiple personality disorder] patients typically experience themselves as persons distinctly different from each other, ESD ego states tend to experience themselves as parts of one person. The degree of dissociation is the degree to which a person defines various self-stimuli (affect, cognition, impulse, identity, behavior, memory, motivation) as 'not-me,' ranging from the relatively complete disowning of self-characteristics in MPD to the milder and less disruptive exclusions in ESD." I am using Tournier terms with his meanings to be true to his earlier contributions.

4. Keith Miller and Andrea Wells Miller, *The Single Experience* (Waco, Tex.: Word Books, 1981), 59.

5. Ibid., 59-60.
6. Ibid., 53.

CHAPTER 5: *The Many Faces of "Child Abuse"*

1. See Mellody, Wells Miller, and Miller, *Facing Co-dependence,* 61-115.
2. For a more complete description of boundaries, see Appendix A, Boundaries.
3. A. Philip Parham, *Letting God* (San Francisco: Harper & Row, 1989), August 30th entry.
4. For a thoughtful look at the plight of the child sports star, see Emily Greenspan's *Little Winners* (Boston: Little, Brown and Company, 1983).

CHAPTER 7: *The Person-Dialogue*

1. Much of the information about the Person-dialogue in this chapter came from hearing Dr. Tournier lecture and from personal conversations through an interpreter. To read more about Tournier's thinking on this subject, read *The Meaning of Persons* and *Secrets.* For a list of some of Paul Tournier's books that relate to subjects in this book see References and Suggested Reading.

CHAPTER 8: *The 12 Steps*

1. For a more detailed description of the sponsoring process, getting a sponsor and ways to tell if the sponsorship is working, see Miller, *A Hunger for Healing,* Appendix p. 219.

CHAPTER 9: *Steps 1, 2, and 3*

1. For a description of the 12 Steps with suggestions about how to work each step, see Miller, *A Hunger for Healing,* 82.

CHAPTER 10: *Steps 4, 5 and 6*

1. For a way to do this, see Miller, *A Hunger For Healing,* 82.
2. See Pia Mellody and Andrea Wells Miller, *Breaking Free* (San Francisco: Harper & Row, 1989) 303-309, for a description of this exercise.
3. For some interesting views on the relation of control and sharing and physical illness, see Bernie Siegel, *Love, Medicine and Miracles* (Boston: G.K. Hall & Co., 1988) and Tournier, *The Healing of Persons.*

CHAPTER 11: Steps 7, 8 and 9

1. *Alcoholics Anonymous*, 83-84.

CHAPTER 12: Steps 10, 11 and 12

1. For specific ways to do Steps 10, 11 and 12, see Miller, *A Hunger for Healing*, 163-215.

CHAPTER 13: Getting Reparented

1. Many counselors have groups in which reparenting can take place, and of course some very important reparenting goes on in most good one-on-one counseling.

2. For a specific way to go back and recover your history, see Mellody and Wells Miller, *Breaking Free*, a workbook to be used in connection with Mellody, Wells Miller, and Miller, *Facing Co-dependence*, Part 1, 1-22.

CHAPTER 14: Re-approaching Your Loved One

1. For more information about interventions, see Vernon E. Johnson, *I'll Quit Tomorrow* (San Francisco: Harper & Row, 1980), 48. You can also contact a counselor or treatment center dealing with addictions and/or co-dependence.

CHAPTER 15: Relearning to Communicate

1. For what I believe to be a sound therapeutic approach to this recovery process for counselors or individuals, see Mellody and Wells Miller, *Breaking Free*.

2. This problem may require one or both parties to go into therapy. One party may always be less able than the other to share because of serious abuse issues or natural differences in approaches to communication.

CHAPTER 16: Making it Real

1. See M. Scott Peck, *The Road Less Traveled: A New Psychology of Love, Traditional Values and Spiritual Growth* (New York: Walker & Co., 1985), 81-85.

2. See Mellody, Wells Miller, and Miller, *Facing Co-dependence* and the accompanying workbook, *Breaking Free*, for a more comprehensive discussion of boundaries and exercises for learning how to set functional boundaries in your relationships. Also see "Appendix A: Boundaries" in this book.

3. *Ibid.*

CHAPTER 18: An Outward Sign of Intimacy

1. If this failure to perform sexually persists, the couple may want to counsel with a sex therapist who specializes in helping couples solve some of the problems caused by issues discussed in this chapter.

2. See Pat Mellody's chapter on relationships in Mellody, Wells Miller, and Miller, *Facing Love Addiction* for elaboration of this idea.

3. For more information, see Eric Berne, *Games People Play* (New York: Grove Press, 1964).

CHAPTER 19: Learning to Live

1. For an audiocassette of the musical album *Home is Where You Are,* by Keith Miller and Tommy Pierce, tracing the process of recovery in story and songs, send $12.20 to Villa Publishers, P.O. Box 26645, Austin, TX 78731.

APPENDIX A: BOUNDARIES

1. This discussion on boundaries is taken from Mellody, Wells Miller, and Miller, *Facing Co-dependence,* and from Appendix B in Miller, *A Hunger for Healing,* 235.

2. See Mellody and Wells Miller, *Breaking Free,* 316-353, for a specific approach to building functional boundaries and examples of specific boundary-setting exercises.

REFERENCES AND SUGGESTED READING

Abramson, Edward E. "The Counselor as a Machiavellian." *Journal Of Clinical Psychology*, no. 3 (1973): 348-349.

Alcoholics Anonymous, 3d ed. New York: Alcoholics Anonymous World Services, 1976.

Berne, Eric. *Games People Play.* New York: Grove Press, 1964.

Bloch, James. *Assessment and Treatment of Multiple Personality and Dissociative Disorders.* Sarasota, Fla.: Professional Resource Press, 1991.

Bradshaw, John. *Healing the Shame that Binds You.* Deerfield Beach, Fla.: Health Communications, Inc., 1988.

Brenner, Elizabeth. *Winning by Letting Go.* New York: Bantam Books, 1983.

Christie, R., and Florence L. Geis, *Studies in Machiavellianism: Social Psychology.* Edited by Festinger & Schacter. New York and London: Academic Press, 1986.

Forward, Susan and Joan Torres. *Men Who Hate Women and the Women Who Love Them.* New York: Bantam Books, 1986.

Fromm, Eric. *The Art of Loving.* New York: Harper & Row, 1956.

————. "Man Is Not a Thing." *Saturday Review*, 1957: 9-11 March.

Glasser, William. *Take Effective Control of Your Life.* New York: Harper & Row, 1984.

Goodall, Jane. *Through a Window.* Boston: Houghton Mifflin Company, 1990.

Hermanowicz, Urszula. "Effect of 'Authenticity' and Machiavellian Attitudes on Communication Styles." *Psychological Bulletin*, no. 1 (1982): 13, 45-51.

Johnson, Vernon E. *I'll Quit Tomorrow.* San Francisco: Harper & Row, 1980.

Laing, R.D. *Knots.* New York: Pantheon Books, 1970.

Leman, Kevin. *The Pleasers: Women Who Can't Say No and the Men Who Control Them.* New York: Dell Publishing, 1988.

Lerner, Harriet Goldhor. *The Dance of Anger: A Woman's Guide to Changing the Patterns of Intimate Relationships.* New York: Perennial Library, 1985.

————. *The Dance of Intimacy: A Woman's Guide to Courageous Acts of Change in Key Relationships.* New York: Harper & Row, 1989.

Machiavelli, Niccolo. *The Prince.* Chicago, Ill.: University of Chicago Press, 1985.

Mason, Avonne, and Virginia Blankenship. "Power and Affiliation Motivation, Stress and Abuse in Intimate Relationships." *Journal of Personality and Social Psychology*, no. 1, 52 (1987): 203-210.

McAdams, Dan P. and Joseph Powers. "Themes of Intimacy in Behavior and Thought." *Journal of Personality and Social Psychology*, no. 3, 40, (1981): 573-587.

McClelland, David C. *Power: The Inner Experience.* New York: Irvington Publishers, Inc., 1975.

Mellody, Pia and Andrea Wells Miller, *Breaking Free.* San Francisco: Harper & Row, 1989.

Mellody, Pia, Andrea Wells Miller, and J. Keith Miller,. *Facing Co-dependence: What It Is, Where It Comes From, How It Sabotages Our Lives.* San Francisco: Harper & Row, 1989.

—————. *Facing Love Addiction.* San Francisco: Harper & Row, 1989.

Miller, J. Keith. *Hope in the Fast Lane: A New Look at Faith in a Compulsive World.* San Francisco: HarperCollins, 1990.

—————. *A Hunger for Healing: The 12 Steps as a Classic Model for Christian Spiritual Growth.* San Francisco: Harper & Row, 1991.

Miller, J. Keith and Andrea Wells Miller. *The Single Experience.* Waco, Tex.: Word Book, 1981.

Norwood, Robin. *Women Who Love Too Much: When You Keep Wishing and Hoping He'll Change.* New York: Pocket Books, 1986.

Parham, A. Philip. *Letting God.* San Francisco: Harper & Row, 1989.

Peck, M. Scott. *The Road Less Traveled: A New Psychology of Love, Traditional Values and Spiritual Growth.* New York: Walker & Co., 1985.

Rogers, Carl. *On Becoming a Person.* Boston: Houghton Mifflin, 1972.

Shostrum, Everett L. *Man the Manipulator: The Inner Journey from Manipulation to Actualization.* Nashville, Tenn.: Abington Press, 1967.

Shostrum, Everett L. and James Kavanaugh. *Between Man and Woman: The Dynamics of Intersexual Relationships.* Los Angeles: Nash Publishing, 1972.

Shreeve, James. "Machiavellian Monkeys." *Discover,* June, 1991: 69-73.

Siegel, Bernie S. *Love, Medicine and Miracles: Lessons Learned About Self-Healing from a Surgeon's Experience with Exceptional Patients.* Boston: G.K. Hall, 1988.

Siegel, Judith. "Money and Marriage: A Transparency to the Struggles of Intimacy." *Journal of Independent Social Work,* no. 4 (1990): 51-60.

Steininger, Marion, and Ellen Eisenberg. "On Different Relationships Between Dogmatism and Machiavellianism Among Male and Female College Students." *Psychological Reports,* no. 6 (1976): 779-782.

Stewart, Abigail, J., and Zick Rubin. "The Power Motive in the Dating Couple." *Journal of Personality and Social Psychology* no. 2 (1976): 305-309.

Symonds, Martin. "The Psychodynamics of Violence-Prone Marriages." *American Journal of Psychoanalysis* 38, no. 3 (1978): 213-222.

Thayer, Stephen. "Close Encounters." *Psychology Today* 22, no. 3 (1988): 30-36.

Tournier, Paul. *The Adventure Of Living.* New York: Harper & Row, 1965.

—————. *Guilt & Grace.* New York: Harper & Row, 1962.

—————. *The Healing of Persons.* New York: Harper & Row, 1965.

—————. *The Meaning of Persons.* New York: Harper & Row, 1957.

—————. *A Place for You.* New York: Harper & Row, 1968.

—————. *Secrets.* Richmond, Va.: John Knox Press, 1965.

—————. *The Strong and the Weak.* Philadelphia: Westminster Press, 1963.

Woititz, Janet. *Struggle for Intimacy.* Deerfield Beach, Fla.: Health Communications, Inc., 1985.

ABOUT THE AUTHOR

J. Keith Miller is one of the nation's most widely known and respected inspirational speakers and authors. He is an oil entrepreneur-turned-author with degrees in business administration, theology and psychological counseling. Miller has more than 20 books to his credit with over 4 million copies in print. His books include *Facing Co-dependence* and *Facing Love Addiction,* both of which he coauthored with Pia Mellody and Andrea Wells Miller; *A Hunger for Healing; Hope in the Fast Lane;* his classic spiritual guide, *The Taste of New Wine;* and his forthcoming book, *The Secret Life of the Soul.*

Compelled to Control is the result of Miller's search to isolate the causes and cures of painful breakdowns in intimate relationships. In this book he explores the process of recovery from the "control disease" and describes how to make your way back to intimate, reality-oriented and loving relationships with spouses, lovers, children, parents, friends and associates.

"The recovery process," Miller states, "can bring with it the courage to live sanely—with serenity and hope."

To contact J. Keith Miller about speaking engagements, write
Michael McKinney
McKinney Associates, Inc.
P.O. Box 5162
Louisville, KY 40205
or call (502) 583-8222